Transportation and Land Development

**INSTITUTE
OF
TRANSPORTATION ENGINEERS**

Transportation and Land Development

Vergil G. Stover
Texas A & M University

Frank J. Koepke
The Traffic Institute, Northwestern University

Prentice Hall, *Englewood Cliffs, New Jersey 07632*

Library of Congress Cataloging-in-Publication Data

STOVER, VERGIL G.
    Transportation and land development.

    At head of title: Institute of Transportation Engineers.
    Includes bibliographies and index.
    1. Traffic engineering. 2. Land use, Urban. 3. Building sites — Planning. I. Koepke, Frank J.
II. Institute of Transportation Engineers. III. Title. HE335.S76   1988   625.7′25   87-11419
ISBN 0-13-930413-4

Editorial/production supervision
and interior design: *Carolyn Fellows*
Cover design: *Edsal Enterprises*
Manufacturing buyer: *Rhett Conklin and Gordon Osbourne*

 © 1988 by Prentice Hall
A Division of Simon & Schuster
Englewood Cliffs, New Jersey 07632

Printed in the United States of America
10   9   8   7   6   5   4   3

ISBN 0-13-930413-4   025

Prentice-Hall International (UK) Limited, *London*
Prentice-Hall of Australia Pty. Limited, *Sydney*
Prentice-Hall Canada Inc., *Toronto*
Prentice-Hall Hispanoamericana, S.A., *Mexico*
Prentice-Hall of India Private Limited, *New Delhi*
Prentice-Hall of Japan, Inc., *Tokyo*
Simon & Schuster Asia Pte. Ltd., *Singapore*
Editora Prentice-Hall do Brasil, Ltda., *Rio de Janeiro*

The Institute of Transportation Engineers is an international, individual member, scientific, and educational association. The purpose of the Institute is twofold: to enable engineers and other professionals with knowledge and competence in transportation and traffic engineering to contribute individually and collectively toward meeting human needs for mobility and safety; and to promote professional development of members, by the support and encouragement of education, stimulation of research, development of public awareness, exchange of professional information, and maintenance of a central point of reference and action.

The Institute's programs include publications, technical committees, professional development seminars, training, local, regional, and international meetings, and standards. For current information on the Institute's programs, please contact:

INSTITUTE OF TRANSPORTATION ENGINEERS
525 School Street, S.W., Suite 410
Washington, D.C. 20024
(202) 554-8050

Contents

Contents

Preface

Transportation and Land Development unites transportation and land use in an exciting and timely discussion of the planning and design of circulation systems from the standpoint of site development. In transportation, the design goal is to provide for the movement of people and goods between and among land uses. In land development, the design goal is to achieve a functional and profitable project. These goals at all times are highly interdependent and sometimes are in conflict.

The underlying assumption throughout this book is that the processes of transportation and land development are inextricably bound: land development cannot occur without transportation; transportation facilities serve no economic purpose without development. The text is organized on the basis that good planning precedes good design.

Part I deals with the planning process inherent to both transportation and land development. The text moves from a discussion of general planning principles to a discussion of transportation and site planning principles, and finally, to the point at which the two processes meet in the site traffic analysis.

Part II deals with specific design considerations of transportation and land development. The organization of Chapters 4, 5, and 6 divides this highly related material to group topics logically within each chapter while maintaining chapters which are of somewhat similar size. Chapter 4 discusses hierarchical movement systems—the basis of functional design criteria, which are equally applicable to public streets and private developments. It also offers information on traffic-circulation considerations in residential development. This discussion is directed toward traffic issues which have broad implications; it does not attempt to deal with the details of subdivision design.

Drive-in facilities present unique traffic-circulation problems and have been the object of specific data collection. Also, drive-thru operations can be subjected to quantitative analysis. Chapter 8 therefore deals expressly with the parking and circulation issues involved with this type of development.

ACKNOWLEDGMENT

The authors wish to express their appreciation to the following, who have been of considerable help in the production of this manual. The ITE Publications Committee was instrumental in identifying the need for this publication. Members of the committee were: Richard L. Peterson, Chairman, John R. McCarthy, John P. Braaksma, Kenneth G. Courage, Alan T. Gonseth, Robert E. Spicher, Bo E. Peterson, Michael A. Powills, Neilon J. Rowan, Harold D. Vick, Walter H. Kraft, and James L. Pline. We are especially appreciative of the committee's recommendation to the ITE International Board of Direction that we be asked to author this manual.

The support and encouragement provided to the authors by Thomas W. Brahms, Executive Director, in this endeavor is gratefully acknowledged.

The following ITE members reviewed the manuscript and provided many helpful suggestions: John J. DeShazo, DeShazo, Starek & Tang, Dallas, Texas; John L. German, P. E., Franklin Savings, Austin, Texas; Nazir Lalani, P. E., City of Santa Rosa, California; William S. Pollard Jr., University of Colorado, Denver, Colorado; and Michael A. Powills, Barton-Aschman Associates, Evanston, Illinois. The authors are very appreciative of their efforts.

Special recognition is given to Ms. Emily Braswell for her editorial work on the second draft. Her suggestions for improvements in sentence structure and wording are reflected in the final manuscript.

Finally, we gratefully recognize the word processing assistance provided by Ms. Ruth Davis, Mrs. Latitia Hedrick, and Ms. Sylvia Garza.

ABOUT THE AUTHORS

Vergil G. Stover has been in the professional practice of transportation engineering and planning for thirty years, including university level teaching, research, consulting, and highway construction. He has extensive experience in the areas of urban transportation studies, access design and management, and site traffic analysis and design. Dr. Stover holds a joint appointment as a Professor in the Department of Civil Engineering and Urban Regional Planning at Texas A & M University and as a Research Engineer with the Texas Transportation Institute. He is also active as a consultant to municipalities and private clients.

Frank J. Koepke, formerly Director of Transportation Engineering with The Traffic Institute, Northwestern University, has over thirty years of experience in traffic engineering. He currently is vice-president of Metro-Transportation Group, Inc., in Bloomingdale, Illinois. Mr. Koepke specializes in transportation planning, the conducting of traffic impact analyses, and site access and parking design. He is a Fellow member of the Institute of Transportation Engineers and a member of the Transportation Research Board.

Transportation
and
Land Development

Part One
PLANNING

1

Transportation and Urban Development

TRANSPORTATION AND LAND USE

Throughout history, transportation and land development have been closely bound. As people settled, and cities and towns began to grow, new and more sophisticated modes of transportation developed. Faster and more flexible transportation, in turn, stimulated land development. In the early days, walking and movement by horse-drawn vehicles provided travel speeds of less than 4 mph. Urban population densities were very high, and land uses were mixed. Except for the wealthy who could afford private carriages, or the commuters who came from nearby towns (after the availability of steam-powered commuter rail service), most people lived in close proximity to the primary earner's work location. Residences were often above some ground-floor commercial activity.

As the use of rail and trolly became more widespread and affordable, the much higher speeds of electric traction, about 12 mph, enabled an increasing number of affluent urban families to establish residences at substantial distances from places of employment. As the segregation of residence and other land uses began to occur, the convenience retail and service activities relocated in response to the changing residential pattern. While densities in the electric-trolley corridors were high by comparison to today's suburban development patterns, they were lower than previous urban densities. The higher travel speeds also permitted a substantial increase in the central city's land area as well as its population.

The automobile offered higher travel speeds as well as greater convenience and flexibility. Use of automobiles led to a decrease in density and a marked increase in the

1

potential size of the urbanized area. This greatly increased the number of locations suitable for a variety of commercial retail, office, light industrial, and service uses. It is interesting to note the difference in urban patterns exhibited among cities settled during different periods of transportation development. Cities that developed before the advent of the automobile tend toward greater densities and less urban sprawl. Cities that developed primarily after World War I, after the advent of the automobile, tend toward lower densities and consequently more urban sprawl.

THE TRANSPORTATION–LAND USE CYCLE

The construction of a new arterial street, or major reconstruction of an existing thoroughfare, modifies the accessibility of an area; this, in turn, leads to development and increased traffic demands. The strip development along major arterials, with closely spaced or poorly designed access, creates numerous and overlapping conflict points. This results in reduced capacity, traffic delays, high levels of motorist discomfort, accidents, and reduced levels of traffic service. In order to better accommodate the increased traffic demand, further roadway improvements are required, and a cycle of events occurs which requires continuing capital investment for arterial improvements or relocation as illustrated in Figure 1-1.

Reconstruction to increase the level of service of an existing arterial is generally very costly and, without careful access management, will provide only temporary relief. The improved service will stimulate increased business activity, which in turn will generate more traffic, resulting in an ultimate decrease in traffic service. Furthermore, the shallow property depth, proximity of buildings to the right-of-way line, multiplicity of ownership, and right-of-way limitations generally preclude good access and site circulation design, even when substantial expenditures are made for reconstruction. In the more severe cases,

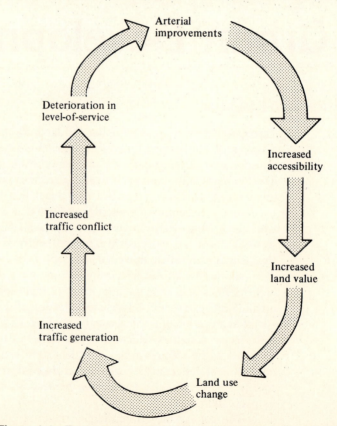

Figure 1-1 Transportation and land development cycle. SOURCE: Vergil G. Stover [4].

the arterial must be relocated because of functional obsolescence, and the process starts all over again in a new location.

Changes in arterial street level of service can also lead to unstable land use patterns as the relative accessibility of different locations changes.

The type of land use as well as the layout of the development may generate problems which adversely impact the public street system. Poor site design and the traffic generated by a development can have an impact at critical intersections at a substantial distance from the development as well as close to the site.

The forces which influence the dynamics of land development are many and complex. The following is not an exhaustive list but is sufficient to point out the multifaceted nature of the problem:

- Governmental policy and programs at the national, state, and local levels
- Changes in family income
- Changing family and personal preferences
- Transportation technology and cost structure
- Transport system changes
- Level-of-service provided by the urban transport system

Although little can be done in shaping the forces of income and general market tendencies, the transportation and land development professionals can play a significant role in the development of governmental policy and programs, particularly at the local level. The three primary tools available at the local government level are the *comprehensive plan,* the *zoning ordinance,* and *subdivision regulations.*

In the absence of strong, realistic comprehensive planning, zoning can be only partially effective in integrating transportation and land use. The reason is that zoning does not directly deal with the type and volume of traffic generated by a development; the land use of any given site is likely to change a number of times over the life of an arterial; and, as commonly administered, zoning is often changed without consistent, comprehensive consideration of the consequences.

Because subdivision regulations are subject to the same limitations as zoning, it is critical that the comprehensive planning process and the day-to-day administration of zoning and subdivision regulations be tightly integrated. Case studies illustrate the interdependence of transportation and land use planning, and the delicate and ever-changing balance between transportation and land use development.

One conceptual dilemma is whether one can define the points in time when the land development and transportation system will be in balance. One new roadway may provide the capacity for thousands of vehicles per day, while residential and commercial activities are developed just a few units at a time. Furthermore, travel flows vary from hour to hour, day to day, and month to month. Consequently, it is better to think of the balance as being represented by a tolerance range, as illustrated in Figure 1-2. The tolerance range accounts for both (1) the inability to precisely and accurately measure and predict traffic and (2) the variability of traffic flows.

Accessibility

The transportation system is the basic infrastructure element which influences the pattern of urban development. This influence can be illustrated by the following example.

Change in System Level-of-Service.   The change in peak-period travel time for the San Diego, California, central business district (CBD) is apparent in the comparison of the 1957 and 1970 travel-time contours shown in Figure 1-3. In this period, 166 miles of freeway were constructed with an additional 26 miles under construction. Although vehicle registrations in San Diego County nearly doubled (from approximately 375,000 to over 725,000), the area accessible to the San Diego CBD from within 20 minutes approximately tripled.

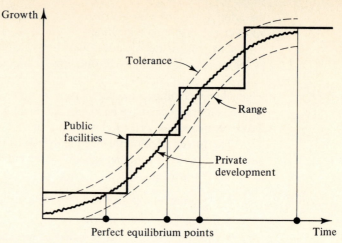

Figure 1-2 Balance between increments of development and improvements in transportation facilities. SOURCE: Robert M. Winick [7].

Unfortunately, the reverse can also be true. The improved accessibility provided by extensive arterial street improvements stimulates increased development, which in turn results in increased traffic volumes and property values. Unless access management and design are carefully addressed, the level-of-service will be seriously degraded. The result will be a decrease in market area and a decrease in property value.

By way of hypothetical example, consider that the primary trade area for a large retail center is 20 minutes. If the average speed on the street system is a uniform 45 mph, then the shopping radius is 15 miles and the primary trade area is 706 square miles. If the level-of-service decreases to 30 mph owing to poor access management, the market area will have a radius of 10 miles or an area of about 314 square miles, as illustrated in Figure 1-4. Thus, a one-third reduction in speed will reduce the market area to about 45% of its former size. A gridiron arterial system will produce a trade area as illustrated schematically in Figure 1-5. The same change in speed produces the same reduction in market area.

The actual size of the market area will be different for different-sized generators, since the travel distances are different. However, the change in market area that will result from a uniform decrease in speed is the same. Unless the monetary size of the market is offset by increased population (increased density) and/or increased family income, the sales volume at the center can be expected to decrease as shown in Table 1-1.

In actual practice the street system is rarely a classical gridiron, nor are the speeds uniform on all sections of the street system. Consequently, the actual shape of the market area will be irregular, such as schematically illustrated in Figure 1-6. In such cases, the travel-time contours must be determined and the areas obtained by planimeter.

Change in Shopping-Center Market Area. Wheaton Plaza is a regional shopping center in the suburban Maryland portion of the Washington, D.C., metropolitan area. When opened, it contained 1 million square feet of retail floor area plus a multistory office tower. The street system in the metropolitan area was radial in nature. Radial freeways were also existing, under construction, and programmed. Circumferential streets were discontinuous or nonexistent prior to the construction of the National Capital Beltway — a circumferential freeway.

Studies [5] show that about 70% of the traffic to a regional center comes from within 20 minutes travel distance. The primary trade areas for Wheaton Plaza prior to and after the Beltway opening are illustrated in Figure 1-7. Since the opening of the entire Beltway occurred in a short period of time, the impact on shopping patterns was quite dramatic. Shopper interviews [6] at suburban Maryland shopping centers revealed that few shoppers visited more than one center when making a major shopping trip prior to the opening of the Beltway. After its opening, the majority of customers reported shopping, or intending

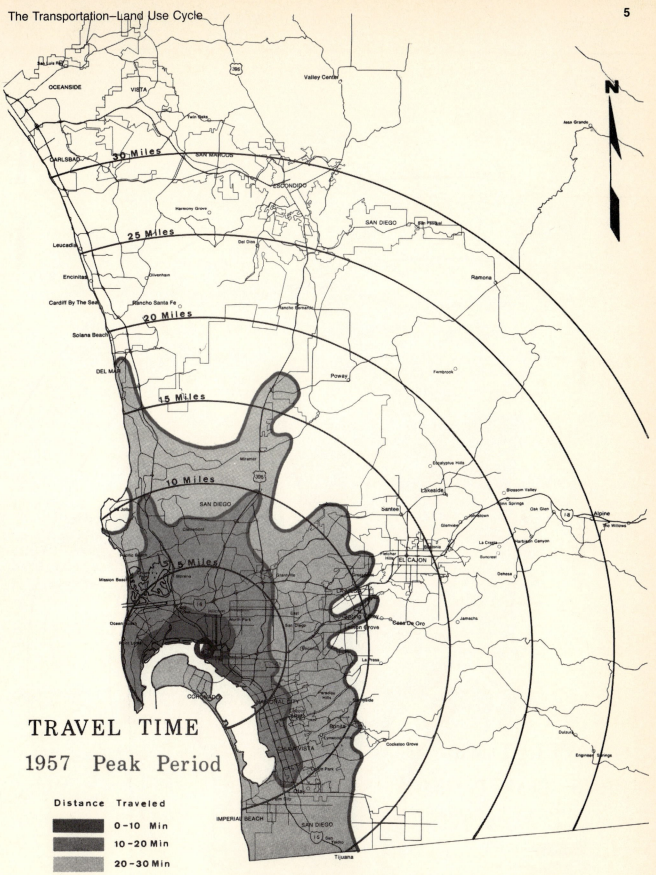

Figure 1-3 San Diego travel-time contours: (a) 1957, (b) 1970.
SOURCE: California DOT, San Diego Travel-Time Study [1].

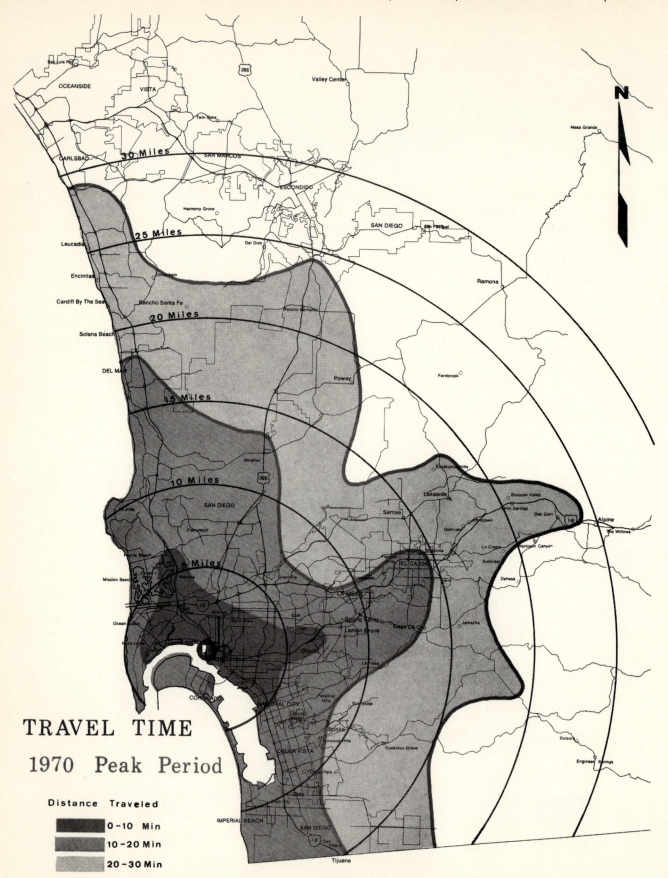

TRAVEL TIME
1970 Peak Period

Distance Traveled

0-10 Min
10-20 Min
20-30 Min

Figure 1–3 (continued)

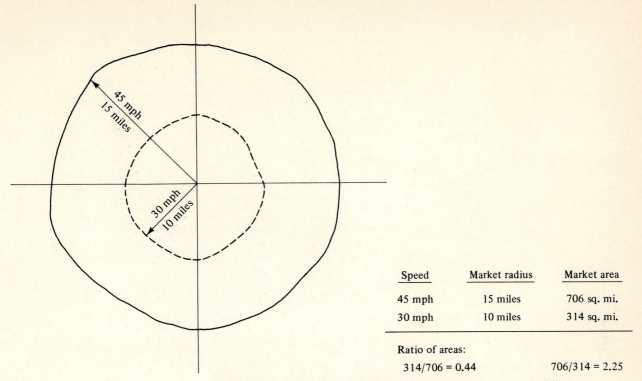

Speed	Market radius	Market area
45 mph	15 miles	706 sq. mi.
30 mph	10 miles	314 sq. mi.

Ratio of areas:

314/706 = 0.44   706/314 = 2.25

Figure 1-4 Theoretical market areas with street system providing equal movement in all directions.

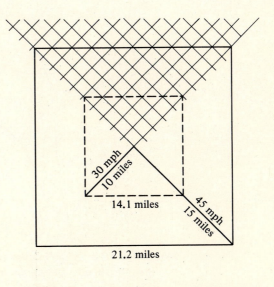

Speed	Market range	Market area
45 mph	15 miles	450 sq. mi.
30 mph	10 miles	200 sq. mi.

Ratio of areas:

200/450 = 0.44   450/200 = 2.25

Figure 1-5 Theoretical market areas with grid iron street system.

TABLE 1-1

Reduction in Market Area as a Function of Reduced Travel Speed

Reduction in Average System Speed	Market Area Relative to Previous Size
0%	100%
10%	81%
20%	64%
33%	45%
40%	36%
50%	25%

Note: Smaller activity centers attract trips from shorter distances. For example, about 70% of the traffic to a regional shopping center comes from within 20 minutes travel, whereas for a community shopping center about 70% of the traffic comes from within 12 minutes and for a neighborhood center from within 7 minutes. Thus while their primary trade areas are of different sizes, for a given reduction in speed each will suffer the same percentage reduction in market area.

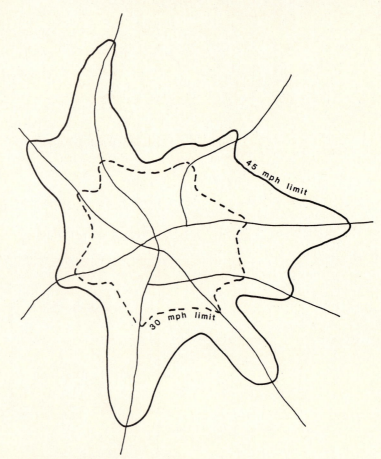

Figure 1-6 Schematic market areas with radial street system and non-uniform speeds for various routes.

to shop, at one or two other regional centers. About 30% indicated that the origin of the trip to the regional shopping center at which they were interviewed was some other regional shopping center.

Migration of Primary Retail Location.   The twin cities of Bryan/College Station, Texas, provide an example of changing growth patterns that resulted in deterioration in the level-of-service of the primary arterials and a significant change in site desirability [3] over a 20-year period. During this period from 1960 to 1980, new residential development, an

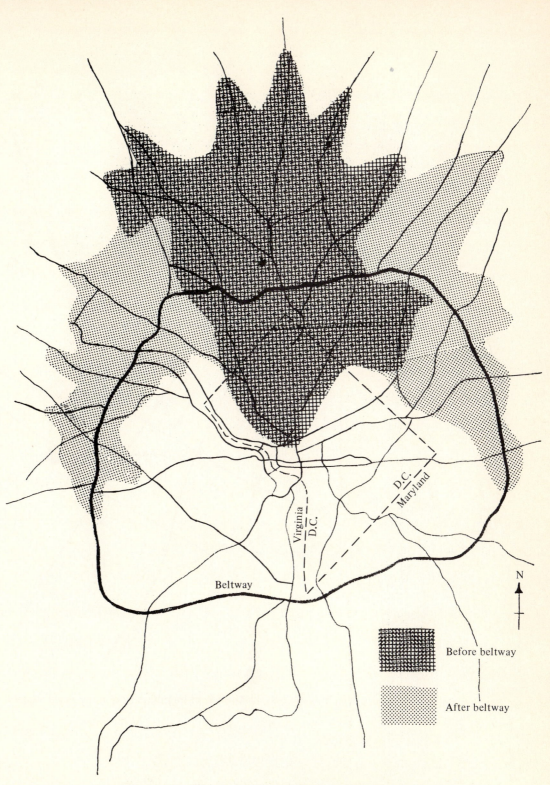

Figure 1-7 Wheaton Plaza market area before and after opening of the capitol beltway. SOURCE: Vergil G. Stover [3].

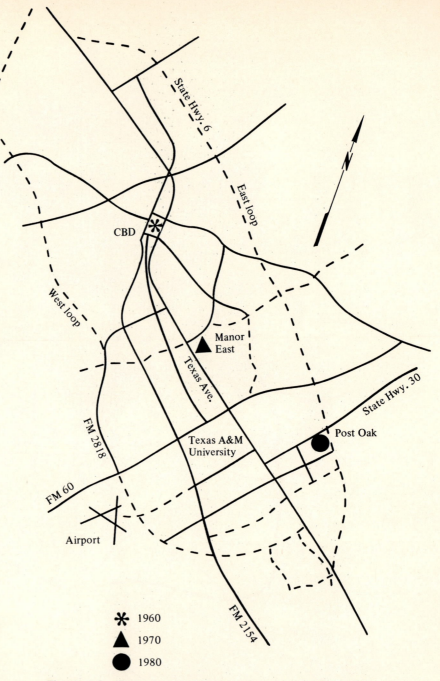

Figure 1-8   Illustration of migration of primary retail location.

increase in population, and an increase in the number of higher-income families occurred in the east and south sections of the metropolitan area. The principal north-south arterial, Texas Avenue, experienced a severe deterioration in level-of-service as a result of strip development and poorly designed access points. Travel time between the historical CBD and the growth area to the south became greater, and travel between the two became less. A freeway constructed along the east side of the urban area dramatically improved the accessibility of the rapidly developing, high-income areas along the east and south sides of the urbanized area. A second north-south loop constructed along the west side also facilitated north-south movement.

The location of the CBD, the 1960 primary retail location, and the locations of two more recently developed retail malls (Manor East, which opened in 1969, and Post Oak, which opened in late 1981) are shown in Figure 1-8. This illustration shows the major street system as it existed in 1960 and 1980. In the 1970s, the Manor East location replaced the historical CBD as the primary retail location. By 1980, the changes in street system and growth pattern combined to result in the development of Post Oak Mall, located about 5.7 miles southeast of the historical CBD.

TRANSPORTATION PLANNING VERSUS SITE PLANNING

The traditional urban transportation planning process diagrammed in Figure 1-9 was developed to evaluate alternative land use–transportation plans. The process was intended to:

- Identify major travel corridors and provide projections of the approximate volume of traffic within these corridors
- Identify major potential problem areas in the proposed network
- Provide a basis for planning and programming major network improvements

The process also provides information (major desire lines and mean trip length) by which the compatibility of the future land use and transportation assumptions can be

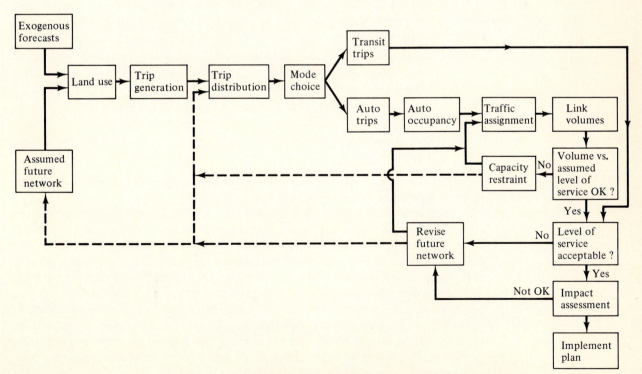

Figure 1-9 Urban transportation planning process.

evaluated. It can also be used to evaluate the relative accessibility of the existing transportation–land use pattern, to identify changes in accessibility that would result with different transportation systems, and to see if proposed large commercial or industrial concentrations are situated at locations which have, or will have, a high level of accessibility.

The urban transportation planning process, which relies heavily upon computer models, is a macroscopic tool which uses an abstract computerized representation of the street and highway network in the traffic assignment. It cannot be used at the microscopic or site-planning level because it does not provide:

- Reliable projections of turn movements at individual intersections or access drives
- Reliable projections of the traffic volumes on individual street segments
- Reliable estimates of traffic volumes at access drives as for different access locations and/or designs
- The effect of numerous access points to an arterial as opposed to only a few direct access points
- Left-turn and right-turn requirements
- Effects of changes in lane use
- Effects of modest changes in the location of activities; e.g., the positioning of 250,000 square feet of retail floor area on each of the 4 quadrants of an intersection versus the location of all 1 million square feet in one quadrant
- Reliable estimates of the traffic on the frontage roads separate from that or the main lanes of a freeway or at-grade arterial

Both the general urban (comprehensive) planning process and the urban transportation planning process commonly utilize a single 20-year time horizon in which permanent elements, 20-year requirements, and short-term needs are conglomerated in a single large study. In order to deal more effectively with transportation and land use development, the planning process should be stratified into the following four planning horizons or levels:

1. An infinite or at least a very long range horizon for strategic planning of major transportation corridors land use patterns and other permanent elements of the urban environment.

2. An intermediate 20-year horizon for the planning of significant changes in transportation facilities, water, waste water, and other major infrastructure elements and land use patterns.

3. A short-range horizon (5 to 10 years) for planning and programming of major development.

4. Design and construction of individual public works projects and private developments.

The successive stages should constitute a progression of planning design with an increasing degree of refinement and detail at each successive stage.

The Level 1 and 2 plans should provide general policy guidance for public and private development decisions. These are the shortest time horizons for which application of the urban transportation modeling process was intended. Level 3 needs to provide effective coordination of public-sector infrastructure decisions and coordination between the public sector and private sector development decisions. Level 4 should help ensure that each proposed development relates to existing and anticipated conditions.

Site planning is essentially a Level 3 activity. It involves analysis of the traffic impact of specific proposed development, the adequacy of the access drives, and the suitability of the on-site circulation and parking. Such analyses are site-specific and micro-scale. Consequently, different analytical procedures are involved. A general framework for site-specific analysis is diagrammed in Figure 1-10.

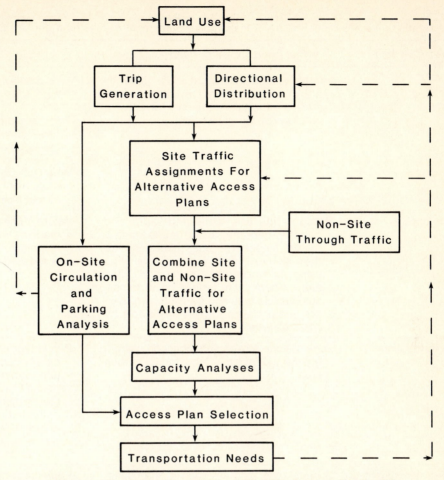

Figure 1-10   Site-traffic analysis. SOURCE: Frank J. Koepke [2].

TABLE 1-2

Comparison of the Traditional Urban Transportation Study and the Site Plan and Traffic Analysis

Analysis Element	Urban Transportation Planning Study	Site Plan and Traffic Analysis
Land use	Mix of general categories of land use in each traffic analysis/assignment zone. No definition as to location of existing or future buildings and other physical improvements.	Specific types of existing and proposed activities are known. Locations of existing and proposed improvements are known for a specific tract of land.
Transportation system	The street and transit systems are abstractly represented.	Specific information as to right-of-way width, paved section, existing traffic characteristics, and existing traffic control are known or can be obtained. Specific information on transit use, if any, is known or obtainable.
Trip generation	Total 24-hour trips are projected for each zone using general categories of trips (i.e., home-based work, home-based non-work, non-home based.) Trips are projected by Productions and Attractions for each zone.	Trips are estimated for the peak hour of the adjacent street and peak hour(s) of the proposed development. For certain developments, such as shopping centers, both the weekday and weekend peaks are used. Traffic is estimated by direction on the street system and for each access point of the proposed development. The

TABLE 1-2

Comparison of the Traditional Urban Transportation Study and the Site Plan and Traffic Analysis *(continued)*

Analysis Element	Urban Transportation Planning Study	Site Plan and Traffic Analysis
	Interzonal and intrazonal trips generally are obtained with gravity model using zone-to-zone, and intrazonal travel times obtained by trip generation.	commonly used trip-generation rates are auto trips. Trips are projected by direction: into the development (destination) or out from the development (origin). When a large development is mixed-use (e.g., retail and office), the number of trips to and from the site must be adjusted.
Mode choice	Person trips are "split" into auto and transit—generally using some mathematical model. The auto mode trips are then converted to auto/vehicle trips using auto occupancy factors. In urban areas where there is little or no transit, auto/vehicle trips and transit trips (if any) are most appropriately obtained by direct generation.	Where some of the trips are expected to be made by transit, the number of transit trips is projected and the number of auto trips is reduced using auto occupancy rates.
Trip distribution	Zone-to-zone movements obtained using a gravity model calibrated for the urban area.	Percentage of traffic to/from the site obtained by: (1) geographical distribution of clientele within the primary trade zones—manual analysis using judgment, or (2) gravity model application—computerized or manual methods, or (3) analogy—appropriate in situations where a similar business is already located in close proximity to the proposed development.
Traffic assignment	Zone-to-zone trips assigned to the coded, abstract network using minimum paths, all-or-nothing, or multiple-path "capacity" restrained assignment.	Percentage of traffic using each access point is projected. Traffic volume at each access point by movement. Traffic added by the proposed development projected by movement for each street segment and intersection adjacent to and within the traffic influence area of the proposed development. If computerized, thorough, detailed analysis of the results is essential.
Use of results	Assess the internal consistency of a land use–transportation plan. Evaluate and compare mutually exclusive land use–transportation plans. Identify major problem areas in the transportation plan given a land use plan. Identify movement corridors and project the approximate volume within each corridor. Identify major system deficiencies in the existing transportation system in comparison to the adopted land use–transportation plan.	Identify the selected peak-hour demands at individual access points of a proposed development. Assess the capacity of the proposed access and its adequacy to accommodate the projected demand. Evaluate the layout of the on-site circulation and parking, building location, and location and design of the access in relation to the adjacent street(s). Identify the need for street improvements such as additional through lanes, turn lanes, and traffic control adjacent to and within the area of traffic influence of the proposed development.

SOURCE: Vergil G. Stover [4].

Much of the terminology used in urban transportation planning and in site planning is similar. However, the applications and uses are very different, as indicated in Table 1-2. The site-specific nature of traffic analyses of individual proposed development projects requires more detailed methods and techniques than those which are suitable for the evaluation of land use–transportation alternatives, which is the objective of the urban transportation study.

REFERENCES

1. California Department of Transportation, State of California, *Travel-Time Study, San Diego, California,* January, 1971.

2. Koepke, Frank J., Course Notes, The Traffic Institute, Northwestern University.

3. Stover, Vergil G., "Accessibility and Access Considerations in the Planning and Design of Urban Activity Centers," paper presented at the Transportation Research Board Workshop on Transportation Requirements for Urban Activity Centers, Phoenix, Arizona, 27–28 September, 1984.

4. Stover, Vergil G., Course Notes for CE 612, Texas A&M University.

5. Urban Land Institute, *Parking Requirements for Shopping Centers: Summary Recommendations and Research Study Report,* 1982, p. 43.

6. Smith, Wilbur, and Associates, *Maryland National Capitol Beltway Impact Study,* 1965.

7. Winick, Robert M., "Balancing Future Development and Transportation in a High Growth Area," *Compendium of Technical Papers,* Institute of Transportation Engineers, 1985.

2

Site Planning

THE SITE-PLANNING PROCESS

The site-planning and design process presently in common use begins with decisions relative to the building size and shape and its placement on the site. The placement decision is commonly based upon visual concerns (e.g., located on the high point on the site or oriented parallel to the arterial) and building shape. The parking and on-site circulation are then designed around the building. Finally, the intersections of the access drives with the adjacent street are established, with little or no consideration being given to the impact on the arterial street.

When inadequate attention is given to the location and design of access, the following problems result:

- Inadequate access capacity
- On-site congestion or
- Congestion on the public street system
- High accident experience
- Limited flexibility to adjust the design or operation to changed conditions

As indicated in Figure 2-1, the design process presently in common use first locates the building footprint, and then the parking and on-site circulation are designed. Little consideration is given to the functional relationship which must exist between the public and private components of an effective and efficient urban circulation system. From an access location and design standpoint, the design process could be reversed. In actuality,

Building
Location & Design

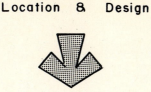

On - Site
Parking & Circulation

Access
Location & Design

Figure 2-1 Schematic representation of the prevalent site-design process. SOURCE: Vergil G. Stover [2].

the building location, on-site circulation, and access are highly interrelated. Therefore a more sophisticated process illustrated in Figure 2-2 needs to be utilized.

Often site traffic problems are discovered after the financial feasibility study has been completed and the investment decision has been made. A preliminary traffic study prepared in conjunction with the market study will avoid such problems by addressing the following:

1. Any existing traffic and other roadway conditions that would limit the development of the site under consideration.
2. Possible/probable changes in traffic conditions, traffic operations, or roadway design that will influence the amount or nature of the development that can be accommodated on the site or the site design.
3. The traffic-generation characteristics of the activities identified in the market feasibility study.
4. Comparison of the traffic that might be generated by the development with an estimate of the access capacity that can be expected to be available. If the access capacity is insufficient, the market feasibility study should investigate other options (scaled-down project, different mix of uses, or another site) before significant investment decisions are made.

Functional design criteria of the surrounding roadway network need to be used as the basis for access location and design.

Improved access design results when access location and design are based on a hierarchy of streets, and the access location and design does not interfere with the movement function of the arterial street. The design process needs to incorporate access and on-site circulation considerations at an earlier stage and in a more comprehensive manner than is common at present. Many times, it is the access location and design, not the site traffic volume per se, which create the traffic problem. Furthermore, the traffic problems which might have been created by a proposed development can be avoided or minimized through the evolution of better access location and/or design.

Since building location, functional on-site circulation, and access are highly interrelated, the traffic engineer should be a part of the design team from the inception of the

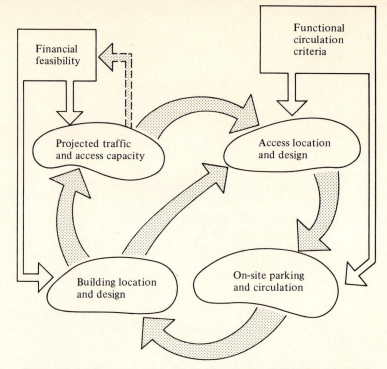

Figure 2-2 Systems approach to site design. SOURCE: Vergil G. Stover [2].

project. In many cases the traffic engineer can identify problems ahead of time, allowing better usage to be made of the site, the adjacent streets, the access, and the on-site circulation and parking. The sooner traffic circulation problems are identified, the more easily and inexpensively they can be resolved. Once construction has been completed, it is generally expensive and often impossible to satisfactorily resolve site circulation and access problems; this situation can damage marketability and the return on investment for the developer.

PROPOSED DEVELOPMENT REVIEW

A Proposed Development Review (PDR) process is the most effective way of dealing with the off-site and on-site traffic and other aspects of any major land development or redevelopment. In this manner, the location and design of access, on-site circulation, and off-site traffic consequences can be addressed as a whole in the site design process. The PDR should consist of the following related studies:

1. A financial feasibility study to determine the demographic/geographic suitability of the proposed land use.
2. A site-plan review, including the access location and design, on-site circulation (pedestrian as well as vehicular), and parking. This review should also consider a variety of other site-plan details including drainage, landscaping, utility locations, fire protection, loading docks, and solid waste collection.
3. A traffic impact analysis (TIA), which estimates the volume of traffic the development can be expected to generate and provides quantitative evaluation of the impact of this traffic on the public street system and on the ultimate development, together with an identification of off-site improvements that may be needed as a result of the development.

Financial Feasibility

A marketing feasibility report is necessary for any major land use development. Its purpose is to determine the market area of influence, the projected build-out/lease-out period, and the potential short- and long-term return on investment. It is a specialized study and should be prepared by real estate marketing and financial professionals. The results of this study are critical in shaping the transportation and development decisions that follow this initial exploratory report.

Site-Plan Review

An approved site plan should be required for all proposed development or redevelopment whether or not a traffic impact analysis (TIA) may be required. The site plan should be prepared at a scale ranging from one inch equals 20 feet to one inch equals 100 feet, depending upon the size of the site. The smallest scale used to determine sight distances and evaluate maneuver areas at intersections and driveways should be one inch equals 40 feet. Elements that should be shown on the site plan include:

- The location and shape of all buildings
- The location and design of all access points
- The right-of-way and cross section of the adjacent streets
- The location and design of any intersections — private (access drives) or public — in close proximity to the site
- Parking layout — stall size, aisle, and "wall-to-wall" dimensions, end-island shape and dimensions
- Width of circulation roadways and radius of horizontal curves
- Sidewalks
- Existing and proposed utilities (including fire hydrants)
- Loading docks and solid waste collection locations
- Storm drainage
- Landscaped areas

The approved site plan should serve as the basis for the administrative issuance of all the necessary governmental permits, including curb cut, building, and utility connection. However, some time limit should be established within which application must be made for all necessary permits. A period of 12 months is suggested for incorporation in municipal ordinance. The following items should be checked during the site-plan review:

Access Location and Design
- Spacing to adjacent public and private access
- Angle
- Curb return radii
- Throat cross section
- Throat length
- Channelization, medial and marginal
- Length, width, and taper of turn bays
- Sign location
- Sight distances
- Visibility of access drive
- Profile

On-Site Circulation and Parking
- Vehicular conflict points
- Vehicular–pedestrian conflicts
- Sight distances

- Channelization
- Delineation of internal circulation roadways
- Widths of internal circulation roadways
- Potential for high speeds adjacent to building
- Potential for high-speed, random vehicular movements in parking area
- Convenience of parking with respect to building entrances
- Parking dimensions
- Location of curbs/wheel stops relative to front of parking stall
- Location and design of handicapped parking stalls
- Building entrances and pedestrian circulation between the entrances and the parking areas
- Sidewalk widths
- Fire lanes
- Delivery/truck docks
- Access to solid waste containers
- Visibility of obstructions such as curbed end islands, barriers, and light posts
- Delineation of edge of development from adjacent streets

Other Elements

- Existing and proposed utilities, including fire hydrant locations
- Surface drainage
- Location and type of landscaping
- Location of light poles
- Location of any on-site items such as any kiosks and U.S. Postal Service drop boxes
- Fences and/or landscaping to screen development from adjacent property
- Location and angle of exterior lighting when development is adjacent to residential development or where lighting might interfere with driver's vision

Traffic Impact Analysis (TIA)

A traffic impact analysis (TIA) is a specialized study of the impact a certain type and size of development will have on the surrounding transportation system. Depending on the type and size of development, the TIA may range from a cursory inspection of the site, the projected traffic volumes, and the adjacent streets to a full-blown alternatives analysis that includes adjacent streets, regional thoroughfares, and transit systems.

The traffic impact analysis should be an integral part of the development impact review process. It is specifically concerned with the generation, distribution, and assignment of traffic to and from a proposed development. The purpose of a TIA is to determine what impact that traffic will have on the existing and proposed roadway network, and what impact the existing and projected traffic on the roadway system will have on the proposed development.

A complete traffic impact analysis should be performed in each of the following situations:

1. All development which can be expected to generate more traffic than some specified threshold (such as 100 vehicles in the peak hour of the adjacent street or generator) or for a lesser volume when review of the site plan indicates that such additional data are desirable.
2. All applications for rezoning.
3. Any change in the use of an existing commercial or industrial site.
4. Cases in which the original TIA is more than two years old or where increased land use intensity will result in an increase in traffic generation by more than 15% or a directional distribution in the site traffic by more than 20%.

The responsible jurisdiction should establish the requirements for the TIA by ordinance. It is suggested that the ordinance should specify a maximum review period. Desirably the review period should be 5 to 10 working days where the review and acceptance of the TIA is at the local (city or county) level and 10 to 20 working days when the state highway agency is also involved in the review.

The ordinance should designate a responsible city staff person for administration of the ordinance and the development and maintenance of a manual on requirements and procedures. While the manual needs to contain specific guidelines which can be consistently and equitably applied, it needs to allow the traffic analyst performing the TIA reasonable latitude to tailor the TIA to the specific situation. Examples of inappropriate rigidity which can unnecessarily increase the cost of a TIA include:

- Requirements for extensive traffic counts adjacent to and in the vicinity of the site when present traffic volumes are well below capacity
- A requirement that a detailed intersection capacity analysis be performed whenever a signalized intersection is adjacent to or in the vicinity of the site
- A requirement that traffic assignment packages for a microcomputer be used

The traffic consultant should discuss the project with the city staff at a very early stage in the study. Topics which should be discussed include: available traffic data, any city plans for street improvements in the vicinity of the site, traffic counts to be made, intersections at which capacity using critical lane analysis is appropriate, and projected volumes when the area becomes fully developed.

The specific content of a TIA will vary depending upon the site and the prevailing conditions. The guidelines for preparing TIAs should specify the format and general contents. The following suggested guidelines represent a minimum standard:

1. Existing Conditions
2. Trip Generation and Design Hour Volumes
3. Trip Distribution and Traffic Assignment
4. Existing and Projected Traffic Volumes
5. Capacity Analysis
6. Traffic Accidents
7. Traffic Improvements
8. Conclusions
9. Summary of Findings and Recommendations

A more complete discussion of methodology and sources for the traffic impact analysis will be presented in Chapter 3.

PLANNING SCALES

The development of an efficient site circulation system requires that traffic analysis and site design progress from broad-scale concerns through specific details. These elements can be categorized as being *corridor, project,* or *site* planning issues, as summarized in Table 2-1. At the corridor level (Figure 2-3), issues would include placement of major facilities such as arterials or collectors in developing areas, or the impact of a major development on the existing primary arterials and collectors in a redeveloping area. Project-level issues include development impacts on adjacent properties and roadways and the placement of access (Figure 2-4). Site-specific issues revolve around the placement and design of internal features such as parking, building footprint, and site circulation (Figure 2-5).

TABLE 2-1
Development Planning Scales

Corridor Scale	Project Scale	Site Scale
1. Create shared marginal access to simplify highway movement and reduce number of access points.	1. Parking access system should be clear and simple, form circulation loops, and avoid dead ends.	1. Parking modules should alternate with planted areas to break up parking expanse, provide safe pedestrian zones, and help define the vehicular circulation system.
2. Highway access points must be 400 ft. minimum distance from a channelized intersection.	2. Parking modules should be used to break up parking lot expanse, and create simple circulation patterns for parking search.	2. Parking module location can facilitate safe pedestrian movement if modules are oriented perpendicular to building entrance facades, to minimize the number of traffic aisles a pedestrian must cross.
3. Avoid "dog leg" situation by locating access point directly opposite another access point or at least 150 ft. away. (This applies at every level of scale.)	3. If parking is shared by two or more buildings, each should have equally convenient pedestrian and vehicle links to the parking area.	3. Circulation within modules should be simple and continuous. Avoid situations where driver must leave site and re-enter to repeat parking search.
4. Site access should be shared whenever possible to reduce pavement, avoid duplication of roads, and create efficient circulation.	4. Building forms should be used to define and emphasize entrances, which must be visible and easily accessible from related parking areas.	4. Delivery areas should be separate from parking area. Service drives should not enter parking modules.
5. Parking lots should be shared to reduce parking area. Adjacent uses which have different operating hours or peak times should share parking.	5. Provide a continuous pedestrian system which links building entrances along a direct path, separate from vehicular right-of-ways, and connects to pedestrian routes beyond the project.	5. Pedestrian walkways should be separate from vehicular right-of-ways, and should follow direct routes between buildings or from parking area to building.
6. Separate incompatible uses with buffer zone or screen.	6. A system of bicycle routes should also be created, separate from auto traffic if possible, and linked to a community-wide bicycle system. Areas for convenient storage of bicycles should be provided.	
7. Size, shape and orientation of buildings should be designed to make them easily visible from highway, at highway speeds.	7. Buildings should be oriented to take advantage of pleasant views and to capture highway visibility.	
8. Locate buildings, parking areas, and open space to create strong and varied mass/space relationships when viewed from highway.	8. Appropriate screens should be used to hide undesirable views.	
9. Site signage must be located where it is easily visible to highway traffic.	9. Some areas of natural open space should be created to provide relief from and contrast to built-up areas.	
10. Site uses along corridor should be land use types which benefit from highway visibility and complement adjacent corridor uses.	10. Use "green" space as a buffer zone between less compatible uses.	
11. Uses should take advantage of vistas and pleasant views where they are available.		
12. Uses adjacent to natural features must not endanger or encroach upon the feature.		

SOURCE: Frank J. Koepke [1].

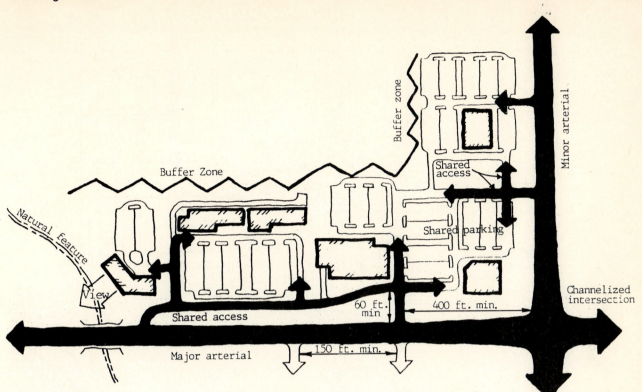

Figure 2-3 Corridor scale. SOURCE: Frank J. Koepke [1].

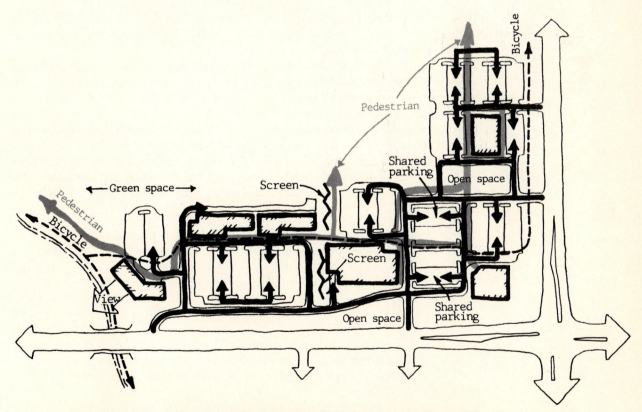

Figure 2-4 Project scale. SOURCE: Frank J. Koepke [1].

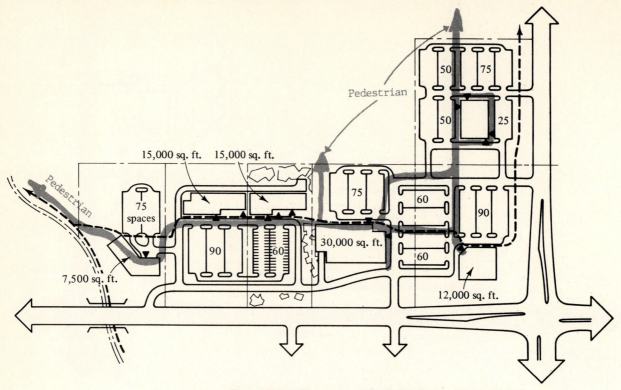

Figure 2-5 Site scale. SOURCE: Frank J. Koepke [1].

Conceptual Site Plan: An Example

A major corporate developer asked that a conceptual land use and circulation plan be developed for a large (740-acre) tract, located in the midst of a stable and growing metropolitan suburban market.

The site is complex. It is affected by airport flight patterns and two freight rail lines. Part of the site has been used by surrounding communities as a sanitary landfill. A creek runs through the property, and some of the land lies within this creek's floodplain.

The tract is bisected by two four-lane arterial highways which provide good connections to regional expressway facilities. The predominant population distribution is to the north and west of the site. The local market will support a variety of residential, industrial and office, and commercial uses. A market feasibility analysis has been completed, and a development program has been proposed for testing and evaluation. The feasibility study suggests the following types and amounts of land use which the market can support:

Residential Land Uses	*Acres*
1. Single-family detached houses	150
2. Townhouses/medium density	153
3. Garden apartments	35
4. High-rise apartments	15

Commercial Land Uses	
5. Community shopping center of approximately 240,000 square feet of gross leasable floor area. The center should include a major food store, major discount store, and other retail shops.	24
6. Highway commercial uses including an auto parts outlet, restaurants, drive-in bank, garden supply store, realty office, and service outlets	10

7.	The development will support two gas stations.	1
8.	A 250-room hotel	8

Employment Areas

9.	General office use	20
10.	Corporate headquarters (campus type)	50
11.	Restricted industrial uses	30

Institutional Uses

12.	Art center serving the entire community	4
13.	Schools:	
	2 elementary schools	5 each
	1 junior high school	10
14.	Community recreation center	5
15.	Open space	215

Follow three essential criteria in assigning land uses to subareas:

1. Match land uses with level of accessibility.
2. Locate uses so they are compatible with adjacent uses.
3. Match land uses to the characteristics of the land.

Figure 2-6 locates the site with respect to the area roadnet.
Figure 2-7 lists the major land use planning determinants.
    Figure 2-8 is a worksheet summarizing site characteristics of six subareas. This sheet is used to determine a preliminary distribution of land use.

Methodology

Step 1.   Using a base map of the area, locate the various land use areas as follows:

   a.   Match area offering the highest level of accessibility with uses which require direct and a high level of accessibility.

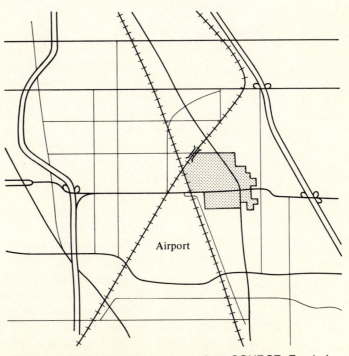

Figure 2-6   Site-location area roadnet. SOURCE: Frank J. Koepke [1].

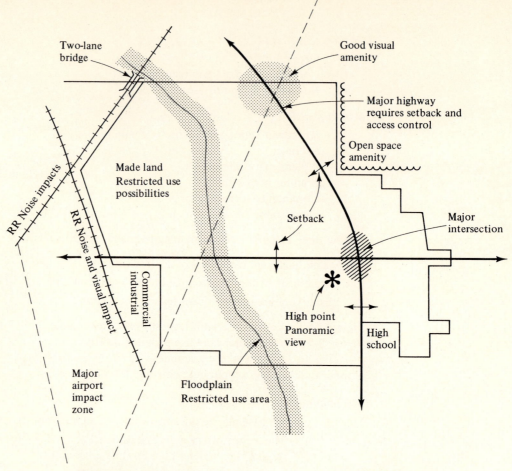

Figure 2-7 Major land use planning determinants. SOURCE: Frank J. Koepke [1].

Methodology

b. Match items on the development program to areas on the site that seem most suitable and take advantage of special site opportunities.

c. Mark out areas which cannot or should not be developed at all.

d. Check for incompatibilities between areas. Can uses be successfully mixed?

Step 2. Prepare a base map of the site showing the adjacent circulation system, including any access drives or nearby properties, then:

a. Establish a circulation framework. Where can the site be entered? Where is it restricted? Are certain road links already dictated by existing conditions?

b. Try to fit a workable circulation system to the land use distribution. Are accessibility levels matched with access needs?

c. Can utilities be provided? Think through how public services and deliveries will be provided.

A scale of one inch equals 20 or 25 feet is suggested if any dimensions are to be scaled off the site plan. For very large developments it is convenient to use two different scales: one showing overall concept of the circulation system (one inch equals 50 to 100 feet) and another showing details. While Step 1 can be at a smaller scale than Step 2, use of the same base map(s) is suggested for convenience.

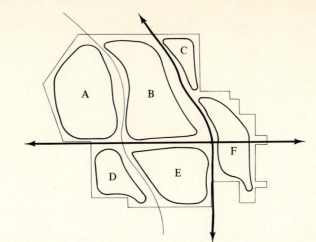

Area	Criteria	Uses	Area	Criteria	Uses
A	• Poor accessibility • Landfill • Noise impact • Airport impact • Water		D	• Moderate accessibility • Adjacent to industry and commercial • Airport impact • Water amenity • Floodplain	
B	• Good accessibility • Water amenity • Soil problems • Floodplain problems • No adjacent uses		E	• High accessibility • No adjacent development (three sides) • Water amenity • Trailer park • Floodplain	
C	• Moderate accessibility • Adjacent to open space • Wooded area		F	• High accessibility • Adjacent to single family • Adjacent to schools • Soil problems	

Figure 2-8   Site analysis by area. SOURCE: Frank J. Koepke [1].

REFERENCES

1. Koepke, Frank J., Course Notes, The Traffic Institute, Northwestern University.
2. Stover, Vergil G., "Accessibility and Access Considerations in the Planning and Design of Urban Activity Centers," paper presented at the Transportation Research Board Workshop on Transportation Requirements for Urban Activity Centers, Phoenix, Arizona, 27–28 September, 1984.

3

Traffic Analysis

Traffic planning for the circulation system external to the site involves two components:

- *Site-oriented traffic:* trips which have an origin or destination on the site
- *Non-site traffic:* trips which do not have an origin or destination on the site of the proposed or existing development

SITE-ORIENTED TRAFFIC

Site-oriented traffic is much easier to estimate than non-site-oriented traffic because:

1. The land use activities (or mix of land use activities) are (is) known.
2. The number of trips expected to be generated by the proposed development can be determined in a rather straightforward manner. (ITE and other sources provide substantial data on traffic generation.)
3. The present and future directional distribution can be estimated.

Traffic Generation

The characteristics of trips generated by a development vary with the type of land use and the intensity of the activity. Five primary characteristics are significant in the analysis of site-generated traffic:

1. The total number of trips generated, commonly calculated as the product of the appropriate trip-generation rate per unit of activity (e.g., 1,000 square feet) and the amount of activity (e.g., floor area divided by 1,000).
2. The number of trips to and from the site during the peak hours of the adjacent street.

3. The number of trips to and from the site during the peak(s) of the generator. The peak volume to the site commonly is at a different time than the peak volume from the site for some generators. For example, a regional shopping center has a weekday entering peak at about 6:45 to 7:45 p.m. and an exiting peak at about 9:15 to 9:45 p.m. when the closing time is 10:00 p.m.

4. Daily variation. Offices, for example, experience little day-to-day variation, while Friday typically is the highest weekday for retail activities.

5. Monthly variation. Traffic generation by retail activities, restaurants, and motels may vary considerably, especially when there is a substantial seasonal tourist trade. On the other hand, general offices are subject to very little variation throughout the year.

The unit used as the base variable for trip-generation rates must

- Be functionally related to the volume of traffic generated
- Be relatively easy to establish/measure
- Provide consistent and transferable rates

For example, dollar sales and employees are highly correlated with trip generation by retail activities but are virtually impossible to project. Gross leasable area (GLA) is an expedient compromise variable. It is easily determined for existing and proposed development and produces unit rates which are transferable. Typical trip-generation units are given in Table 3-1.

The ITE report *Trip Generation* [9] is the principal source of trip-generation rates used in site traffic analysis. The major advantages of this source are:

- The data are presented in a relatively detailed manner (see Figure 3-1, p. 39).
- The data are periodically updated and additional information added through the efforts of an ITE Committee.

Prior to using the data contained in this report, the companion document entitled *"Using the ITE Trip Generation Report"* [3] should be carefully reviewed.

A second major source of secondary data is the report "Development and Application of Trip Generation Rates" [11]. These summary trip-generation data are presented in Table 3-2, pp. 30–38. In addition to the average, minimum, and maximum trip-generation rates, this report provides statistical information as to the variability of the observed data. For example, for the land use generator shopping centers over 1 million square feet (ITE Codes 827 and 828) the standard deviation is 16.13 ($s = 16.13$) and the standard deviation of the mean is 3.80 ($s/\sqrt{n} = 16.13/\sqrt{18} = 3.80$) for trips per 1,000 square feet. The application of these statistics is explained a few pages further on, in a section on reliability and transferability.

Problems which are common to trip-generation data are:

1. *Age of data base:* The data base extends back to the early 1960s. Mehra and Keller [11] divided the data into pre-1973 and post-1973 data sets and tested for a significant difference in the mean trip-generation rate when there were a sufficient number of observations. They concluded, at the 5% significance level, that there is no difference in the mean trip-generation rates for all land uses except apartments.

2. *Daily variations:* Average weekday, together with Saturday and Sunday, trips are reported. Many generators, however, such as banks, shopping centers, and restaurants, exhibit substantial daily variation. In many cases the highest weekday, rather than the average weekday, trip rate should be used in a traffic impact analysis, since the higher rates and associated traffic problem will occur several times per year. For example, in an area where there are a large number of

TABLE 3–1
General Guide on Trip End Generation Rates by Land Use

Type of Land Use	Type of Development	No. of Studies	Weekday Trip End Generation Rates	
			Average*	Range
RESIDENTIAL	Subdivision	21	9.5 TE per Occupied Dwelling Unit	6.4–12.7
	Apartment	17	5.7 TE per Occupied Dwelling Unit	3.1–7.9
	Condominium	21	5.1 TE per Occupied Dwelling Unit	3.1–12.2
	Mobile Home Park	17	5.4 TE per Occupied Dwelling Unit	2.8–6.8
	Retirement Community	5	3.3 TE per Occupied Dwelling Unit	2.9–4.9
MAJOR INSTITUTION	College (4 yrs.)	5	2.2 TE per Student	1.9–3.3
	College (2 yrs.)	4	1.3 TE per Student	1.1–1.6
	High School	5	1.3 TE per Student	1.1–2.1
	Elementary School	9	1.0 TE per Student	0.7–1.2
	Hospital	8	9.4 TE per Bed	4.5–14.9
	Library	4	58.4 TE per Employee	37–82
	Government Office Building	11	64.6 TE per 1000 Sq. Ft. floor area	25–272
COMMERCIAL	Shopping Center (Regional)	4	315 TE per Net Acre	149–671
	Shopping Center (Neighborhood)	3	949 TE per Net Acre	800–1064
	Commercial Store (free-standing)	6	48 TE per 1000 Sq. Ft. floor area	35–330
	Commercial Office Building	10	15 TE per 1000 Sq. Ft. floor area	8.8–23.6
	Furniture Store	8	6.3 TE per 1000 Sq. Ft. floor area	3.7–12.5
	Lumber/Home Improvement	6	30.6 TE per 1000 Sq. Ft. floor area	21.1–68.9
	Medical Office	4	41 TE per Doctor	31–53
	Motel	10	10.1 TE per Occupied Unit	4.7–14.6
	Restaurant (Quality)	15	14.1 TE per Employee	9–28
	Coffee Shop	2	29 TE per Employee	22–37
	Bank, Savings and Loan	6	43 TE per Employee	31–76
	Service Station	2	57 TE per Employee	41–79
	Nurseries	12	22.2 TE per Employee	10.7–53.9

		Number of Studies	Rate	Range
INDUSTRIAL	Various Types of Industry	27	79 TE per Net Acre	9–350
	Industrial Park	4	64 TE per Gross Acre	52–140
	Warehouse	10	81 TE per Net Acre	28–256
	Mass Production	8	93 TE per Net Acre	38–191
	Administration	8	60 TE per Net Acre	28–229
	Research and Development	9	31 TE per Net Acre	20–127
	Specialty Production	7	39 TE per Net Acre	9–159
	Truck Terminals	4	56 TE per Net Acre	43–128
RECREATIONAL	Picnicking	26	0.8 TE per Total Acre	0.1–35
	Winery with Tasting Room	1	11 TE per Employee	—
	Golf Course (18-Hole)	7	6.4 TE per Acre	2.5–10.9
			816 TE per Golf Course	237–1524
	Golf Course (9-Hole)	1	176 TE per Golf Course	—
	Bowling Lane	1	33 TE per Lane	—
	Marina	3	4.8 TE per Berth	3.2–10
	Ocean Beaches	13	56 TE per 1000 Ft. of Beach	8.0–345
	Swimming	6	7.4 TE per Total Acre	1.7–20
	Hiking Trails	17	0.5 TE per Total Acre	0.1–10.3
	Overnight Camping	10	0.3 TE per Total Acre	0.1–15.6
	Tennis Club	4	27 TE per Tennis Court	20–51
	Handball Club	3	105 TE per Handball Court	56–313
MISCELLANEOUS	General Aviation (Airport)	9	9.8 TE per Acre	1.0–16.2
	Church	6	44 TE per Employee (Sunday)	30–191
	Car Wash	1	33 TE per Employee	
	Transit Station (Suburban)	1	1.5 TE per Daily Patron	
	Rental Storage	6	0.28 TE per Vault	0.13–0.46

SOURCE: California Department of Transportation, District 4 Trip Ends Generation Research Counts. Except for Fresno State College, all studies were taken within the San Francisco Bay Area.

*Average rates are weighted from the total number of studies for each type of development with ranges shown. They will be updated periodically as more studies are made. Average rate for developments with limited number of studies may be drastically changed.

TABLE 3–2

Summary of Trip-Generation Rates

LAND USE GENERATOR (DESCRIPTION & ITE CODE)	UNITS	VEHICLE TRIPS PER DAY TO & FROM LAND USE (Rate/Unit as noted)			STATISTICS			VEHICLE TRIP RATES IN PEAK HOUR								
								AM			PM			PEAK HOUR OF GENERATOR		
		MEAN	MIN	MAX	STD DEV.[a]	STD DEV. OF MEAN[b]	OBS. IN SAMPLE	IN	OUT	TOTAL	IN	OUT	TOTAL	IN	OUT	TOTAL
PORTS & TERMINALS (000)																
Water Ports 010	BOSBER	171.52	38.60	338.57	112.98	42.70	7	*	*	*	*	*	*	*	*	*
	ACRE	11.95	4.95	19.47	5.45	2.06	7	*	*	*	*	*	*	*	*	*
Air Ports 020	CFL/DY	70.85	51.33	78.44	13.59	7.85	3	2.86	1.95	4.81	4.16	4.42	8.58	3.33	3.33	6.66
	FLT/DY	3.05	0.96	31.38	8.83	2.66	11	0.17	0.13	0.30	0.22	0.23	0.45	0.25	0.25	0.50
	EMP	21.45	11.55	284.29	102.29	38.66	7	1.32	1.03	2.35	1.69	1.81	3.50	0.98	0.98	1.96
	ACRE	4.77	0.99	24.89	8.25	2.49	11	0.23	0.18	0.41	0.30	0.31	0.61	0.31	0.31	0.62
Comm Airport 021	CFL/DY	122.21	99.50	138.74	22.55	13.02	3	3.57	2.86	6.43	3.72	3.17	6.89	4.26	4.98	9.24
	FLT/DY	8.34	1.62	122.97	60.71	35.05	3	0.24	0.20	0.44	0.25	0.22	0.47	0.29	0.34	0.63
	EMP	15.39	14.11	22.94	6.25	4.42	2	0.45	0.37	0.82	0.44	0.36	0.80	0.54	0.67	1.21
	ACRE	11.48	9.13	16.22	3.63	2.10	3	0.33	0.27	0.60	0.35	0.30	0.65	0.40	0.47	0.87
Gen Avi Airport 022	FLT/DY	2.50	*	*	NA	NA	*	*	*	0.30	*	*	0.26	*	*	0.39
	EMP	6.50	*	*	NA	NA	*	*	*	0.77	*	*	0.68	*	*	1.02
	ACRE	3.60	*	*	NA	NA	*	*	*	0.43	*	*	0.38	*	*	0.57
Truck Terminals 030	IK SF	9.86	NA	NA	NA	NA	1	0.36	0.54	0.90	0.35	0.47	0.82	0.36	0.54	0.90
	EMP	6.99	4.22	47.29	30.45	21.53	2	0.27	0.39	0.66	0.26	0.29	0.55	0.27	0.39	0.66
	ACRE	81.86	66.20	100.08	23.96	16.94	2	3.12	4.62	7.74	3.05	3.41	6.46	3.12	4.62	7.74
INDUSTRIAL (100)																
Gen Lght Indus 110	1K SF	6.98	1.58	16.88	4.44	1.05	18	0.82	0.13	0.95	0.19	0.69	0.88	0.35	0.66	1.01
	EMP	4.50	1.53	10.42	2.12	0.49	19	0.45	0.07	0.52	0.10	0.37	0.47	0.53	0.08	0.61
	ACRE	76.03	5.21	159.38	43.90	10.07	19	7.51	1.35	8.86	1.80	6.12	7.92	7.63	2.63	10.26
Gen Heavy Indus 120	1K SF	1.50	0.58	1.84	0.69	0.40	3	*	*	0.51	*	*	0.19	*	*	0.69
	EMP	2.05	0.75	11.05	4.99	2.50	4	*	*	0.51	*	*	0.89	*	*	0.89
	ACRE	15.62	1.66	55.13	24.71	12.36	4	*	*	1.98	*	*	2.16	*	*	6.41
Indus Park 130	1K SF	7.00	0.91	36.97	7.71	1.12	47	0.71	0.22	0.93	0.24	0.75	0.99	0.24	0.75	0.99
	EMP	3.59	1.37	8.80	1.92	0.29	45	0.42	0.15	0.57	0.14	0.38	0.52	0.42	0.15	0.57
	ACRE	62.82	13.87	1272.63	209.24	32.68	41	7.79	2.45	10.24	8.26	2.65	10.91	8.26	2.65	10.91
Manufact 140	1K SF	3.85	0.50	52.05	6.90	0.89	60	*	*	0.78	0.43	0.32	0.75	0.52	0.26	0.78
	EMP	2.09	0.60	6.66	1.21	0.16	60	*	*	0.43	0.22	0.17	0.39	0.17	0.29	0.46
	ACRE	38.88	2.54	396.00	69.43	9.28	56	*	*	7.35	4.78	3.50	8.28	6.10	3.05	9.15
Warehouse 150	1K SF	4.88	1.51	17.00	3.76	0.97	15	*	*	0.66	0.62	1.01	1.63	2.19	2.69	4.88
	EMP	3.89	1.47	15.71	3.74	0.97	15	*	*	0.50	0.49	0.79	1.28	0.61	0.76	1.37
	ACRE	56.08	20.23	255.80	59.64	15.94	14	*	*	9.56	7.07	11.70	18.77	9.01	11.01	20.02

RESIDENTIAL (200)

Land Use	Unit															
S-F Det Hous 210	DU	10.03	4.31	21.90	2.37	0.13	313	0.21	0.54	0.75	0.64	0.36	1.00	0.64	0.36	1.00
	ACRE	26.18	1.82	275.19	31.15	2.82	122	0.61	1.50	2.11	1.70	1.03	2.73	1.70	1.03	2.73
Urban	DU	11.28						0.24	0.61	0.84	0.72	0.41	1.13	0.72	0.41	1.13
	ACRE	29.45						0.69	1.69	2.37	1.91	1.16	3.07	1.91	1.16	3.07
Suburban	DU	9.06						0.19	0.49	0.68	0.58	0.33	0.90	0.58	0.33	0.90
	ACRE	23.64						0.55	1.35	1.91	1.54	0.93	2.47	1.54	0.93	2.47
Rural	DU	9.73						0.20	0.52	0.73	0.62	0.35	0.97	0.62	0.35	0.97
	ACRE	25.40						0.59	1.46	2.05	1.65	1.00	2.65	1.65	1.00	2.65
Apartment 220	DU	6.11	0.54	12.34	1.92	0.17	122	0.09	0.46	0.55	0.49	0.22	0.71	0.49	0.22	0.71
	ACRE	23.79	1.82	361.83	67.98	8.37	66	0.36	0.90	1.26	1.40	0.81	2.21	1.40	0.81	2.21
Urban	DU	6.87						0.10	0.52	0.62	0.55	0.25	0.80	0.55	0.25	0.80
	ACRE	26.76						0.41	1.01	1.42	1.58	0.91	2.49	1.58	0.91	2.49
Suburban	DU	5.52						0.08	0.42	0.50	0.44	0.20	0.64	0.44	0.20	0.64
	ACRE	21.48						0.33	0.81	1.14	1.26	0.73	2.00	1.26	0.73	2.00
Rural	DU	5.93						0.09	0.45	0.53	0.48	0.21	0.69	0.48	0.21	0.69
	ACRE	23.08						0.35	0.87	1.22	1.36	0.79	2.14	1.36	0.79	2.14
Condomin 230	DU	5.40	0.57	11.79	2.28	0.31	55	0.07	0.37	0.44	0.36	0.18	0.54	0.36	0.18	0.54
	ACRE	68.04	14.81	337.66	74.29	17.04	19	0.76	4.50	5.26	4.41	2.16	6.57	4.66	2.52	7.18
Urban	DU	6.08						0.08	0.42	0.50	0.41	0.20	0.61	0.41	0.20	0.61
	ACRE	76.55						0.86	5.06	5.92	4.96	2.43	7.39	5.24	2.84	8.08
Suburban	DU	4.88						0.06	0.33	0.40	0.33	0.16	0.49	0.33	0.16	0.49
	ACRE	61.44						0.69	4.06	4.75	3.98	1.95	5.93	4.21	2.28	6.48
Mobile Home 240	DU	4.78	2.29	7.60	1.44	0.28	26	0.05	0.37	0.42	0.38	0.19	0.57	0.38	0.19	0.57
	ACRE	39.13	15.86	85.89	17.19	3.19	29	0.59	3.03	3.62	3.10	1.81	4.91	3.23	1.81	5.04
Retire Comm 250	DU	3.30	2.80	9.90	NA	NA	3	*	*	0.40	*	*	0.40	*	*	*
Plan Unit Dev 270 (Suburban)	DU	7.49	5.23	14.38	2.62	0.70	14	0.13	0.43	0.56	0.46	0.24	0.70	0.46	0.26	0.72
	ACRE	46.78	41.85	50.80	4.24	2.12	4	0.67	2.21	2.88	2.66	1.39	4.05	2.64	1.49	4.13

LODGING (300)

Land Use	Unit															
Hotel 310	ROOM	8.70	5.31	9.58	1.58	0.60	7	0.44	0.26	0.70	0.36	0.31	0.67	0.56	0.35	0.91
	EMP	14.34	8.85	24.47	6.13	2.74	5	0.40	0.29	0.69	0.36	0.27	0.63	0.52	0.45	0.97
	ACRE	1430.19	755.38	1663.55	395.72	197.86	4	7.05	4.90	11.95	47.31	46.42	93.73	65.28	54.57	119.85
Urban	ROOM	8.68						0.44	0.26	0.70	0.36	0.31	0.67	0.56	0.35	0.91
	EMP	14.31						0.40	0.29	0.69	0.36	0.27	0.63	0.52	0.45	0.97
	ACRE	1427.33						7.04	4.89	11.93	47.22	46.33	93.54	65.15	54.46	119.61
Suburban	ROOM	9.34						0.47	0.28	0.75	0.39	0.33	0.72	0.60	0.38	0.98
	EMP	15.39						0.43	0.31	0.74	0.39	0.29	0.68	0.56	0.48	1.04
	ACRE	1534.59						7.56	5.26	12.82	50.76	49.81	100.57	70.05	58.55	128.60
Motel 320	ROOM	6.13	4.17	10.04	2.54	0.90	8	0.32	0.20	0.52	0.27	0.27	0.54	0.41	0.24	0.65
	EMP	12.81	7.20	41.00	10.69	3.38	10	0.51	0.31	0.82	0.30	0.30	0.60	0.69	0.42	1.11
	ACRE	180.71	38.41	364.44	106.57	32.13	11	12.03	7.32	19.35	6.39	6.39	12.78	11.03	6.45	17.48
Resort Hotel 330	ROOM	18.40	7.11	52.41	14.33	5.07	8	*	*	0.24	*	*	0.50	*	*	0.57
	EMP	10.27	NA	NA	NA	NA	1	*	*	0.34	*	*	0.73	*	*	0.82
	ACRE	237.96	33.42	1811.11	568.51	201.00	8	*	*	16.72	*	*	35.63	*	*	40.18

Table 3-2 (continued)

LAND USE GENERATOR — DESCRIPTION & ITE CODE	UNITS	VEHICLE TRIPS PER DAY TO & FROM LAND USE (Rate/Unit as noted) MEAN	MIN	MAX	STATISTICS STD DEV.[a]	STD DEV. OF MEAN[b]	OBS. IN SAMPLE	AM IN	AM OUT	AM TOTAL	PM IN	PM OUT	PM TOTAL	PEAK HOUR OF GENERATOR IN	OUT	TOTAL
RECREATION (400)																
Parks 410	PRKSPC	7.81	2.93	24.28	6.74	2.25	9	*	*	*	*	*	*	*	*	*
	EMP	96.17	42.35	183.62	59.56	29.78	4	*	*	*	*	*	*	*	*	*
	ACRE	30.37	2.99	214.55	62.22	16.07	15	*	*	*	*	*	*	*	*	*
City Parks 411	PRKSPC	6.50	1.91	12.55	5.51	3.18	3	*	*	0.43	*	*	0.60	*	*	1.00
	EMP	51.10	47.06	66.67	9.97	5.76	3	*	*	2.32	*	*	3.21	*	*	5.37
	ACRE	3.66	1.04	129.83	55.36	24.76	5	*	*	2.43	*	*	3.37	*	*	5.63
County Parks 412	PRKSPC	2.18	0.42	21.00	5.58	1.61	12	*	*	*	*	*	0.22	*	*	*
	EMP	26.46	23.33	183.33	50.32	13.96	13	*	*	*	*	*	2.17	*	*	*
	ACRE	5.09	0.17	81.24	21.12	5.12	17	*	*	*	*	*	7.50	*	*	*
State Parks 413	PRKSPC	1.15	0.40	3.13	0.97	0.34	8	*	*	*	*	*	*	*	*	*
	EMP	60.20	21.93	183.33	67.14	20.24	11	*	*	2.35	*	*	4.60	*	*	5.45
	ACRE	0.69	0.05	16.67	6.51	1.81	13	*	*	0.64	*	*	0.06	*	*	1.49
Marinas 420	BOSBER	2.96	1.91	10.04	2.33	0.70	11	*	*	0.09	*	*	0.17	*	*	0.20
	EMP	251.47	231.50	276.67	24.13	12.06	4	*	*	9.75	*	*	18.00	*	*	31.75
	ACRE	20.92	10.32	75.45	32.64	18.84	3	*	*	*	*	*	*	*	*	*
Golf Course 430	PRKSPC	5.32	1.75	16.39	3.47	0.87	16	0.22	0.06	0.28	0.13	0.20	0.33	*	*	*
	EMP	20.63	10.90	75.00	18.27	5.07	13	*	*	*	*	*	*	*	*	*
	ACRE	6.91	2.33	22.78	4.42	0.94	22	0.21	0.06	0.27	0.12	0.27	0.39	*	*	*
INSTITUTIONS (500)																
Military Base 501	EMP	1.80	*	*	NA	NA	*	*	*	*	*	*	*	*	*	*
	DEFEMP	2.20	*	*	NA	NA	*	*	*	*	*	*	*	*	*	*
	CIVEMP	7.10	*	*	NA	NA	*	*	*	*	*	*	*	*	*	*
Day Care Cen 511 (Suburban)	STDNT	4.98	4.10	7.10	1.22	0.55	5	0.53	0.41	0.94	0.44	0.47	0.91	0.59	0.46	1.05
	1K SF	79.14	57.20	125.10	26.40	11.81	5	8.38	6.47	14.85	6.94	7.45	14.40	9.36	7.32	15.68
	EMP	33.20	25.60	50.40	12.73	5.70	5	3.52	2.71	6.23	2.91	3.13	6.04	3.93	3.07	6.60
Elem School 520	STDNT	1.02	0.45	1.82	0.35	0.06	40	0.12	0.07	0.19	*	*	0.03	0.12	0.07	0.19
	EMP	13.10	4.47	26.37	5.28	0.84	40	1.86	1.08	2.94	*	*	0.28	2.34	1.05	3.39
	ACRE	33.69	3.72	123.80	28.41	4.49	40	10.71	6.24	16.95	*	*	1.60	5.96	2.75	8.71
High School 530	STDNT	1.38	0.71	2.49	0.52	0.10	27	0.23	0.10	0.33	0.07	0.14	0.21	0.23	0.10	0.33
	EMP	16.79	4.28	32.87	6.52	1.26	27	1.47	0.64	2.11	0.28	0.55	0.83	2.64	0.94	3.58
	ACRE	23.81	1.02	103.20	26.71	5.97	20	6.01	2.61	8.62	1.13	2.25	3.38	8.70	3.09	11.79
Jr Comm Coll 540	STDNT	1.58	0.94	27.52	5.65	1.23	21	0.16	0.02	0.18	0.05	0.07	0.12	0.16	0.02	0.18
	EMP	10.06	NA	NA	NA	NA	1	*	*	*	*	*	*	*	*	1.73
	ACRE	11.90	NA	NA	NA	NA	1	*	*	*	*	*	*	*	*	2.04

	C1	C2	C3	C4	C5	N	C7	C8	C9	C10	C11	C12	C13	C14	C15
Universit 550 STDNT	2.41	1.40	3.89	0.92	0.37	6	*	*	*	*	*	*	*	*	*
EMP	14.35	NA	NA	NA	NA	1	*	1.00	*	*	4.44	3.57	*	3.17	1.77
ACRE	107.28	NA	NA	NA	NA	1	*	11.56	*	*	51.33	24.70	*	22.13	13.20
Libraries 590 EMP	49.51	36.80	81.91	19.65	9.83	4	*	*	*	*	*	*	*	*	6.74
ACRE	343.78	221.65	909.00	296.91	148.46	4	*	*	*	*	*	*	*	*	46.83

MEDICAL (600)

	C1	C2	C3	C4	C5	N	C7	C8	C9	C10	C11	C12	C13	C14	C15
Hospital 610 BED	11.84	3.00	32.83	7.46	1.49	25	0.72	0.29	1.01	0.38	0.79	1.17	0.44	0.92	1.36
EMP	5.03	2.17	11.11	2.35	0.49	23	0.17	0.08	0.25	0.10	0.19	0.29	0.23	0.34	0.57
ACRE	167.73	24.07	1012.50	229.97	51.42	20	7.67	3.50	11.17	3.70	10.02	13.72	5.21	9.13	14.34
Urban BED	13.08						0.80	0.32	1.12	0.42	0.87	1.29	0.49	1.02	1.50
EMP	5.56						0.19	0.09	0.28	0.11	0.21	0.32	0.25	0.38	0.63
ACRE	185.34						8.48	3.87	12.34	4.09	11.07	15.16	5.76	10.09	15.85
Suburban BED	11.21						0.68	0.27	0.96	0.36	0.75	1.11	0.42	0.87	1.29
EMP	4.76						0.16	0.08	0.24	0.09	0.18	0.27	0.22	0.32	0.54
ACRE	158.86						7.26	3.31	10.58	3.50	9.49	12.99	4.93	8.65	13.58
Nurs Home 620 BED	2.60	1.88	3.97	0.57	0.13	18	*	*	0.05	0.16	0.21	0.17	0.19	*	0.36
EMP	4.03	2.53	9.69	1.99	0.47	18	*	*	*	*	*	*	*	*	0.44
Clinics 630 BED	15.96	NA	NA	NA	NA	1	0.30	0.15	0.45	0.46	0.66	1.12	0.65	0.65	*
EMP	5.89	NA	NA	NA	NA	1	*	*	*	*	*	*	*	*	1.30
ACRE	91.19	NA	NA	NA	NA	1	*	*	*	*	*	*	*	*	*

OFFICE (700)

	C1	C2	C3	C4	C5	N	C7	C8	C9	C10	C11	C12	C13	C14	C15
Gen Off Bldg 710 1K SF	12.43	3.60	28.80	6.03	0.97	39	1.76	0.22	1.98	0.31	1.62	1.93	1.76	1.62	1.98
EMP	3.54	2.42	6.22	1.16	0.24	23	0.43	0.05	0.48	0.08	0.38	0.46	0.43	0.38	0.48
ACRE	250.64	50.75	299.70	580.16	116.03	25	19.46	2.61	22.07	4.41	17.21	21.62	18.46	21.62	22.07
Urban 1K SF	10.33						1.46	0.18	1.65	0.26	1.35	1.60	1.46	1.46	1.65
EMP	2.94						0.36	0.04	0.40	0.07	0.32	0.38	0.36	0.36	0.40
ACRE	208.28						16.17	2.17	18.34	3.66	14.30	17.97	15.34	15.34	18.34
Suburban 1K SF	14.81						2.10	0.26	2.36	0.37	1.93	2.30	2.10	2.10	2.36
EMP	4.22						0.51	0.06	0.57	0.10	0.45	0.55	0.51	0.51	0.57
ACRE	298.64						23.19	3.11	26.30	5.25	20.51	25.76	22.00	22.00	26.30
Med Off Bldg 720 1K SF	39.83	38.68	42.55	2.74	1.94	2	0.64	0.21	0.85	0.89	3.05	3.94	2.55	1.65	4.20
EMP	12.20	NA	NA	NA	NA		0.18	0.06	0.24	0.58	0.99	1.57	0.58	0.99	1.57
ACRE	6666.67	NA	NA	NA	NA	1	100.00	33.33	133.33	316.67	540.00	856.67	543.33	540.00	1083.33
Urban 1K SF	33.10						0.53	0.17	0.71	0.74	2.53	3.27	2.12	1.37	3.49
EMP	10.14						0.15	0.05	0.20	0.48	0.82	1.30	0.48	0.82	1.30
ACRE	5540.00						83.10	27.70	110.80	263.15	448.74	711.89	451.51	448.74	900.25
Suburban 1K SF	47.46						0.76	0.25	1.01	1.06	3.63	4.69	3.04	1.97	5.00
EMP	14.54						0.21	0.07	0.29	0.69	1.18	1.87	0.69	1.18	1.87
ACRE	7943.34						119.15	39.71	158.86	377.31	643.41	1020.72	647.38	643.41	1290.79

Table 3-2 (continued)

LAND USE GENERATOR DESCRIPTION & ITE CODE	UNITS	VEHICLE TRIPS PER DAY TO & FROM LAND USE (Rate/Unit as noted)			STATISTICS			VEHICLE TRIP RATES IN PEAK HOUR						PEAK HOUR OF GENERATOR		
		MEAN	MIN	MAX	STD DEV.[a]	STD DEV. OF MEAN[b]	OBS. IN SAMPLE	AM IN	AM OUT	AM TOTAL	PM IN	PM OUT	PM TOTAL	IN	OUT	TOTAL
Gov Off Bldg 730	1K SF	67.72	NA	NA	NA	NA	1	4.83	0.95	5.78	*	*	*	8.06	2.78	10.84
	EMP	11.95	NA	NA	NA	NA	1	0.85	0.17	1.02	*	*	*	1.42	0.49	1.91
	ACRE	66.25	NA	NA	NA	NA	1	4.80	0.85	5.65	*	*	*	7.88	2.72	10.60
Urban	1K SF	56.28						4.01	0.79	4.80	0.00	0.00	0.00	6.70	2.31	9.01
	EMP	9.93						0.71	0.14	0.85	0.00	0.00	0.00	1.18	0.41	1.59
	ACRE	55.05						3.99	0.71	4.70	0.00	0.00	0.00	6.55	2.26	8.81
Suburban	1K SF	80.69						5.75	1.13	6.89	0.00	0.00	0.00	9.60	3.31	12.92
	EMP	14.24						1.01	0.20	1.22	0.00	0.00	0.00	1.69	0.58	2.28
	ACRE	78.94						5.72	1.01	6.73	0.00	0.00	0.00	9.39	3.24	12.63
Civic Center 740	1K SF	25.00	NA	NA	NA	NA	1	2.00	0.25	2.25	0.89	1.97	2.86	0.89	1.97	2.86
	EMP	6.09	NA	NA	NA	NA	1	0.49	0.06	0.55	0.22	0.48	0.70	0.22	0.48	0.70
Off Parks 750	1K SF	20.65	9.40	30.30	11.68	6.74	3	2.30	0.34	2.64	0.40	1.96	2.36	2.30	0.34	2.64
	EMP	3.33	2.92	3.53	0.32	0.19	3	0.55	0.08	0.63	0.09	0.45	0.54	0.55	0.08	0.63
	ACRE	276.38	153.68	340.87	93.86	54.19	3	45.83	6.78	52.61	7.57	37.12	44.69	45.83	6.78	52.61
Urban	1K SF	17.16						1.91	0.28	2.19	0.33	1.63	1.96	1.91	0.28	2.19
	EMP	2.77						0.46	0.07	0.52	0.07	0.37	0.45	0.46	0.07	0.52
	ACRE	229.67						38.08	5.63	43.72	6.29	30.85	37.14	38.08	5.63	43.72
Suburban	1K SF	24.60						2.74	0.41	3.15	0.48	2.34	2.81	2.74	0.41	3.15
	EMP	3.97						0.66	0.10	0.75	0.11	0.54	0.64	0.66	0.10	0.75
	ACRE	329.31						54.61	8.08	62.68	9.02	44.23	53.25	54.61	8.08	62.68
Research Cen 760	1K SF	5.34	1.78	12.98	4.02	1.42	8	1.11	0.10	1.21	0.12	0.81	0.93	2.28	0.21	2.49
	EMP	2.37	0.96	5.33	1.29	0.43	9	0.45	0.03	0.48	0.43	0.03	0.46	0.03	0.55	0.58
	ACRE	57.25	15.61	1323.08	525.95	214.72	6	21.58	1.13	22.71	1.27	20.18	21.45	21.58	1.13	22.71
Urban	1K SF	4.44						0.92	0.08	1.01	0.10	0.67	0.77	1.89	0.17	2.07
	EMP	1.97						0.37	0.02	0.40	0.36	0.02	0.38	0.02	0.46	0.48
	ACRE	47.57						17.93	0.94	18.87	1.06	16.77	17.82	17.93	0.94	18.87
Suburban	1K SF	6.36						1.32	0.12	1.44	0.14	0.97	1.11	2.72	0.25	2.97
	EMP	2.82						0.54	0.04	0.57	0.51	0.04	0.55	0.04	0.66	0.69
	ACRE	68.21						25.71	1.35	27.06	1.51	24.04	25.56	25.71	1.35	27.06
Hi-Tech Off Bldg 770	1K SF	7.28	4.08	8.71	2.18	1.26	3	1.39	0.10	1.49	0.08	1.27	1.35	1.39	0.10	1.49
	EMP	2.76	2.39	3.27	0.47	0.27	3	0.53	0.04	0.57	0.03	0.48	0.51	0.53	0.04	0.57
Urban	1K SF	6.05						1.16	0.08	1.24	0.07	1.06	1.12	1.16	0.08	1.24
	EMP	2.29						0.44	0.03	0.47	0.02	0.40	0.42	0.44	0.03	0.47
Suburban	1K SF	8.67						1.66	0.12	1.78	0.10	1.51	1.61	1.66	0.12	1.78
	EMP	3.29						0.63	0.05	0.68	0.04	0.57	0.61	0.63	0.05	0.68

Land Use	Unit															
Twnhs Off Bldg 780	1K SF	23.47	19.06	24.78	4.94	2.85	3	2.22	0.49	2.71	0.66	1.54	2.20	2.22	0.49	2.71
Urban	1K SF	19.50						1.84	0.41	2.25	0.55	1.28	1.83	1.84	0.41	2.25
Suburban	1K SF	27.96						2.65	0.58	3.23	0.79	1.83	2.62	2.65	0.58	3.23
RETAIL (800)																
Disc Shop Ctr 815	1K SF	70.13	25.53	106.88	27.83	10.52	7	*	*	0.51	*	*	4.43	*	*	6.97
	EMP	32.53	28.08	35.46	3.10	1.38	5	*	*	0.37	*	*	3.17	*	*	4.54
	ACRE	456.31	127.64	480.63	302.57	135.31	5	*	*	5.27	*	*	45.70	*	*	63.73
Shp Ctr (<100k sf) 820,821	1K SF	83.43	18.10	270.89	45.47	5.29	74	1.50	1.33	2.83	4.89	5.08	9.97	5.72	5.69	11.41
	EMP	38.18	17.68	82.05	16.71	3.28	26	0.72	0.66	1.38	2.28	2.42	4.70	2.42	2.28	4.70
	ACRE	786.72	303.55	2277.27	528.25	99.83	28	13.48	12.47	25.95	46.01	50.00	96.01	46.01	50.00	96.01
Sh Ctr(100k,500k) 822,823,824,825	1K SF	49.64	2.80	116.14	22.26	1.84	146	0.89	0.53	1.42	2.59	2.65	5.24	2.35	3.05	5.40
	EMP	28.40	15.45	53.05	10.13	1.85	30	0.45	0.33	0.78	1.58	1.55	3.13	1.58	1.55	3.13
	ACRE	462.40	46.94	1431.67	268.74	40.06	45	6.55	5.14	11.69	25.57	25.57	51.14	25.57	25.57	51.14
Sh Cr(500k,1000k) 826	1K SF	34.44	10.30	61.18	11.38	1.42	64	0.47	0.22	0.69	1.61	1.59	3.20	1.93	1.87	3.80
	EMP	16.72	3.20	53.62	11.35	2.32	24	0.21	0.12	0.33	0.81	0.80	1.61	0.91	0.89	1.80
	ACRE	405.22	119.10	1178.12	251.48	51.33	24	5.83	3.27	9.10	19.92	19.47	39.39	24.87	24.40	49.27
Sh Ctr(>1000k sf) 827,828	1K SF	29.59	11.99	72.82	16.13	3.80	18	0.47	0.16	0.63	1.17	1.42	2.59	1.59	1.54	3.13
	EMP	12.50	6.14	42.41	14.60	5.16	8	0.10	0.03	0.13	0.30	0.34	0.64	0.40	0.32	0.72
	ACRE	268.31	62.17	1259.74	376.87	125.62	9	3.35	0.92	4.27	9.57	10.93	20.50	12.79	10.33	23.12
Qual St Dwn Rest 831	SEAT	2.95	1.77	5.50	1.16	0.32	13	*	*	0.03	0.14	0.06	0.20	0.16	0.11	0.27
	1K SF	97.27	48.56	139.33	30.81	8.54	13	*	*	0.94	4.57	1.57	6.14	5.95	4.40	10.35
	EMP	14.53	9.16	29.98	5.93	1.65	13	*	*	0.13	0.68	0.26	0.94	0.76	0.72	1.48
	ACRE	478.44	223.21	806.32	201.42	60.73	11	*	*	5.08	25.89	9.67	35.56	28.94	26.93	55.87
Fast Food Restau 833	SEAT	22.25	8.88	35.78	8.21	2.28	13	0.30	0.25	0.55	0.65	0.55	1.20	1.59	1.65	3.24
	1K SF	685.61	284.00	1359.50	280.14	77.70	13	8.18	6.82	15.00	21.84	19.28	41.12	58.95	58.27	117.22
	EMP	54.78	28.40	90.63	22.05	6.37	12	0.52	0.44	0.96	1.68	1.54	3.22	3.97	4.28	8.25
	ACRE	2985.22	2772.22	3298.57	268.22	154.86	3	4.02	3.37	7.39	100.49	89.73	190.22	172.90	189.75	362.65
New Car Sales 841	1K SF	47.52	15.45	79.00	36.15	20.87	3	2.12	1.76	3.88	1.26	2.82	4.58	*	*	*
	EMP	24.04	10.82	38.55	13.94	8.05	3	1.08	0.90	1.98	0.34	0.69	1.03	*	*	*
	ACRE	385.57	162.25	526.67	206.84	119.42	3	16.42	13.58	30.00	15.93	25.50	41.43	22.27	24.09	46.36
Service Stations 844	PUMP	*	*	NA	NA	NA	*	*	*	10.76	*	*	14.36	*	*	17.24
	STN	*	*	NA	NA	NA	*	*	*	74.00	*	*	98.75	*	*	118.50
Food Store 850	1K SF	*	*	NA	NA	NA	*	0.38	0.16	0.54	4.54	4.28	8.82	3.47	3.64	7.11
	ACRE	*	*	NA	NA	NA	*	9.86	4.20	14.06	92.12	86.06	178.18	92.12	86.06	178.18
Conv Market 851	1K SF	756.44	396.00	1438.00	334.23	118.17	8	32.65	32.29	64.94	25.77	25.09	50.86	32.65	32.29	64.94
	EMP	275.07	158.40	359.50	24.02	67.95	8	11.87	11.74	23.61	9.25	9.01	18.26	11.69	12.63	24.32
	ACRE	289.70	221.33	419.50	74.37	33.26	5	42.73	42.27	85.00	11.94	11.63	23.57	*	*	*

Table 3-2 (continued)

LAND USE GENERATOR DESCRIPTION & ITE CODE	UNITS	VEHICLE TRIPS PER DAY TO & FROM LAND USE (Rate/Unit as noted)			STATISTICS			VEHICLE TRIP RATES IN PEAK HOUR								
								AM			PM			PEAK HOUR OF GENERATOR		
		MEAN	MIN	MAX	STD DEV.[a]	STD DEV. OF MEAN[b]	OBS. IN SAMPLE	IN	OUT	TOTAL	IN	OUT	TOTAL	IN	OUT	TOTAL
SERVICES (900)																
Walk-in-Bank 911	1K SF	169.00	NA	NA	NA	NA	1	*	*	4.40	8.34	8.34	16.68	17.01	17.99	35.80
	EMP	44.47	NA	NA	NA	NA	1	*	*	1.16	3.16	3.16	6.32	4.47	4.93	9.40
	ACRE	1056.25	NA	NA	NA	NA	1	*	*	27.50	231.67	231.67	963.33	255.00	255.00	510.00
Drive-in-Bank 912	1K SF	291.11	134.67	1520.00	391.06	117.91	11	3.71	3.23	6.94	15.30	15.85	31.15	20.47	19.75	40.22
	EMP	79.79	31.85	380.00	101.75	30.68	11	0.96	0.84	1.80	3.92	4.16	8.08	5.86	5.65	11.47
	ACRE	849.30	414.00	1647.50	545.77	272.88	4	24.17	2.71	26.88	96.24	104.17	200.41	96.24	104.17	200.41
Walk-in Sv & Ln 913	1K SF	61.00	NA	NA	NA	NA	1	*	*	1.33	*	*	5.33	*	*	9.67
	EMP	30.50	NA	NA	NA	NA	1	*	*	0.67	*	*	2.67	*	*	4.83
	ACRE	261.42	NA	NA	NA	NA	1	*	*	5.71	*	*	22.86	*	*	41.43
Drive-in Sv & Ln 914	1K SF	74.17	NA	NA	NA	NA	1	*	*	1.00	*	*	6.83	*	*	9.67
	EMP	49.44	NA	NA	NA	NA	1	*	*	0.67	*	*	4.56	*	*	6.44
	ACRE	1483.33	NA	NA	NA	NA	1	*	*	20.00	*	*	136.67	*	*	193.33

LEGEND FOR UNITS:

			VEHICLE TRIPS PER ...
1K SF	1,000 SQ. FT. GFA	CFL/DY	COMMERCIAL FLIGHT PER DAY	ROOM	HOTEL/MOTEL ROOM
ACRE	ACRE	CIVEMP	CIVILIAN EMPLOYEE	SEAT	RESTAURANT SEAT
BED	HOSPITAL BED	DEFEMP	DEFENSE FORCES EMPLOYEE	STDNT	STUDENT
BOSBER	BOAT OR SHIP BERTH	DU	DWELLING UNIT	STN	GAS (OR DIESEL) STATION
		EMP	EMPLOYEE		
		FLT/DY	FLIGHT PER DAY		
		PRKSPC	PARKING SPACE		
		PUMP	GAS (OR DIESEL) PUMP		

SOURCE: Joe Mehra and C. Richard Keller [11].

[a]The standard deviation of the sample is $s = \sqrt{\Sigma(x_i - \bar{x})^2/(n-1)}$, where x_i is an individual observation; $\bar{x}$ is the mean of all the observations ($\bar{x} = \Sigma x_i/n$), and n is the number of observations.

[b]The standard deviation of the mean, S_x, is $s/\sqrt{n}$.

SUMMARY OF TRIP GENERATION RATES

Land Use/Building Type <u>Shopping Center over 1,250,000 G.S.F.</u>   ITE Land Use Code <u>828</u>

Independent Variable—Trips per <u>1,000 Gross Square Feet of Leasable Area</u>

			Average Trip Rate	Maximum Rate	Minimum Rate	Correlation Coefficient	Number of Studies	Average Size of Independent Variable/Study
Average Weekday Vehicle Trip Ends			34.1	72.8	18.9		7	1394
Peak	A.M.	Enter	0.36	0.52	0.16		4	1357
Hour	Between	Exit	0.13	0.21	0.09		4	1357
of	7 and 9	Total	0.49	0.73	0.25		4	1357
Adjacent	P.M.	Enter	1.10	1.31	0.89		6	1404
Street	Between	Exit	1.41	1.95	0.89		6	1404
Traffic	4 and 6	Total	2.51	2.88	1.79		6	1404
Peak	A.M.	Enter	1.20	1.32	1.07		2	1259
Hour		Exit	1.39	2.60	0.66		3	1283
of		Total	1.94	2.14	1.74		2	1259
Generator	P.M.	Enter	1.42	1.87	1.05		6	1405
		Exit	1.76	3.30	1.16		7	1394
		Total	2.93	4.12	2.21		6	1404
Saturday Vehicle Trip Ends			39.0	62.4	22.5		6	1377
Peak		Enter	1.83	2.04	1.66		3	1343
Hour of		Exit	2.23	2.88	1.64		4	1340
Generator		Total	3.84	4.30	3.30		3	1343
Sunday Vehicle Trip Ends			23.5	40.3	12.5		5	1352
Peak		Enter	1.48	1.50	1.47		2	1259
Hour of		Exit	1.85	2.42	1.38		3	1283
Generator		Total	3.03	3.21	2.84		2	1259

Source Numbers _____ 13, 42, 48, 100, 110

ITE Technical Committee 6A-6—Trip Generation Rates

Date: _____ 1975, 1979, Rev. 1982

G.S.F. = Gross Square Feet

Figure 3-1 Example of the ITE trip-generation data. SOURCE: Institute of Transportation Engineers [9].

persons who are paid on Fridays biweekly, the Friday payday traffic-generation rate should be used in a TIA for a bank.

3. *Location variation:* Nearly all the data contained in the ITE *Trip Generation* manual were collected at suburban locations. Also, the data are from throughout the United States and Canada. Specific site conditions, such as proximity to the development, the availability of transit, and walk-in traffic, can result in vehicular traffic-generation rates which are much different.

4. *Passer-by traffic:* Some generators attract traffic from the passing traffic stream (e.g., fast-food restaurants). In such cases, the volume of traffic added to the adjacent street(s) is less than the driveway volume on and off the site. This problem is specifically addressed a few pages further on, in a section entitled "Passer-by Traffic."

5. *Mixed-use Development:* All the trip-generation rates are from isolated stand-alone developments. When several uses are included in the same development, the traffic added to adjacent streets may be less than the sum of the individual

trip-generation volumes. The reduction would be attributable to trips being made internal to the development.

6. *Vehicular trips:* The generation rates are vehicular trips for "average" vehicle occupancy.

7. *Variability in rates:* Inspection of the minimum and maximum rates, the standard deviation of the sample data, or plots of the data such as illustrated in Figure 3-2 clearly indicates that there is substantial variation in trip-generation rates from one development to another.

8. *Sample size:* For some types of generators, the sample size is extremely small — in some cases only one or two studies. Three observations is generally considered a minimum for any statistical inference.

Variation in Traffic Volumes.   The time at which peak traffic occurs, as well as the duration, depends upon the city size and activity patterns. For example, in a city of 100,000 population, most work trips will be less than 15 minutes in length. Residential areas will generate peak outbound traffic about 7:20 to 7:45 a.m. and peak inbound at about 5:00 to 5:30 p.m. A suburban "bedroom" community in a large urban area will generate peaks at about 6:30 to 7:30 a.m. (outbound) and 5:30 to 6:30 p.m. (inbound). In a small city, the peaks typically extend from about 7:30 to 8:00 a.m. and 5:00 to 5:30 p.m. In a large urban area, the morning peak might extend from about 6:45 to 8:15 a.m. and the evening peak from 4:30 to 6:30 p.m., or longer.

Site-oriented traffic generally exhibits substantial hourly variation. Therefore, in most cases it is necessary to analyze the traffic impact at two different time periods: (1) the peak traffic period of the street and (2) the peak traffic-generation period of the proposed generator. Typical traffic-generation periods for general types of land uses are as follows:

Residential: The peak periods of site-generated traffic coincide with the peak periods of the street system. The peak outbound movement coincides with the a.m. peak traffic period on the street and the peak inbound movement coincides with the p.m. peak traffic period.

Neighborhood commercial: The peak of the generation coincides with the peak of the adjacent street.

Regional retail: The peak inbound generation occurs between about 7:00 to 8:00 p.m. The peak outbound occurs between about 9:15 to 9:45 p.m. for a 10:00 p.m. closing. Approximately two-thirds of the hourly volume will occur in a half-hour period. Therefore, if the exiting trip rate for the p.m. peak of the generator is 1.8 trips per 1,000 square feet, the flow rate will be about 2.4 trips per 1,000 square feet: (1.8 trips per hr) (2/3) (60 min./hr − 30 min.). The weekend peaks are less pronounced than the weekday peak, since the peak period is extended over a longer period of time. A two- to three-hour peak period normally occurs during midafternoon. Regional retail centers will generate substantial traffic during the peak period of the adjacent streets. Figures 3-3 and 3-4 give examples of various traffic conditions at Regional Shopping Centers. See pages 42–43.

Office: Office developments characteristically have peaks which coincide with the peak periods on the street system. Flex-time and staggered hours spread the site-oriented traffic over longer time periods, and in large cities, where the interval between the earliest and latest hours exceeds one hour, may also reduce the peak-hour generation rates (both for peak of generation and peak of street). In some cases where little interface is needed outside the organization, the work hours may be scheduled to avoid the peak street traffic. Peak directional movement of office and traffic is the reverse of residential traffic, i.e., inbound in the a.m. and outbound in the p.m.

Industrial: The peak traffic periods of manufacturing and assembly plants may or may not coincide with the traditional a.m. and p.m. peak periods of the arterial street

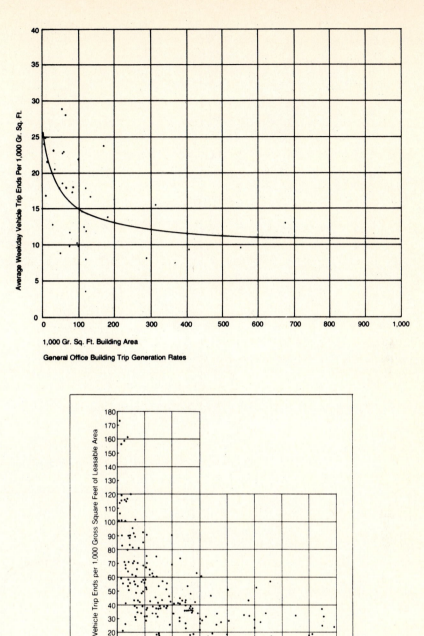

General Office Building Trip Generation Rates

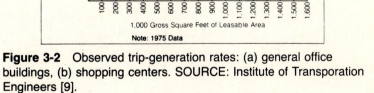

Note: 1975 Data

Figure 3-2 Observed trip-generation rates: (a) general office buildings, (b) shopping centers. SOURCE: Institute of Transporation Engineers [9].

system. In densely developed areas, shifts are commonly scheduled to avoid these peak traffic periods. However the trip-generation characteristics of some very high-tech sites may be similar to those of offices.

Urban arterials experience two peaks, as shown in Figure 3-5 (p. 43). The morning and evening peaks include approximately the same work trips; however, since considerably more nonwork trips are made in the afternoon, the evening peak is generally the larger of the two. Figure 3-6 (p. 44) shows that between 8% and 12% of the 24-hour

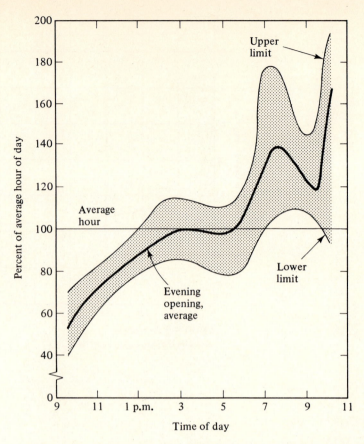

(a) Total traffic entering and leaving regional shopping centers on weekdays

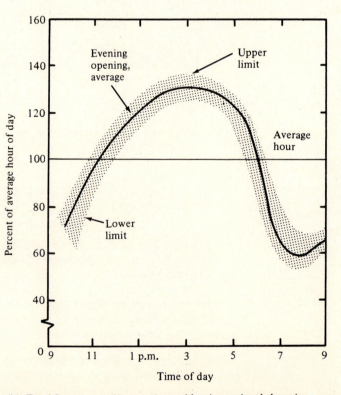

(b) Total Saturday traffic entering and leaving regional shopping center

Figure 3-3 Examples of hourly variation in regional shopping-center traffic.
SOURCE: adapted from Donald E. Cleveland and Edward E. Mueller [5].

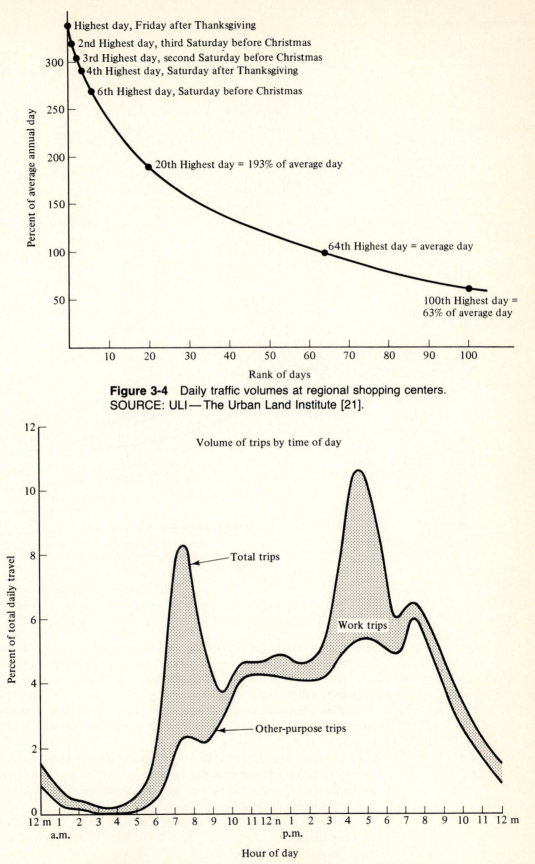

Figure 3-4 Daily traffic volumes at regional shopping centers.
SOURCE: ULI—The Urban Land Institute [21].

Figure 3-5 Typical variation in hourly volumes on urban streets.
SOURCE: The Traffic Institute, Northwestern University [19].

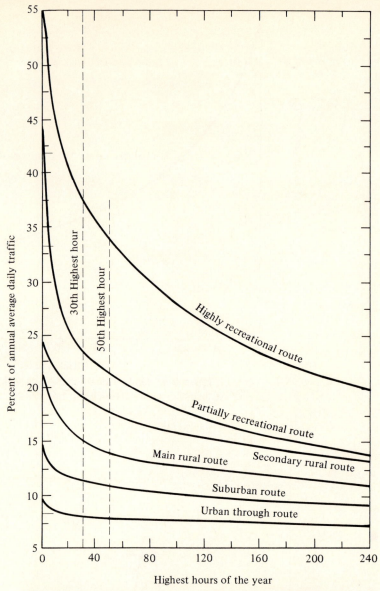

Figure 3-6 Hourly volumes on various types of traffic routes.
SOURCE: The Traffic Institute, Northwestern University [19].

weekday traffic on an urban street is carried in the highest one-hour period of the day. The percentage of the 24-hour traffic decreases as city size and congestion increase. Ten percent is typical for small and medium-size cities and for the less congested streets in large metropolitan areas. Where the peak period is two to three or more hours in duration, the highest one-hour period will be about 8.5% of the 24-hour traffic volume. Under these conditions, approximately the same percentage of the 24-hour traffic will be carried in several hours of the day.

In urban areas having a diversified and stable economy, arterial streets are subject to very little weekday or seasonal variation. On the other hand, areas which have large recreational or tourist activities may experience considerable seasonal variation in arterial traffic volumes. In these cases, the site-design and traffic impact analysis should not be based on the annual average daily traffic (ADT); rather, the 30th to 50th highest hour of the year should be used. Figure 3-6 compares hourly volumes on several types of traffic routes.

Reliability and Transferability of Trip-Generation Rates from Various Sources.
Comparison of trip-generation data from various sources indicates that similar land use
activities in the United States and Canada have similar trip-generation characteristics.
Regional variation is very small compared to the variation between individual establishments within the same area; however, significant differences in generation rates have been
found for similar land uses located in different areas of a city (i.e., a downtown apartment
complex compared to a suburban complex; or a downtown commercial development
compared to a suburban shopping center).

The common practice is to use the mean trip-generation rates in traffic impact
analysis. When only a few observations are available (see the column headed "Number of
Studies" in the ITE Report, *Trip Generation*), the information should be used only with
extreme caution. Even when a substantial number of observations were available in
calculating the mean trip-generation rate, it should be recognized that there is substantial
variation in land use activities of the same type and that it is very unlikely that a specific
proposed development will in fact be "average."

The statistics presented in the report "Development and Application of Trip Generation Rates" [11] provide information which is useful in dealing with this problem. Again,
shopping centers over 1 million square feet (ITE Codes 827 and 828) will be used as an
example. Recall that the standard deviation of trips per 1,000 square feet for this land use
generator is $s = 16.13$ and that the standard deviation of the mean is $s/\sqrt{n} = 3.80$.

Using standard statistical techniques, the variability in trip generation can be evaluated using the t values of the standard normal distribution (large single sizes, generally
assumed to be 30 or more for practical purposes) or the Student t distribution (where the
sample size is less than 30). These t values can be found in any statistics text; selected
values are presented for convenience in Table 3-3.

The confidence limits on the mean trip-generation rate are found by

$$CL = \bar{x} \pm t\left(\frac{s}{\sqrt{n}}\right)$$

For shopping centers over 1 million square feet the upper and lower 80% confidence
limits are

$$\text{lower 80\% CL} = 29.59 - (1.33)(3.80) = 24.54, \text{ say } 24.5$$
$$\text{upper 80\% CL} = 29.59 + (1.33)(3.80) = 34.64, \text{ say } 34.6$$

Thus, we can say there is an 80% chance that the true mean for such shopping centers is
bracketed by 24.5 trips per 1,000 square feet and 34.6 trips per 1,000 square feet. Or, there
is a 20% chance that the true mean is outside these limits. With such precision in
measurement of the true mean trip-generation rate, the common practice of making
adjustments for small differences in auto occupancy or transit use is highly questionable.

TABLE 3-3

The t Statistic for the Normal Distribution

Sample Size n	In One-Tail				In Two-Tail			
	0.05	0.10	0.15	0.20	0.05	0.10	0.15	0.20
5	2.13	1.53	—	—	2.78	2.13	—	1.53
10	1.83	1.38	—	—	2.26	1.83	—	1.38
15	1.76	1.34	—	—	2.14	1.76	—	1.34
20	1.73	1.33	—	—	2.10	1.73	—	1.33
25	1.71	1.32	—	—	2.06	1.71	—	1.32
30 or more	1.64	1.28	1.04	0.85	1.96	1.64	1.44	1.28

The likelihood that a development might generate more, or less, traffic than average can also be assessed using

$$x = \bar{x} \pm ts$$

Continuing with the shopping-center data and calculating the 85th percentile trip-generation rate,

$$x = 29.59 + (1.04)(16.13) = 46.36, \text{ say } 46.4$$

It can then be concluded that there is only a 15% chance that if the mean is 29.59 trips per 1,000 square feet, such a center will generate more than about 46 trips per 1,000 square feet.

Passer-by Traffic.   Land use activities such as offices, industrial parks, hotels, high-quality restaurants, and residential development generate traffic which intends to have a trip end at the particular site and therefore constitutes new traffic on the street system. However, a sizable portion of the traffic generated by fast-food restaurants and gas stations is already on the adjacent street and merely stops at the establishment in passing by (i.e. passer-by traffic).

The data presented in Table 3-4 suggest that a high percentage of the traffic generated by small shopping centers, service stations, and fast-food restaurants is otherwise on the adjacent street. On the other hand, most of the traffic generated by banks, hardware stores, and large shopping centers consists of new traffic.

The shopping-center data summarized in Table 3-4 show that, on the average, smaller centers attract a larger percentage of their traffic from passer-by traffic. Such a pattern is to be expected. However, the available data exhibit substantial variation for centers of similar size. Several factors in addition to differences between individual centers may account for much of this variation. For example, the data presented in Table 3-5 show considerable variation in the percent passer-by traffic by the time of day. This, and logic, suggests that data on passer-by traffic should be obtained for both weekdays and Saturdays as well as for peak of the street and peak of the generator.

TABLE 3-4

Trips Attracted from Passing Traffic

Generator	Percent of Site Traffic	Source
Banks with drive-thru windows	14%	(d)
Supermarkets	28%	(d)
Hardware stores	8%	(d)
Convenience stores	16%	(d)
	45%	(a)
Fast-food restaurants	45%	(c)
Service stations	58%	(b)
Shopping centers, sq. ft. GLA:		(e)
> 1 million, 2 centers, range 12%–25%	19%	
800 to 1 million, 3 centers, range 9%–25%	15%	
600 to 799,999, 2 centers, range 14%–23%	19%	
400 to 599,999, 6 centers, range 5%–48%	32%	
200 to 399,999, 4 centers, range 17%–36%	41%	
100 to 299,999	—	
< 100,000, 4 centers, range 51%–72%	60%	

SOURCES: (a) Carl H. Buttke [3]

(b) Joe Mehra and C. Richard Keller [11]

(c) The Traffic Institute, Northwestern University [19]

(d) Nazir Lalani [10]

(e) Developed from a composite of data from the following references: Steven A. Smith [15], Louis J. Slade and Federick E. Gorove [14], Carl H. Buttke [4]

TABLE 3-5

Percentage of Average Weekday Shopping-Center Trips Which Are Attracted from Traffic on Adjacent Streets

NAME	TGLA	LOCATION	2–9 p.m.	4–5 p.m.	5–6 p.m.
Meriden Square	500	Meriden, Conn.	5%	10%	6%
Enfield Square	660	Enfield, Conn.	14%	18%	26%
Cristal Mall	845	Waterford, Conn.	9%	18%	9%
Westfarms	1,059	W. Hartford, Conn.	12%	15%	20%
Composite			11%	16%	20%

SOURCE: Connecticut Department of Transportation, "Transportation Characteristics of Regional Shopping Malls within Connecticut," June 1985, p. 16.

Buttke [4] presents previously unpublished information which indicates that the percentage of passer-by trips is slightly less on Saturdays than on the average weekday (22% on Saturdays compared to 27% on weekdays, see Table 3-6).

Mixed-Use Development. When an activity center is developed with a mix of different land uses (e.g., retail and office), there are fewer trips on and off the site than if the retail and office activities are developed on separate sites. In a mixed-use development, some individuals will complete two or more purposes without leaving the site. For example, some of the lunch and shopping trips by office workers will be satisfied at the on-site retail establishments. Some visitors to the offices also will complete shopping trips within the development. Unfortunately, there are limited data relative to the magnitude of the trip reduction for different-sized developments and mixes of activities. The traffic generation is often taken to be the sum of the "free-standing" traffic generations. This practice produces an estimate of the traffic impact which is biased toward the conservative (worst-case) side. With small developments the difference is not significant, because the opportunity for "dual-purpose" trips diminishes as the size of the development decreases. In short, the number of dual-purpose trips is less than the error involved in the estimation of total trip ends.

Unpublished data collected at a mixed-use (office, retail, and hotels) development in southern California which contains approximately 5 million square feet indicated that total trip generation was nearly 20% less than the number of trips which would be generated by the same uses developed stand-alone.

The Colorado-Wyoming Section of ITE conducted surveys at mixed-use centers ranging in size from just over 91,000 square feet to 1.25 million square feet [6]. The developments consisted of a wide range of uses, including office, retail, hotel/motel, supermarkets, banks, and restaurants. Interviews of 1,132 persons indicated that 77% came for a single purpose. Thus, the trip generation of mixed-use developments might be 20% or 25% lower than stand-alone development. The average total trip generation for

TABLE 3-6

Percentage of Trips Attracted from Traffic on Adjacent Streets: Saturday versus Average Weekdays

Gross Leasable Area × 1,000 sq. ft.	Saturday		Weekday	
	Time Period	Percent from Passing Traffic	Time Period	Percent from Passing Traffic
720	11:00–4:00	23	3:00–7:00	23
890	11:00–4:00	5	3:00–8:00	12
402	9 a.m.–10 p.m.	38	4:00–6:00	48
430	1:00–9:00	22	1:00–9:00	24

SOURCE: Carl H. Buttke [4, p. III-4].

the combined sites studied was only 8% less than that which would be expected using the average ITE trip-generation rates. Therefore, many of the secondary trips may occur because of the availability of multiple opportunities in close proximity to primary destinations. If the secondary destinations were not so located, the secondary trips might not occur at all or would occur at much lower rates.

As shown in Table 3-7, most of the interviewees went to a particular mixed-use development for a single purpose; theaters, restaurants, and banking especially reflect this tendency. As might be expected, persons making work trips expressed the greatest propensity to complete additional trip purposes on the site (less than 70% made the trip for the primary purpose only). However, it is interesting to note that most made only one additional trip.

A survey of employees at the North Park East Complex in Dallas, Texas [7] indicated that a.m. peak-hour trips were reduced by 2.6% and p.m. peak-hour trips were reduced by 13.1%. A summary of the mix of uses and trip-generation data is given in Table 3-8.

Satellite Development.   Regional shopping centers attract other commercial retail developments to property surrounding the center. Unpublished data from Barton-Aschman Associates, Inc., indicate that the interaction (shared trips) may be 10% or more of the traffic generated by a satellite development. The data presented in Table 3-9 indicate that the interaction traffic can be substantial.

TABLE 3-7

Distribution of Daily Trips by Number of Trip Purposes and Primary Purpose

	Number of Purposes Reported by Interviewee			
Primary Purpose	1	2	3 +	Total
Bank/Savings & Loan	83%	8%	9%	100%
Hardware Store	76%	22%	2%	100%
Supermarket	77%	17%	16%	100%
Theater	94%	6%	0%	100%
Office/Work Location	68%	30%	2%	100%
Retail Shopping	73%	12%*	15%	100%
Restaurant	85%	9%	6%	100%
Health Club	71%	21%	8%	100%
Post Office	63%	24%	13%	100%
Other	100%	0%	0%	100%

SOURCE: Colorado–Wyoming Section, Institute of Transportation Engineers [6].
*Includes multiple-purpose retail shopping trips.

TABLE 3-8

Summary Data for the Northpark East Complex, Dallas, Texas

Mix of Uses
Office, 912,329 sq. ft.
Restaurants, 36,704 sq. ft.
Other, 67,553 sq. ft.
Employees
Total, 2,585
Survey, random sample of 347
Trips Generated by the 347 Employees Surveyed

	Total Monthly Peak Hour Trips	Monthly Mixed-Use Trips	Mixed-Use Trips As Percent of Total
A.M. peak hour	113	4368	2.6%
P.M. peak hour	529	4040	13.1%

SOURCE: DeShazo, Starek, and Tang, Inc. [7]

TABLE 3-9

Traffic Interaction Between a Regional Shopping Center and Satellite Development

Shopping Center	Type of Satellite Development	Day	Percent of Satellite Traffic Interaction with Shopping Center		
			Average	Peak of Mall	
				Enter	Exit
Valley Vista Mall Harlingen, Tx.	Discount store	Sat.	28%	37%	30%

Example

A 200,000-sq.-ft. GLA discount store is proposed to be located opposite a regional shopping center. The estimated total (entering and leaving) peak-of-generator traffic of a free-standing discount store is calculated to be

$$(200,000 \text{ GLA})(6.9 \text{ trips}/1,000 \text{ GLA}) = 1,380 \text{ trips}$$

Assuming that the inbound and outbound traffic is approximately equal, approximately 690 vehicles per hour (vph) enter and leave the discount store. The number of trips from the discount store to the mall is then established to be

$$(690)(28\%) = 190$$

A similar number of trips (190) would be made from the shopping center to the discount store. The total new traffic to be assigned to the external roadway would be 1,000 trips (1,380–380).

Notice that the number of interacting trips is calculated as a percentage of the satellite development and not of the regional shopping center.

Directional Distribution of Site Traffic

After the site-generated traffic is estimated, the next step in the site traffic analysis is to determine the directional distribution of that traffic. The assumptions and method used in estimating the direction in which traffic will approach and depart the site will vary with several location-specific conditions, such as the following:

- Size of the proposed development
- Type of development (e.g. industrial, commercial, residential, etc.)
- Prevailing conditions on the existing street system
- Available data base

Since a wide range of situations will be encountered, even within a single municipality, ordinances should not require the use of specific techniques or methodology for the conduct of traffic impact analyses. When ordinances specify technique and methodology, the tendency is for approval/disapproval of the TIA to be based on "mechanical method" rather than on the appropriateness of the analysis and the proper interpretation of the potential traffic impacts.

Thus, it is essential that the analyst preparing the TIA be able, and permitted, to exercise appropriate judgment. Various methodologies which have been effectively applied include the following:

- Primary market
- Analogy
- Origin–destination
- Gravity model

Primary Market. The primary-market or area-of-influence method utilizes a unique trade area or area of influence. It is the geographical area from which a high percentage (80%) of the site-generated traffic will be "drawn" to the site. The boundary of the trade area might be identified by one of the following techniques:

Method 1. Delineate the trade area as a regular geometric shape (commonly a circle or square with the site at the center) with a radius of travel appropriate for the type of development.

Method 2. Delineate the trade area by establishing the most distant points that can be reached within some selected travel time over the specific street system.

Method 3. Use Reilly's Law of Retail Gravitation to establish the boundary between competing centers.

Travel time (not distance) and trip purpose are the determinants of trip length. As shown in Figure 3-7, shoppers travel farther to a regional shopping center than to a neighborhood center. For a regional shopping center, the primary trade area is that which is within 30 minutes of the center (20% come from a longer distance).

Maximum travel times for identifying the primary trade area of other land use activities are:

- Community shopping center: 15–20 minutes
- Neighborhood shopping: 10 minutes
- Industrial park: 30 minutes
- Residential: peak-hour trips: 30 minutes
                      other trips: 20 minutes

Table 3-10 lists the determinants with respect to area of influence and the required data base within the area of influence for selected land use activities.

Method 1: Figure 3-8 (p. 52) illustrates the use of a circular area in delineating the primary market of a neighborhood shopping center for the purpose of establishing the direction of approach to a proposed development. The steps in the process are:

1. Select the appropriate maximum trip length for the proposed development (10 minutes in the example).

2. Draw the selected geometric shape (commonly a circle) with the center located over the site.

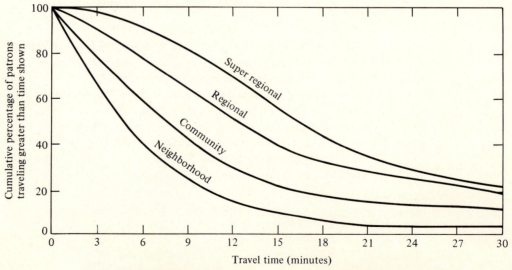

Figure 3-7 Travel distribution to retail centers. SOURCE: ULI — The Urban Land Institute [20].

TABLE 3-10

Information Needed for Determination of Area of Influence and Site Traffic Distribution

Land Use Activity	Factors for Determining Areas of Influence	Data Base within the Area of Influence
Regional shopping center	1. Competing similar commercial developments 2. Travel time—usually a maximum of 30 minutes	Population distribution* (sometimes weighted by projected spendable income in the proposed center)
Community shopping center	1. Competing similar commercial developments 2. Travel time—usually a maximum of 20 minutes	Population distribution* (sometimes weighted by projected spendable income in the proposed center)
Industrial park and office park	Travel time—usually a maximum of 30 minutes or a distance of 10–15 miles is assumed	Population distribution*
Stadium	Travel time–usually a maximum of 40 minutes or more, dependent on the size and character of the stadium	Population distribution* (sometimes weighted by travel time, i.e., the longer travel time is weighted less)
Residential	Travel time—usually a maximum of 30 minutes or a distance of 10 miles is assumed	Employment-opportunity distribution*

SOURCE: The Traffic Institute, Northwestern University [18].
*Projections of population and employment-opportunity data should be used for the design year if possible.

3. Divide the trade area into sections (zones) and determine the amount of activity in each (Figures 3-8 and 3-9).

4. Calculate the proportion of each section (zone) as a percentage of the total primary market area.

5. Identify the most logical route from the centroid of each section (zone) to the site.

6. Calculate the directional distribution by assigning the percentages from step 4 to the minimum paths identified in step 5 (Figure 3-10).

If population is the study activity, the use of census tracts to define each zone is advantageous. However, census data (population) should be weighted by areawide development trends to better estimate future conditions.

Method 2:   This method differs from Method 1 in that the travel distance is calculated along each route using the appropriate maximum travel time and the travel speed(s) on each street. This results in an irregular geometric shape, such as that illustrated in Figure 3-11 (p. 54). Steps 3 through 6 are then the same as for Method 1. Since travel time is a principal factor in determining trip length, this method is used more frequently than Method 1.

Method 3:   Reilly's Law of Retail Gravitation [13] can be used to establish the primary market boundary between competing activity centers. This formulation of the gravity model considers the separation (travel time or distance) between the two competing locations as well as their relative size. Reilly's Law is:

$$d_A = \frac{d_{AB}}{1 + \sqrt{\dfrac{P_B}{P_A}}}$$

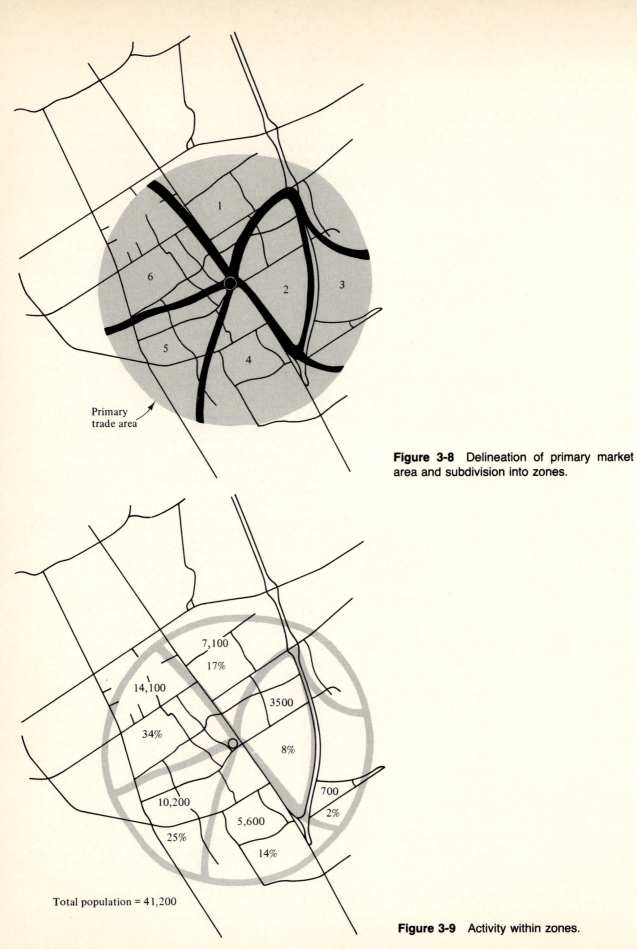

Figure 3-8 Delineation of primary market area and subdivision into zones.

7,100
17%

14,100

3500

34%

8%

10,200

700

25%

2%

5,600

14%

Total population = 41,200

Figure 3-9 Activity within zones.

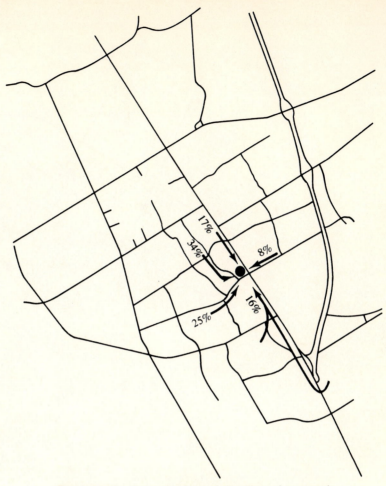

Figure 3-10   Determination of direction of approach.

where:

d_A = distance (in travel time or miles) from center A to its primary market-area boundary with center B

d_{AB} = distance (travel time or miles) from center A to center B

P_A = size of center A

P_B = size of center B, commonly measured in thousands of square feet of gross leasable area

For example, consider a proposed 1.25-million-square-feet shopping center which is located 15 minutes from an existing center of 500,000 square feet:

$$d_{AB} = 15 \text{ minutes}$$
$$P_A = 1,250,000$$
$$P_B = 500,000$$
$$d_A = \frac{15}{1 + \sqrt{\dfrac{500,000}{1,250,000}}} = 10.7$$

Thus, the boundary between the proposed development and an existing competitor is about 11 minutes from the proposed site. Repeating the calculations from all competing centers will yield the "break points," which are then connected to identify the primary-market-area boundary as illustrated in Figure 3-12 (p. 55). The analysis is then followed as in Method 1, Steps 3 through 6.

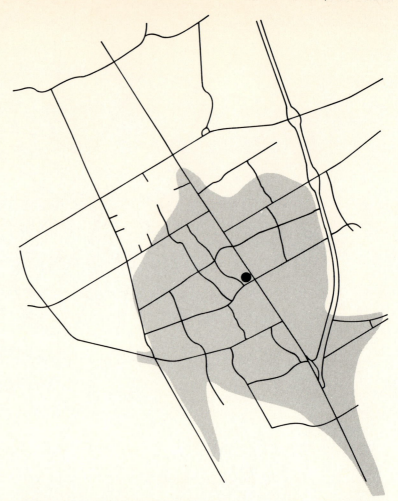

Figure 3-11 Primary trade area using route-specific travel speeds.

Analogy: As with all applications of analogy, the problem is to identify existing situations which have the same characteristics as expected of the subject. A traffic survey of a similar development in close proximity to the subject site follows this methodology. In many cases, a manual count of turn movements is sufficient to obtain the necessary data for analysis of the direction of approach. With a large development where there are several approach streets, a license-plate survey might be used. Applications include:

- A fast-food restaurant where a competing establishment is located near the site
- Service stations where traffic volumes on the adjacent streets are similar to those projected at the site
- A motel site near an existing motel
- Residential developments on the fringe of an urban area
- A site to be developed in residential use, where the tract is one of the few vacant parcels in a developed area
- An occupied office building located in an office complex being developed in phases

The following example will serve to illustrate this method. A multifamily development (condominium) was proposed along an urban arterial. The city denied the request for a change in zoning because of the concern over the traffic volume that would be generated by the development. The specific concern was that left turns at the south access (across from the existing single-family development) would necessitate signalization of

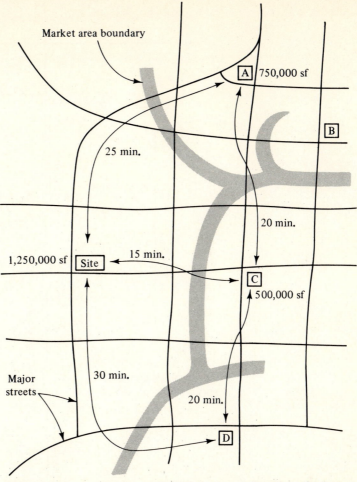

Figure 3-12 Application of Reilly's Law to delineation of primary market area.

the intersection. The developer retained a traffic consultant to determine if this concern was valid. The consultant needed to develop the following information:

- Site-traffic generation
- Directional distribution of the site traffic
- Traffic assignment of the site traffic
- Acceptable gaps in the Main Street traffic

The directional distribution was determined in the following manner.

1. Traffic counts by 15-minute periods were taken at the existing single-family development opposite the proposed site from 7:00 to 9:00 a.m. and 4:00 to 6:00 p.m. in order to obtain a.m. and p.m. peak-hour traffic counts (Figure 3-13).

2. Using the turning-movement counts, the directional distribution of the existing single-family development was determined for the a.m. and p.m. peak hours, as follows:

Exiting traffic, a.m. peak:

$$28 + 32 = 60 \text{ exit to south}$$
$$19 + 14 = \underline{33} \text{ exit to north}$$
$$93 \text{ total exiting traffic}$$
$$60/93 = 65\% \text{ exit to south}$$
$$33/93 = 35\% \text{ exit to north}$$

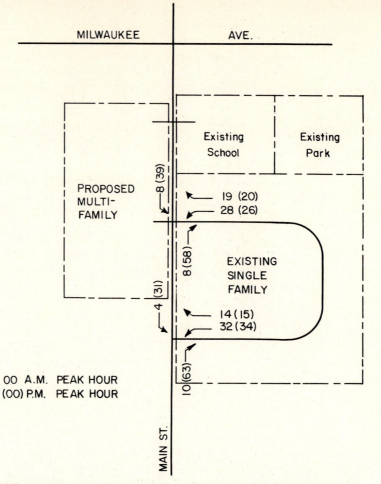

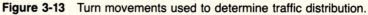

Figure 3-13 Turn movements used to determine traffic distribution.

Exiting traffic, p.m. peak

$$26 + 34 = 60$$
$$20 + 15 = \underline{35}$$
$$95 \text{ total exiting traffic}$$
$$60/95 = 63\%$$
$$35/95 = 37\%$$

Entering traffic, a.m. peak

$$8 + 10 = 18 \text{ enter from south}$$
$$8 + 4 = \underline{12} \text{ enter from north}$$
$$30 \text{ total entry traffic}$$
$$18/30 = 60\% \text{ enter from south}$$
$$12/30 = 40\% \text{ enter from north}$$

Entering traffic, p.m. peak

$$58 + 63 = 121 \text{ enter from south}$$
$$39 + 31 = \underline{70} \text{ enter from north}$$
$$191 \text{ total entering traffic}$$
$$121/191 = 63\%$$
$$70/191 = 37\%$$

3. The multifamily development was assumed to have the same site traffic distribution as the single-family development. For this case, the directions of approach and departure were assumed to be identical for both the a.m. and p.m. peak hours. Thus, 63% of the traffic leaving and entering the proposed multi-family development is expected to be to and from the south, and 37 percent is expected to be to and from the north (see Figure 3-14).

4. This may not be true if the existing and proposed developments are separated by an arterial, such as 1st Avenue in the example. The proximity of an arterial will change travel patterns and the resulting directional distribution factors.

Origin–Destination.   The origin–destination (O–D) method is used infrequently because of the lack of comparable trip origins and destinations. The methodology is sound, but the data are either outdated or inadequate and the cost involved in acquiring new and additional data becomes prohibitive. A data source would be a recent comprehensive transportation study for the municipality. Typical applications are:

- Relocation of an industrial plant or headquarters office when the employees are not expected to change residential location and very few personnel changes are expected.
- Analogy with an existing industry or office located in close proximity to the site and having a very similar labor force or clientele.

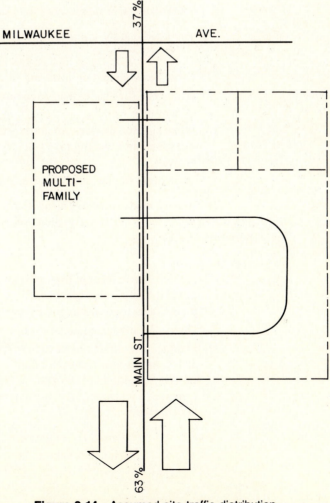

Figure 3-14   Assumed site-traffic distribution.

These cases would assume that the distribution (geographically) of employees will remain the same in future years. Another example would be the relocation of a major sports arena. The area of influence, which normally is very large, should be analyzed with respect to population distribution plus a study of the residential location of season ticket holders. This assumes the current fans will continue to purchase season tickets and that they will remain in their current residences.

Gravity-Model Analysis.   Gravity-model and traffic-assignment techniques can be employed to evaluate the traffic impact of proposed development. The procedure may be performed manually or by computer. In any event, the analyst must have a thorough understanding of the process in order to properly prepare the input and correctly interpret the computer-modeling results. The procedure, both manual and computerized, produces the direction of approach (DOA) information and reduction in site traffic at increased distance from the site. Therefore, the gravity-model and traffic-assignment process is advantageous when it is desired or necessary to evaluate the traffic impact of a proposed development on intersections some distance from the proposed development.

The advantages of the manual analysis are:

1.   The analyst is *forced to think* about the specific problem being analyzed — as opposed to *mechanically* following procedures and accepting the computer output. In simple situations, the manual results are undoubtedly more reliable.
2.   The calculations can be performed by technical/clerical personnel in a reasonable period of time, especially when appropriate forms and calculation procedures have been developed. In simple applications, the total number of man-hours likely will be no more than the computerized process.

It is suggested that the computerized procedure be considered only in the following cases:

1.   Large development projects and extensive street systems and numerous zones.
2.   When the office has extensive computer-modeling expertise which will expedite calculations.
3.   When simpler analyses are not expected by the client or the municipal officials, and the client is willing to pay the fee for the appearance of a more sophisticated analysis.
4.   To impress the client and/or municipal officials.

The gravity-model process (manual and computerized) consists of trip-generation, trip-distribution, and traffic-assignment steps involved in the traditional urban transportation studies.

Trip Generation:

1.   Estimate the number of trips to be generated by the proposed development using the ITE *Trip Generation* manual or other sources. These trip ends will be the productions used in the gravity-model distribution process.
2.   Divide the urbanized area into traffic zones.
3.   Estimate the attractions in each traffic zone based upon each zone's economic and demographic characteristics. It is important to recognize that it is the relative magnitude of the attractions in each zone and not the number of trips generated by a zone that must be determined. Examples of appropriate activity variables are:

Proposed Development	*Activity Variable*
Neighborhood retail	Dwelling units
	Population

Proposed Development	*Activity Variable*
Regional retail	Dollars available to be spent
	Dwelling units
	Population
General office	Labor force
	Population
	Dwelling units
Governmental office	Population
	Dwelling units
Parks/recreation	Population
	Dwelling units
Industrial	Labor force
	Population
	Dwelling units
Residential	Employment

If the number of trip ends are used as the measure of attractiveness, they can be calculated using trip-generation rates. Trip-generation rates can be obtained from the urban transportation study (where such a study has been performed) or from simplified techniques and transferable parameters.

Trip Distribution: Trip ends generated by the proposed development are "distributed" to the several traffic zones using the gravity model in either the friction-factor or the travel-time formulation.

friction-factor formulation

$$T_{si} = P\left[\frac{A_i F_{si}}{\sum (A_i F_{si})}\right]$$

travel-time formulation

$$T_{si} = P\left[\frac{\dfrac{A_i}{t_{si}^x}}{\sum \left(\dfrac{A_i}{t_{si}^x}\right)}\right]$$

where:

- s = the site of the proposed development
- i = a counter identifying the several traffic zones which comprise the analysis area ($= 1, 2, 3, \ldots, n$)
- T_{si} = the trips between the site of the proposed development and zone i
- P = the estimated trips generated by the proposed development
- A_i = the measure of the activity in zone i for the generation of trips to the proposed development
- F_{si} = the friction factor, which is a measure of the resistance to travel
- t_{si} = the travel time between the proposed development and zone i
- x = an exponent which varies with the trip purpose and the travel time

The friction factors may be obtained from the gravity-model calibration when an urban transportation study has been performed for the urban area.

Alternately, the travel time within the site's area of influence may be used directly in the calculations. It has been demonstrated that the exponent of travel time is not a constant but a variable which is a function of both trip purpose and travel time. However, the error involved by assuming a constant value of 2.0 is undoubtedly minor compared to that involved in the range in observed trip-generation rates. If the appearance of greater precision is desired, the analyst can use exponent values which increase with trip time and vary with trip purpose.

Caution is urged against the tendency toward more sophisticated and complex analyses in traffic impact studies for the following reasons:

1. Increased sophistication and complexity add to the cost and do not necessarily contribute to accuracy or precision.

2. The direction of approach is not sensitive to the exponent of travel time; therefore, neither the accuracy nor the precision of the estimated site traffic in close proximity will be improved.

3. The improvement in the estimation of additional traffic at intersections some distance from the site is small compared to the accuracy of mechanical traffic counts and intersection capacity analysis.

Traffic Assignment:

1. The average speed for each segment of the street network is estimated and the travel time calculated.

2. The most logical route between the site and each traffic zone is identified.

3. The travel time between the site and each zone is calculated by summation of the travel time for each segment of the most logical route.
   Alternately, the travel times may be estimated using the airline distance between the site and each traffic zone and using the distance–travel-time curves included in *NCHRP Report No. 187*.

4. The estimated number of trips between the site and each zone is posted to each street segment comprising the most logical route. The estimated site traffic added to each segment of street is then formed by summation of the individual site-to-zone volumes on that segment.

Steps 1, 2, and 3 must be completed prior to performing the trip-distribution calculations.

SITE-TRAFFIC ASSIGNMENT

Once the total site-generated traffic has been determined, it is multiplied by the directional distribution factor and assigned to the street system approaching the site. These external volumes must then be assigned to individual site access points, and turn movements must be estimated. This step-by-step procedure is illustrated in the following example.

An office building containing 190,000 square feet of space is planned for a tract of land for the northeast quadrant of the intersection of 1st and Main. It is anticipated that 40% of site-generated traffic will approach from the south, 30% from the east, 20% from the west, and 10% from the north.

Step 1. Traffic generator:
         P.M. peak hour traffic generation:

inbound trips = 190 (0.5) = 100 vehicles
outbound trips = 190 (2.2) = 420 vehicles

Step 2. Site-traffic direction of approach:

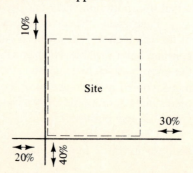

Step 3.   Site-traffic assignment:

Inbound Trips	Outbound Trips
100(.40) = 40	420(.40) = 170
100(.30) = 30	420(.30) = 130
100(.20) = 20	420(.20) = 80
100(.10) = 10	420(.10) = 40
100	420

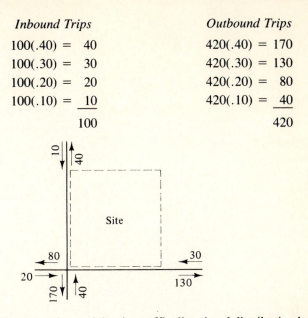

When the site-traffic generation and the site-traffic directional distribution have been determined, the traffic is assigned to individual access points, and turn movements are estimated. Commercial office and retail developments having two or more access drives commonly have inbound movements as illustrated in Figure 3-15. The outbound distribution at the access drives, in general, is more equal than the inbound traffic, as illustrated in Figure 3-16. See page 62.

The turning movements at access drives are influenced by the following factors:

- The type of traffic control at the access intersection (stop sign or traffic signal)
- The volume of through traffic (which influences the number of acceptable gaps)
- Median design (none, continuous two-way left, channelized left — in and/or out, barrier median)

Significance of Site-Traffic Distribution: A Case Study

Two alternative sites were being considered for a 1-million-square-foot regional shopping center. From a land use standpoint, both sites were considered to be equal, and the adjacent land uses are similar. A preliminary evaluation of the site-traffic movements was desired for each site.

The site-traffic distribution in Figure 3-17 (p. 63) was estimated based on the population distribution within the primary market area (within 30 minutes travel time). If the slip ramp from the freeway to the southbound frontage road were relocated to the north, traffic approaching the site on the freeway from the north could enter the site from the frontage road. The volume of traffic to and from Site A which must pass through the signalized intersections of the state road and the freeway frontage roads is listed below:

	Inbound	Outbound
West signal	30%	45 + 30 = 75%
East signal	30%	30 + 15 = 45%

For Site B, the percentages are:

	Inbound	Outbound
West signal	45 + 30 = 75%	45%
East signal	30%	45%

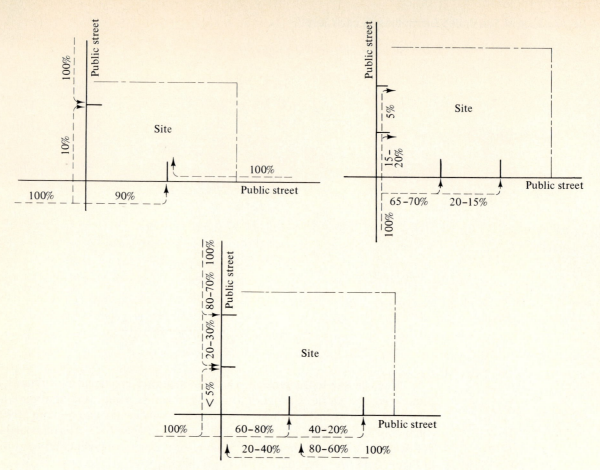

Figure 3-15 Typical distribution of inbound trips at commercial office and retail sites.

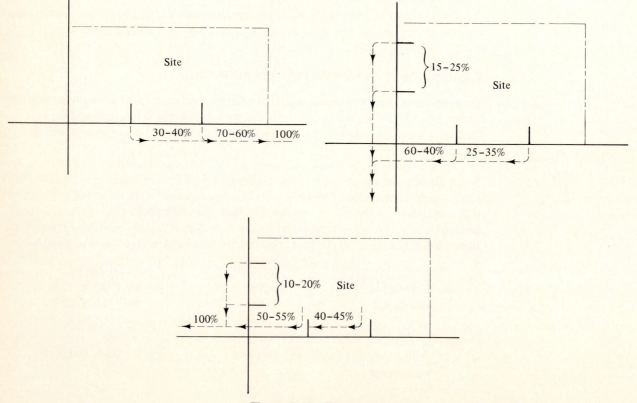

Figure 3-16 Typical distribution of outbound trips.

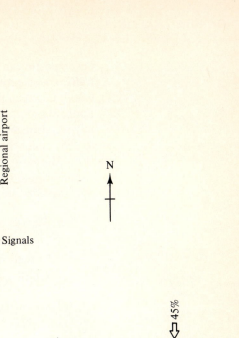

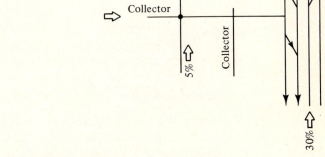

Figure 3-17   Case-study traffic distribution.

The west intersection will experience the highest volume of the shopping-center traffic (75% of the total). For Site A, the southbound traffic could be provided with a channelized free right turn; thus, only the outbound site traffic heading north on the freeway — (1.7 trips/1000 sq. ft.)(1,000,000 sq. ft.)(0.45) = 765 vph — would need to be accommodated through the signal. With Site B, the site traffic through the signalized intersection of the arterial and the west frontage road would be approximately (1.7 trips/1000 sq. ft.)(1,000,000 sq. ft.)(0.75) = 1,275 vph. Of these, about 765 vph would approach Site B on the west (southbound frontage road) and 510 from the east (westbound on the arterial after having exited the freeway northbound). Therefore, given the direction of approach indicated in Figure 3-17, from a traffic standpoint Site A would be the better site.

NON-SITE TRAFFIC

The volume of existing traffic on streets adjacent to and in the vicinity of a proposed development can be readily obtained by conventional traffic-count procedures. However, traffic counts provide little useful information when the present traffic volumes are considerably less than the street capacity—especially when much of the area is undeveloped. Furthermore, it must be realized that traffic counts of one or two days duration are likely to yield average annual daily traffic (AADT) estimates, which have an error of at least 10% to 15% under the best of conditions.

Moreover, the real need in analyzing the situation is to determine what the traffic volume would be in absence of the proposed development. Four methods for addressing this question are:

- Analogy of traffic increase
- Trend analysis
- Growth factor
- Traffic assignment

All projection methods are subject to some error. The magnitude of the error can be expected to become larger as the ratio of present volume to future volume becomes small. In any case, the projection of specific movements of individual intersections is extremely unreliable, and such projections should not be used as the basis for significant decisions.

Analogy of Traffic Increase

Analogy involves the transfer of results from a similar existing location to a future location. Steps in the process include the following:

1. Identify existing location(s) having the same street-design characteristics and development similar to that expected along the subject street.
2. Obtain the historical traffic-count data for the existing location(s).
3. Calculate the annual growth rates and plot the pattern of traffic growth rates for the existing location(s). When two or more existing locations are available, select a "best" estimate of growth pattern for the subject location based on averages and/or subjective evaluation.
4. Apply the growth rate or pattern of growth rates to the counted volume(s) on the subject street.

Trend Analysis

This method is applicable where sufficient count data are available to establish a trend line for the subject street. The simplest procedure is to plot the data and establish the trend line by eye. It should be noted that the use of time-series regression (computer model) will not produce a more reliable projection. It simply will result in different individuals' obtaining the same mathematical result.

Trend analysis is most applicable where extensive count data over a long period of time are available and where the present volume is approaching capacity. It assumes a constant growth rate and no capacity restraints.

Growth Factor

The growth-factor method assumes that traffic volumes are related to, and will follow a pattern similar to that of, some urban growth variable such as population or gross leasable area. For example, in its simplest form, if the population of an area is projected to double, traffic volume would be projected to double as well.

Traffic Assignment

Traffic assignments are commonly available for large urban areas and for some smaller and medium-size urban areas over 50,000 population. In addition to the computerized process, the Federal Highway Administration has produced a graphical process which can be used to project the traffic volumes on an arterial street system.

Computerized Traffic Assignment. The computerized process is certainly the most sophisticated of processes. However, sophistication does not guarantee accuracy. The following research findings [16] should be kept in mind when traffic-assignment results are used:

1. The comparison of assigned link volumes and ground counts is dependent upon:
   a. The correct number of total trip ends in the study area
   b. The correct mean trip length
   c. A reasonable (but not necessarily accurate) geographical distribution of trip ends
2. Increased network detail does not improve the comparison of assigned link volumes to ground counts.
3. Increased network detail results in an increased number of minimum paths which are unrealistic.
4. Assigned turn movements at individual intersections have no correlation to the counted turn movements at individual intersections. The total counted volume of left or right turns at the several intersections along a section of street several miles in length (at least 3 to 5 miles) will bear some comparison to the assigned turn movements.
5. Turn penalties do not produce significant improvement in the comparison of assigned and counted turn movements nor a reduction in illogical minimum paths in a detailed network.

Traffic assignment may be useful where the present traffic volumes are substantially less than capacity. Trend analysis is more appropriate when the present volume begins to approach capacity (say, V/C ratios greater than 0.7).

Graphical Method. A graphical procedure was developed from a series of assignments to the same traffic-assignment network. The procedure is documented in the report, "Land Use and Arterial Spacing in Suburban Areas" [12]. The procedure, as documented, utilizes certain selected capacities per lane per hour for 2-, 4-, 6-, and 8-lane streets and a chart for adjusting for levels-of-service other than LOS C. It is suggested that the analyst performing the traffic impact study select a capacity (vehicles per lane per hour) appropriate for the street cross section, level-of-service, and signal timing. The procedure, as modified, is explained below and illustrated by the following example.

Data for Example
    Subregional density = 3,500 persons per square mile
    Project size: = 4 square miles (2 × 2 miles)
    Density = 5,000 persons per square mile
    Transit use = 3%
    Auto ownership = 1.7 autos per dwelling unit
    Nonresidential/residential mix = 0.5

Street Requirements Based on Gross Density: Chart 1 is used for analysis of land use patterns distributed over a subregional area, considered jointly with the overall development pattern of uniform density in the surrounding region. The minimum development size that can be considered as subregional development is determined primarily by major street system spacing; if an area is so small that it "falls through" the spaces within the major development pattern, then it is better analyzed by the methods described subsequently for major generators. However, even a small project should be analyzed by the subregional development methods if the project, together with its surrounding development, can be considered as a uniform land use pattern extending over a substantial area.

Since the primary direction of flow normally establishes the size of the major street system in both directions, Chart 1 was developed to reflect volumes per mile and street

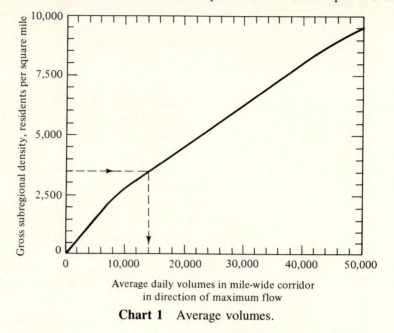

Average daily volumes in mile-wide corridor
in direction of maximum flow

Chart 1   Average volumes.

requirements in the direction of maximum flow or primary direction. Therefore, Chart 1 should be used for estimating primary-direction requirements. If predictions of traffic in the secondary direction are to be developed, the degree of directional imbalance and reduction factor should be estimated from local traffic patterns in the immediate area.

Example: Given a uniform subregional density of 3,500 residents per square mile, Chart 1 indicates that a daily traffic volume of about 14,000 per mile could be expected.

Density Patterns: Uniform residential density may not prevail throughout the subregion; therefore, Chart 2 provides adjustments for various nonuniform density combinations. The relative densities of the subregion and the project are expressed as a series of ratios (4:1, 2:1, 1:1, 1:2, 1:4) which are represented by curves on the chart. The chart should be entered with the ratio of the subregional area density to project area density and the size of the project in square miles. For other density combinations, adjustment factors may be interpolated between the given curves. The adjustment factor is to be applied to the Chart 1 volumes that were determined using subregional density. Note that the simulation runs used in developing Chart 2 were based on regularly shaped areas, and that as the area becomes more irregularly shaped (i.e., further from square-shaped), a greater error is introduced in the volume estimate.

Example — Continued: Given a 2-mile by 2-mile project with a residential density of 5,000 residents per square mile located in a subregion having 3,500 residents per square mile, we obtain a subregion/project ratio of 5,000:3,500 = 1.4:1. Interpolation from Chart 2 gives an adjustment factor of 1.2. When this factor is applied to the volume obtained from Chart 1 (14,000 per mile), a modified volume of 16,800 is obtained.

Transit Utilization: Chart 3 provides volume adjustment factors for variations in transit utilization during peak periods. If only the daily transit utilization is known, a rule of thumb that may be applied is that peak-period transit use is 1.5 to 2.0 times the daily use.

The base condition requiring no adjustment was assumed to be a transit utilization of approximately 7% of all person trips in the peak period for suburban subregional areas.

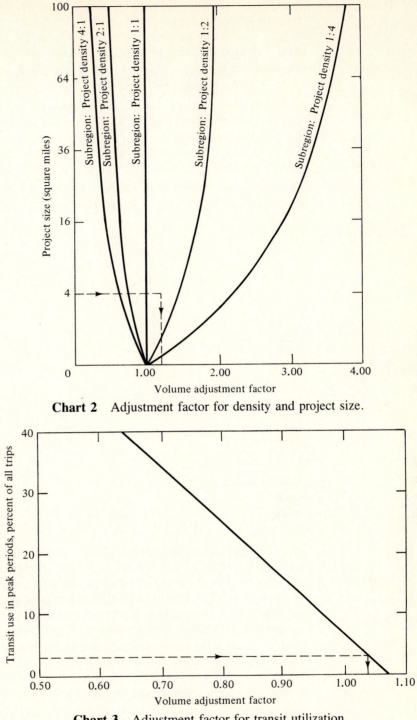

Chart 2 Adjustment factor for density and project size.

Chart 3 Adjustment factor for transit utilization.

Although some big-city downtown areas currently experience much greater peak transit usage (ranging from 25% to 50% and more), transit use in other parts of the urban region drops off sharply. With greater concern and support for public transit in the United States, the percentage share of transit in the future could increase significantly. The effect on traffic volumes and street requirements in suburban subregional areas, however, would be quite limited because of the small amount of current transit use in these areas. For example, if the proportion of peak-period transit use were to triple over that assumed as the base, the corresponding street traffic reduction would be only 15%.

    It should also be noted that transit usage and car ownership are interdependent. Because of this, applying adjustments for both factors is not recommended when substantial (20% or more) transit use is anticipated. In that case, only the Chart 3 adjustment should be applied, rather than both the Chart 3 and Chart 4 adjustments.

Example—Continued: Given a peak period transit use of 3% (independent of the car ownership) for the area, an adjustment factor of 1.05 is determined.

Car Ownership: Chart 4 provides the adjustment factor to account for car ownership variations. Every attempt should be made by the user to assess the level of car ownership for the subregion, since this factor strongly influences travel and street requirements. If car ownership estimates are not available, the U.S. census data on car ownership for a comparable developed area may provide a useful guide.

Example—Continued: Given a car ownership of 1.7 cars per dwelling unit, which has been determined to be independent of transit usage, Chart 4 indicates an adjustment factor of 1.4.

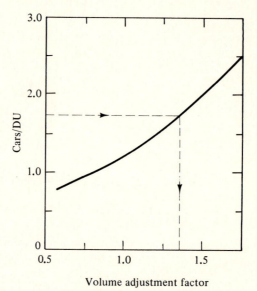

Chart 4   Adjustment factor for car ownership.

Project Nonresidential/Residential Mix: Suburban developments vary from entirely residential to balanced subregional areas that incorporate a mix of employment together with the residential uses. If little employment is provided within the project area for residents, a low mix is used to estimate the volume adjustment factor from Chart 5. On the other hand, if a wide range of opportunities are available, a high mix value is appropriate. (Note that the availability of employment within the project area does not produce actual balanced conditions, since competing external employment still attracts a substantial degree of in–out traffic across the project boundaries.)

    The adjustment factors in Chart 5 are given for three project sizes— 1 mile by 1 mile, 4 miles by 4 miles, and 10 miles by 10 miles. For other project sizes, interpolation is used.

Example—Continued: Given a 2-mile project area containing 20,000 residents, a residential labor force of 10,000 and 5,000 jobs, we calculate a project nonresidential/residential activity mix of 0.5 (5,000 jobs/10,000 labor force). Then, entering Chart 5 with a 0.5 nonresidential/residential rate and a 2 × 2 project area (interpolation required), we obtain an adjustment factor of 0.97.

Freeway Diversion Factor: Freeways can have a significant impact on the traffic carried by arterial streets. On streets parallel to a freeway, traffic volumes are generally decreased by a freeway. This impact is greatest close to the freeway and decreases on streets farther from the freeway. Conversely, on streets perpendicular to the freeway, particularly those

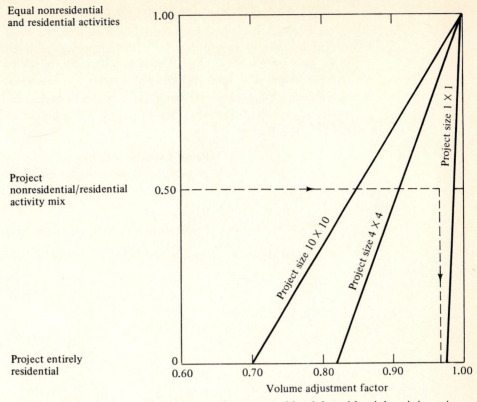

Chart 5   Adjustment factor for project non-residential–residential activity mix.

which serve interchanges, traffic volumes are generally increased by a freeway. The amount of volume increase is greater closer to the freeway.

To account for this influence of freeways, adjustment factors are provided in Chart 6. Note that, in contrast to the other charts in this section, the same adjustment factor is not applied throughout the project area, but a different adjustment factor is applied

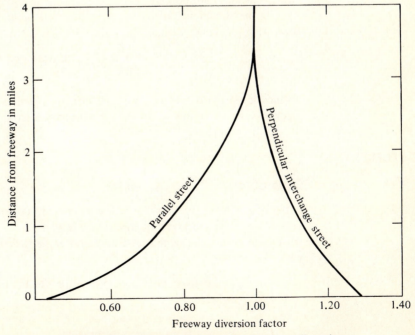

Chart 6   Adjustment factor for freeway diversion.

within each mile-wide corridor. The adjustment factors are a function of the distance from the freeway. It is suggested that this distance be measured as a straight-line distance (airline distance) from the freeway to the midpoint of each milewide corridor. To facilitate the calculations, these adjustment factors should be applied after all the previous adjustment factors have been applied. This approach is illustrated in the following example:

Example—Continued: Given a 2-mile by 2-mile project and a freeway, the effect of the freeway on the surface-street traffic is reflected in the following adjustment factors:

At 1.0 mile:

$$\text{Parallel streets} = 0.75$$
$$\text{Perpendicular interchange streets} = 1.12$$

At 2.0 miles:

$$\text{Parallel streets} = 0.90$$
$$\text{Perpendicular interchange streets} = 1.04$$

Computed Volumes: The adjusted volume per mile-wide corridor is:

Chart 1	14,000
Project size, Chart 2	× 1.2
Transit, Chart 3	× 1.05
Car Ownership, Chart 4	× 1.4
Nonresidential mix, Chart 5	× 0.97
	23,955

An arterial more than three miles from the freeway would not be influenced by the freeway. On parallel arterials two miles from the freeway between 8.5% and 12% of the 24-hour traffic is carried in the peak hour of the day. Assuming 10% for this example:

$$21,500 \times 10\% = 2,150 \text{ vph}$$

and, at 600 vph per lane:

$$2,150 \div 600 = 3.58 \text{ lanes}$$

Thus, four lanes are needed.

If the directional distribution in the peak hour is, say, 60–40, the number of lanes is:

$$2,150 \times 60\% = 1,294 \text{ vph in peak direction}$$
$$1,294 \div 600 = 2.2 \text{ lanes, or 3 lanes, in the peak direction}$$

A suitable design would be four-lane primary arterials at the one-mile intervals and a secondary arterial midway between the primary arterials at one-mile intervals.

CASE STUDIES

Case Study—Shopping Center

A regional shopping center that will contain 918,000 square feet of commercial space is proposed for the southwest quadrant of two major arterials in a large metropolitan area. In order to make a thorough traffic appraisal of the site, the following studies and analyses were undertaken:

1. A field inspection was made of the site and of traffic conditions in the vicinity of the site.
2. Average daily and peak-hour traffic volumes in the vicinity of the site were obtained from local governmental agencies.

3. Current roadway improvement plans and proposals were obtained from local governmental agencies.

4. Data on the size and composition of the development along with a market study that had been conducted for the shopping center were provided by the developer.

5. A travel-time survey was made on existing site approach routes.

6. An estimate was made of site-generated traffic volumes for site-related critical hours.

7. Based on the estimated trade area, roadway travel times, and population data for the trade area, a direction-of-approach analysis was made to determine the distribution of patron traffic.

8. An assignment of future traffic movements was made based on the amount of site traffic, the direction of approach of patron traffic, and the anticipated non-site traffic volumes.

9. Capacity analyses were made at critical roadway intersections and at site entrance–exits.

10. Recommendations for roadway improvements were developed where necessary, based on the above capacity analyses.

Factors Affecting Access: The proposed site has approximately 2,600 feet of frontage along one arterial and 2,000 feet of frontage along the other. Both arterials are currently two lanes wide but are programmed by the city to be improved to six-lane divided facilities in the near future.

The site is also adjacent to a regional east–west freeway that is being constructed as a six-lane facility. A diamond interchange is proposed at its intersection with the north–south arterial that abuts the site. Figure 3-18 illustrates the site location with respect to the area roadnet.

Estimates of Future Traffic Volumes: Future traffic volumes in the vicinity of the site will be composed of traffic generated by the shopping center, forecasted volumes of through traffic bypassing the site, and additional volumes of traffic generated by new development in the vicinity of the site.

Normally, a shopping center experiences three traffic peaks. The first occurs simultaneously with the through-traffic evening peak hour, the second occurs from 7:00 to 8:00 p.m. and is the center's peak inbound period, and the third, from 9:00 to 10:00 p.m., is the center's peak outbound period. The latter two periods assume a 10:00 p.m. closing time for the center. Table 3-11 presents site-generated traffic volumes that can be anticipated on 20 to 30 days per year during peak retail seasons. The volumes are based on 918,000 square feet of gross leasable area and assume that all shoppers will arrive at the site by automobile.

Direction of Approaching Patron Traffic: The directions from which patrons travelling by automobile will approach a shopping center are determined by the population distribution within the center's trade area and the efficiency of the various roadways leading to the site. The potential trade area was determined through a travel-time survey (see Figure 3-19) and by the location of nearby commercial centers.

TABLE 3-11

Estimated Site-Generated Traffic for Shopping-Center Case Study

Hour	Inbound	Outbound
4:30–5:30 p.m.	1,370	1,560
7:00–8:00 p.m.	2,480	1,370
9:00–10:00 p.m.	460	3,120

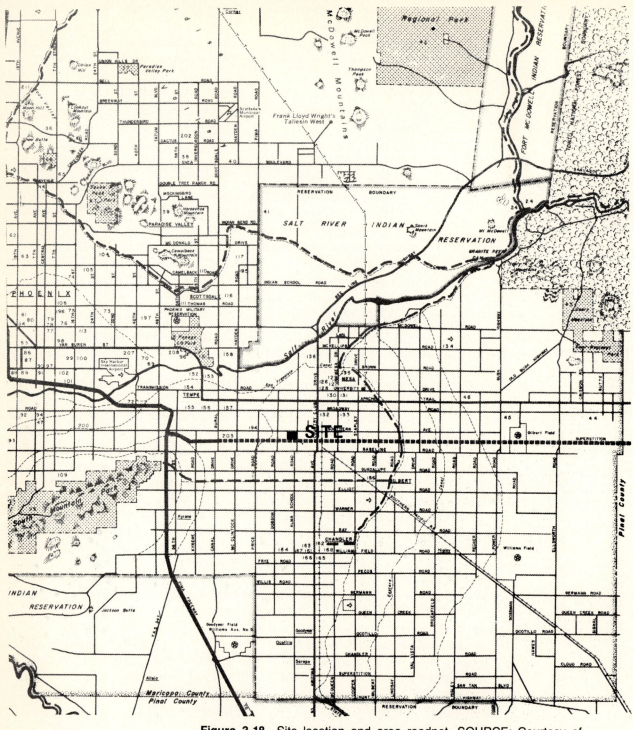

Figure 3-18 Site location and area roadnet. SOURCE: Courtesy of Barton-Aschman Associates.

Analysis of travel times over the roadnet (Figure 3-19) and of population distribution determined that the trade area contains approximately 390,000 persons and that the site is well located with respect to population distribution. Figure 3-20 indicates the anticipated direction of approach of site traffic. Based on the estimates of site-generated traffic and on the analysis as to where they will travel, the volumes were assigned to the area roadnet. A preliminary access scheme was developed for the site, and traffic volumes were assigned to the various driveways. Figure 3-21 (p. 75) illustrates the site traffic assignment.

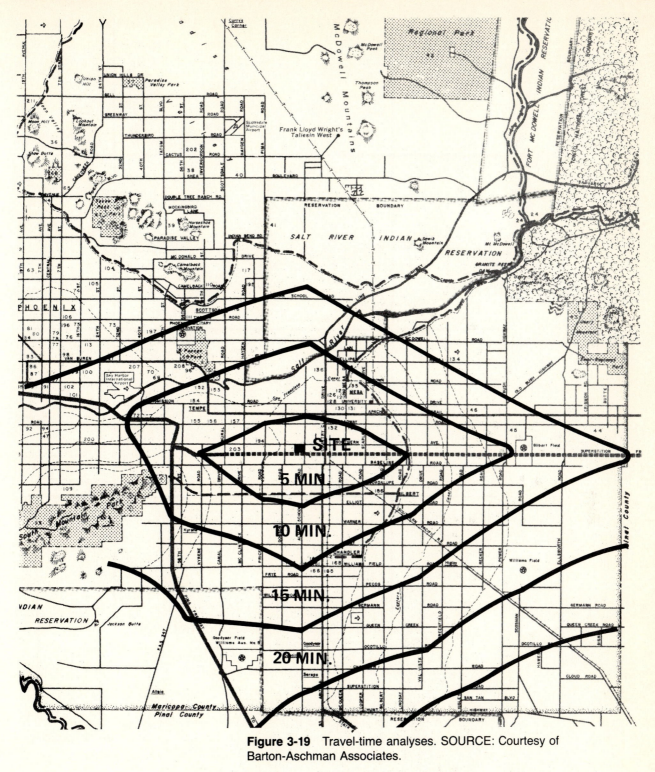

Figure 3-19 Travel-time analyses. SOURCE: Courtesy of Barton-Aschman Associates.

In order to analyze the impact of site-generated traffic volumes on the site access system and on the adjacent roadway system, capacity analyses were conducted. Site traffic volumes were added to through (non-site) volumes anticipated to be on the road system five years after the shopping center opened for business.

Recommended Roadway and Site Access Improvements: In order for a shopping center of this size to function efficiently, the internal and external traffic systems must be

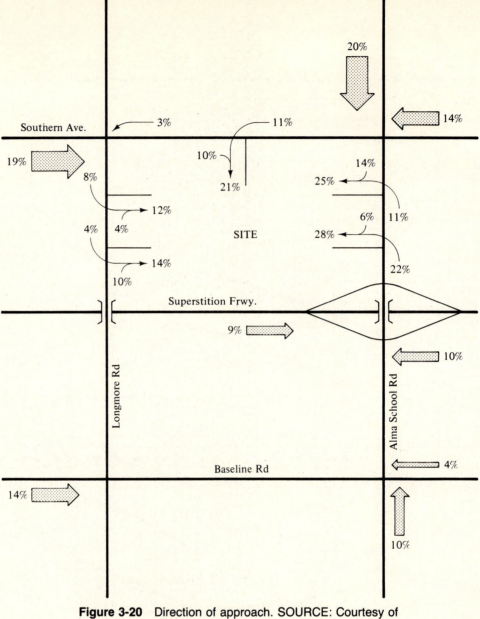

Figure 3-20 Direction of approach. SOURCE: Courtesy of
Barton-Aschman Associates.

coordinated. Roadway and access improvements were recommended to satisfy the following criteria.

1. A system of site access points should be provided in sufficient number to
    maximize the distribution of site-generated traffic on the external roadways.
2. Each access point should be designed to provide adequate capacity as well as
    safe ingress and egress.
3. The site access system and external roadway improvements should be com-
    patible and coordinated in terms of staging and design.
4. The adjacent roadways should be designed to accommodate combined site and
    future non-site traffic volumes.
5. The vehicular system should be designed to provide efficient site access and to
    minimize interference with through traffic on the adjacent roadways.

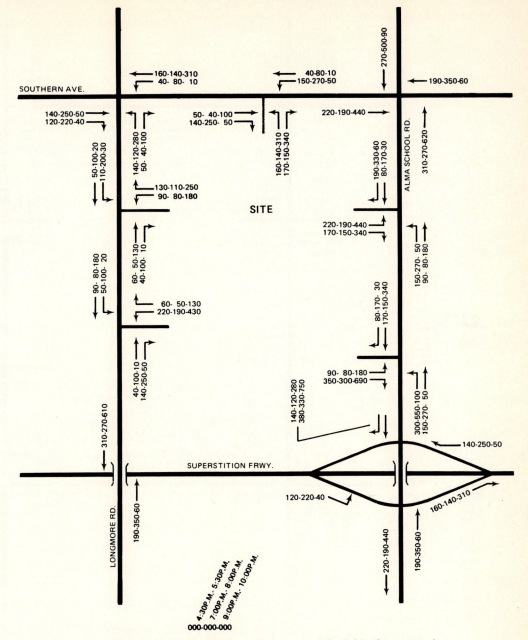

Figure 3-21 Site-traffic assignment. SOURCE: Courtesy of Barton-Aschman Associates.

Based on these criteria, the number of necessary traffic lanes and the recommended traffic control was determined and is illustrated in Figure 3-22.

Conclusion: The proposed site is well located with respect to the area roadnet. With implementation of the recommended roadway improvements, an acceptable level of service can be achieved and maintained on adjacent streets. As recommended, the site will provide safe and efficient ingress and egress for patrons while minimizing description of traffic flow on the area roadnet.

Case Study — Fast-Food Restaurant

A fast-food restaurant with drive-thru facilities is proposed in a rapidly growing suburban area. The restaurant is proposed for a two-acre site in close proximity to a community college and a large light-industrial complex.

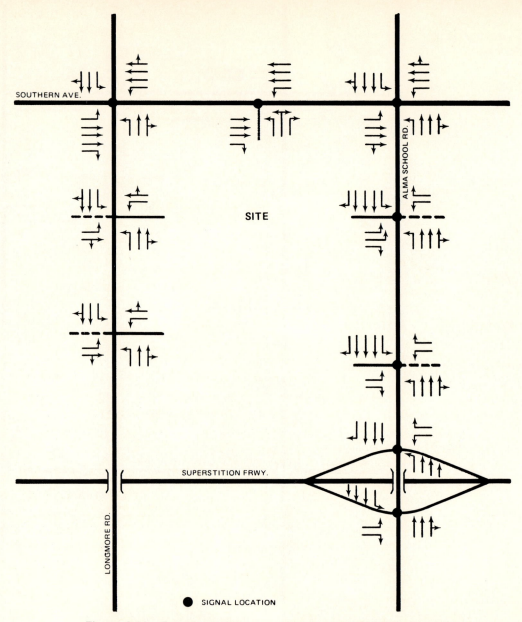

Figure 3-22 Recommended lane requirements. SOURCE: Courtesy of Barton-Aschman Associates.

The proposed site is located along a major four-lane divided suburban arterial that accommodates approximately 25,000 vehicles per day. The area roadnet is illustrated in Figure 3-23. The building itself will have approximately 3,400 square feet of floor area and a seating capacity of 118 people.

There are three specific traffic characteristics of the development which must be analyzed in order to evaluate its impact upon traffic conditions and to determine the adequacy of the site's access system:

1. The time periods of peak site and non-site traffic generation.
2. The traffic volumes generated by the development during the peak periods.
3. The directional distribution of site-generated traffic.

The proposed restaurant will have several peak periods: the noon lunch hour, which is the highest period; and the evening peak hour, usually between 5:00 and 7:00 p.m. The

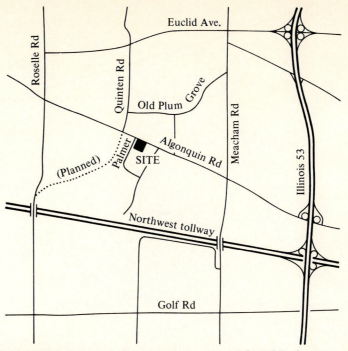

Figure 3-23 Area roadnet and site location. SOURCE: Courtesy of Barton-Aschman Associates.

peak-hour volumes that are expected to be generated to and from the proposed development are listed in Table 3-12. The evening peak hour on the arterial, due to the nearby industrial and college land uses, occurs between 4:00 and 5:00 p.m., and the noon-hour volume is very low.

The directional distribution of site-generated traffic is a function of several variables. These include the distribution of population within the development's area of influence, operational characteristics of the area's street system, and the influence of major traffic generators in close proximity to the site. Because of the configuration of the restaurant's trade area, the major student/employee generators in the area, and the influence of the development on existing traffic in the area, it is anticipated that the directional patterns will vary throughout the day. During the noon hour, it is estimated that approaching site traffic will be equally distributed from the east and west on the arterial roadway. In the evening peak hour, it is estimated that approximately two-thirds of the site traffic will approach from the east.

In order for a high-turnover restaurant to function efficiently, the internal circulation system must be closely coordinated with the external street system. The external street system should efficiently accommodate estimated peak-traffic movements (both site generated and through traffic). The access system serving the development should contain a sufficient number of driveways, located in a manner which best distributes traffic on the street system. The access driveways should be designed to provide adequate capacity for all traffic, and the site access system should be easily understood by the average driver.

Based upon an analysis of the traffic assignment and the site configuration, it is recommended that two access drives be provided to serve the site. The two driveways

TABLE 3-12
Estimated Site-Generated Traffic Volumes for Fast-Food Case Study

Time Period		Inbound	Outbound
Weekday	12:00–1:00 p.m.	300	280
Weekday	5:00–6:00 p.m.	120	110

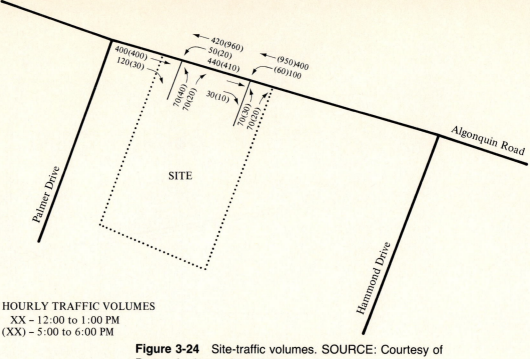

HOURLY TRAFFIC VOLUMES
  XX – 12:00 to 1:00 PM
(XX) – 5:00 to 6:00 PM

Figure 3-24   Site-traffic volumes. SOURCE: Courtesy of
Barton-Aschman Associates.

should be located to either side of the proposed building serving the parking areas around the periphery of the site. Figure 3-24 illustrates the entering–exiting site traffic along with through traffic during the two peak time periods.

Because the arterial is a four-lane, divided roadway with a 16-foot mountable median, it is recommended that no modifications be made to the median strip and that vehicles entering from the east wait in the median until a safe gap in the traffic stream occurs. The noon-hour volumes on the arterial are low, and sample studies in the evening indicate that adequate gaps in traffic occur to allow entering and exiting traffic safe accessibility.

The local community requires that parking be provided at a ratio of 32 spaces per 1,000 square feet of floor area. This ratio would require 109 parking spaces, which should be more than adequate for a high-turnover sit-down and drive-thru facility.

REFERENCES

1. Arizona DOT, *Trip Generation Intercity Factors,* July 1, 1976.

2. Arnold, E. D., "Trip Generation of Special Sites," *ITE Journal,* March 1985.

3. Buttke, Carl H., "Using the ITE Trip Generation Report," Institute of Traffic Engineers, July 1984.

4. Buttke, Carl H., "Trip Generation Update," *A Compendium of Papers* of a National Conference sponsored by the Institute of Transportation Engineers, Orlando, Florida, 23–26 March 1986.

5. Cleveland, Donald E., and Edward A. Mueller, "Traffic Characteristics at Regional Shopping Centers," New Haven, Ct.: Bureau of Highway Traffic, Yale University, 1961.

6. Colorado–Wyoming Section, Institute of Transportation Engineers, "Trip Generation for Mixed Use Developments," *Technical Committee Report,* draft September 1985.

7. DeShazo, Starek, and Tang, Inc., correspondence with V. G. Stover, October 1985.

8. Institute of Transportation Engineers, "Site Development and Transportation Reports," *A Compendium of Papers* of a National Conference held in Orlando, Florida, 23–26 March 1986.

9. Institute of Transportation Engineers, *Trip Generation,* 3rd ed.

10. Lalani, Nazir, "Factoring 'Passer-By' Trips Into Traffic Impact Analyses," *Public Works,* May 1984.

11. Mehra, Joe and Keller, C. Richard, "Development and Application of Trip Generation Rates," *Report No. FHWA/PL/85/003,* prepared by Kellerco, Inc., for the Federal Highway Administration, Final Report, January 1985.

12. Pearson, Frederick C. and George E. Schoener, "Land Use and Arterial Spacing in Suburban Areas," *Report No. FHWA-PL-77016,* prepared by Gruen Associates for the Federal Highway Administration, May 1977, reprinted January 1980.

13. Reilly, William J., "Methods for the Study of Retail Relationships," *Bulletin 2944,* University of Texas, 1929.

14. Slade, Louis J. and Frederick E. Gorove, "Reductions in Estimates of Traffic Impacts of Regional Shopping Centers," *Traffic Engineering,* January 1981.

15. Smith, Steven A., "A Methodology for Consideration of Pass-By Trips in Traffic Impact Analyses for Shopping Centers," *ITE Journal,* August 1986.

16. Stover, Vergil G., J. Buechler, and J. D. Benson, "A Sensitivity Analysis of Traffic Assignment," *Research Report 17-2,* Texas Transportation Institute, November 1974.

17. Sosslan, Arthur B., Hassam, Amin B., Carter, Maurice M., and Wickstrom, George V., Comsis Corporation, "Quick-Response Urban Travel Estimation Techniques and Transferable Parameters," *NCHRP Report No. 187,* Transportation Research Board, 1978.

18. Texas State Department of Highways and Public Transportation, *Special Traffic Generation Study.*

19. The Traffic Institute, Northwestern University, Course Notes.

20. ULI — The Urban Land Institute, *Parking Requirements for Shopping Centers: Summary Recommendations and Research Study Report,* a study conducted under the direction of ULI by Wilbur Smith and Associates, Inc., and sponsored by the International Council of Shopping Centers, 1982.

21. ULI — The Urban Land Institute and the National Parking Association, "Appendix B: Parking Demand at the Regionals," *The Dimensions of Parking,* ULI — The Urban Land Institute and the National Parking Association, 1979.

Part Two
DESIGN

4

Functional Circulation Systems

MOVEMENT HIERARCHY

Functional design recognizes that individual elements of the circulation system do not serve travel independently. Rather, travel involves movement through a network of public and private roadways. Thus, a functionally designed circulation system provides for a series of distinct stages which are involved in making a trip. As illustrated in Figure 4-1, these are: primary movement, collection/distribution, access, and termination. Each trip stage needs to be accommodated by an element which theoretically is designed specifically for it. Each element of a functional hierarchy serves as a collecting/distributing facility for the next higher element of the system. Each functional class should intersect with facilities of the same and adjacent classifications. Thus, for example, theoretically arterials should intersect only with other arterials and collectors or their private-access equivalents.

A hierarchical circulation system provides for the gradation in function from access to movement. Efficient and safe operation of the system requires that specific facilities be designed to serve a specific purpose within this spectrum. The failure to recognize and accommodate, by suitable design, each of the different trip stages of the movement hierarchy is a cause of street and highway obsolescence. Conflicts and congestion occur at the interfaces between public streets and the site circulation of development projects when the transitions are functionally inadequate.

FUNCTIONAL CLASSIFICATION OF CIRCULATION FACILITIES

A functional system of streets and highways must provide for a graduation of traffic flow from the movement function to the access function. The entire system can be schematically classified by relating the proportion of movement function to that of access function. At

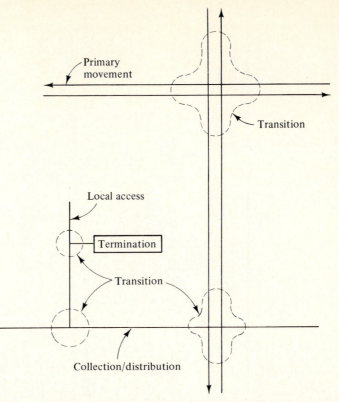

Figure 4-1   Hierarchy of movement in a functional circulation system.
SOURCE: adapted from American Association of State Highway and
Transportation Officials [1].

one extreme is the freeway or expressway which carries no local-access traffic; at the other extreme is the local cul-de-sac street which carries no through traffic. The access function is characterized by the degree of use of the street for access purposes and the decreasing degree of access restriction exercised. Access control ranges from complete control in the case of the freeway to no control in the case of the cul-de-sac.

It is important to note that the classification according to movement and access is a continuum from unrestricted access (no through traffic) to complete access control (no local traffic). While the higher classes of streets, as a group, carry larger traffic volumes than the lower classes, actual (counted) traffic volumes are not an element in functional classification. Once the existing and future street system has been properly classified as to function, there should be no need or justification to change it unless there is a significant change in the urban comprehensive plan.

Figure 4-2 schematically shows the relationship between access and movement. As indicated, three general classes of facilities (arterial, collector, and local) are recognized [1]. Each in turn is subdivided into various facility types and typical cross-sectional designs to meet the specific needs of a particular political jurisdiction or development. In large urban areas, a number of facility types and typical designs will be required; in a small municipality only three to five typical cross sections may be required. The general types of facilities and their characteristics are summarized in Table 4-1 and briefly described in the following. While the terms major and minor are used herein, the terms primary and secondary, respectively, are equivalent and also frequently employed.

Arterials

Freeways serve the function of movement and are therefore properly classified as major arterials, as is the case with the 1984 AASHTO policy. Owing to their unique geometric

TABLE 4–1
Functional Route Classification

Classification	Function	Typical Percent of Surface Street System Mileage	Continuity	Spacing (miles)	Typical Percent of Surface Street System Vehicle-Miles Carried	Direct Land Access	Minimum Roadway Intersection Spacing	Speed Limit (mph)	Parking	Comments
Freeway and Expressway	Traffic movement	NA*	Continuous	4	NA	None	1 mile	45–55	Prohibited	Supplements capacity of arterial street system and provides high speed mobility
Primary Arterial	Intercommunity and intrametro area Primary—traffic movement Secondary—land access	5–10	Continuous	1–2	40–65	Limited—major generators only	1/2 mile	35–45 in fully developed areas	Prohibited	
Secondary Arterial	Primary—intercommunity, intrametro area, traffic movement Secondary—land access	10–20	Continuous	1/2–1	25–40	Restricted—some movements may be prohibited; number and spacing of driveways controlled	1/4 mile	30–35	Generally prohibited	Backbone of street system
Collector	Primary—collect/distribute traffic between local streets and arterial system Secondary—land access Tertiary—interneighborhood traffic movement	5–10	Not necessarily continuous; should not extend across arterials	1/2 or less	5–10	Safety controls; limited regulation	300 feet	25–30	Limited	Through traffic should be discouraged
Local	Land access	60–80	None	As needed	10–30	Safety controls only	300 feet	25	Permitted	Through traffic should be discouraged

(Arterial — includes Primary Arterial and Secondary Arterial)

SOURCE: The Traffic Institute, Northwestern University [29].

*NA = Not applicable.

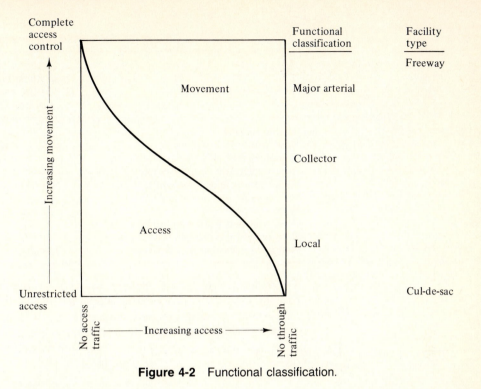

Figure 4-2 Functional classification.

and access design it is a convenient and common practice to identify them as a separate design category distinct from other arterials.

The other, *at-grade,* arterials are commonly further divided into *major* and *minor arterials* (each of which might have a number of different cross-sectional designs). However, it is possible to develop an urban street system which does not utilize the minor arterial category. Rather, selected major collectors are enhanced in the vicinity of major activity centers. Major arterials are intended to provide a high degree of mobility and serve the longer trips. Therefore, they should provide for high operating speeds and levels of service. Since movement, not access, is their principal function, access management is essential in order to preserve capacity. Major arterials provide continuity for the intercity arterials through urban areas; therefore, they serve most of the trips entering and leaving the urban area as well as those trips passing through it. The urban major arterial system interconnects such major developments as the central business district, large suburban commercial centers, large industrial centers, major residential communities, and other major activity centers within the urbanized area.

Desirable and theoretical operating speeds on arterials should be 40–45 mph in the off-peak and 30–35 mph in the peak period. Intersections with other public streets and private access should be designed to limit speed differentials between turning vehicles and other traffic to 10 mph. Signalized intersections should be spaced far enough apart to permit efficient two-way progressive movement of traffic between intersections at the desirable off-peak and peak-hour speeds. Recommended operational criteria for the urban sections of intercity arterials and intracity arterials are given in Table 4-2.

Left- and right-turn bays should be provided at all intersections, public and private, with major arterials and should have the provision for double left turns at all major intersections. Left- and right-turn bays need to be sufficiently long to limit the speed differential and store all turning vehicles with a probability of at least 85%, preferably 95%.

Implementation of such criteria will help ensure that the traffic capacity and level-of-service is maintained. This, in turn, will help preserve the regional accessibility (market area) of private development and help stabilize land use patterns and property values. Thus, preservation of the level-of-service on the arterial system is mutually advantageous to the public and private sectors.

TABLE 4-2
Recommended Operational Criteria for Major At-Grade Arterials

	Sections of Intercity Arterials Within Urbanized Areas	Intraurban Arterials
Off-peak periods:		
Speed (mph)	45 min.	40–45 min.
Design speed differential (mph)	10 max.	15 max.
Progression band cycle length (%)	45 min.	40 min.
Range of cycle lengths (seconds)	45–90	45–90
Peak periods:		
Speed (mph)	30–40 min.	3–35 min.
Design speed differential (mph)	10 max.	10 max.
Progression band cycle length (%)	40 min.	25 min.
Range of cycle lengths (seconds)	90–120	90–120

The minor arterial system interconnects with and augments the major arterial system. It accommodates trips of somewhat shorter length and slightly lower level-of-service. Therefore, operating speeds and traffic-signal progression may be less than on the major arterial. Such a facility interconnects residential, shopping, employment, and recreational activities at the community level. However, as with major arterials, the minors should not penetrate identifiable residential neighborhoods.

Collectors

The collector system provides both land access and movement within residential, commercial, and industrial areas. Collectors penetrate, but should not have continuity through, residential areas.

Operating speeds should be 25 to 30 mph. Since speeds are slower and turning movements are expected, a high speed differential (15 mph) and closer intersection/access spacings can be used than on arterials.

The cross-sectional design of collector streets may involve considerable variation, depending upon the type, scale, and density of the adjacent development. Access spacing (public and private), cross section, alignment, and continuity need to be integrated in the design of the adjacent project designs. Therefore, the designer must exercise a much broader latitude of good judgement than with access to an arterial street.

For a large development such as a regional shopping center, the on-site roadway that interconnects the parking areas and the access drives is the internal-circulation equivalent of a major collector. Speeds should be somewhat slower than on the public collector street system, preferably 30 mph or less.

Locals

Local streets serve to provide land access and can and do exist in any land use setting. In other words, there can be local residential streets, local downtown streets, and local industrial streets. Movement on local streets is incidental and involves traveling to or from a collector facility. Therefore, trip length on the local street is short and as a result volumes may be low and speeds are slow.

On-Site Circulation

The same principles of functional design which apply to streets and highways also apply to on-site circulation systems, and the stages of hierarchical movement are recognizable in an internal circulation system. For example, the aisles leading to individual parking spaces (vehicle terminal) become the equivalent of the local access streets. Thus, a well-designed internal circulation system will accommodate the order of movement and provide an appropriate transition with the public street system. The range of movement hierarchy that will be necessary as part of the on-site circulation system varies with the size of the traffic generator.

With small generators, direct access to a collector, but not to an arterial, is justified. An intermediate collector street should be used to combine the traffic flows from several commercial developments to justify an intersection with the arterial street.

A very small generator, such as a stand-alone convenience grocery, has an on-site circulation system which is the equivalent of a local access street; the driveway is the equivalent of nothing more than a collector.

A regional shopping center will include the full range of circulation elements from primary movement to local access and vehicle terminal. The driveways to such large generators are the functional equivalent of an arterial street. Thus, a signalized intersection with the major arterial street is justified. However, the intersection of such an access drive should have the same spacing and design characteristics as the intersection of two at-grade major arterials.

As the size of a development increases, the internal circulation system will require an increasing range from the hierarchy facilities. A large commercial or industrial development will incorporate the entire spectrum of functional facilities. Smaller developments will include a more limited range of functional facilities. Some parallels between public streets and on-site circulation are:

Classification of public street	Comparable internal circulation
• Local	• Aisle within parking lot
• Minor collector	• Circulation aisles at end of parking rows • Access drive of a small stand-alone business
• Major collector	• Circulation road connecting parking areas within a large development • Access drive of a moderate-size development such as a community shopping center
• Minor arterial	• Access drive of a large development
• Major arterial	• Access drive to a very large mixed-use development or a regional/superregional shopping center

The design standards for on-site circulation roadways should be similar to those of public streets for the same operating speeds. However, operating speeds on the on-site facilities generally will be lower than the comparable class of public street.

Functionally Designed Street Systems

In a street system which has been developed based on functional criteria, about 75% of the vehicle-miles of travel will be carried on the arterial streets, which typically will comprise about 10% of the street mileage. While local streets should comprise about two-thirds of the total street mileage, they should carry less than 10% of the vehicle-miles of travel; a percentage higher than 10% would suggest a deficiency in the arterial street system and/or poor design of residential areas.

The development of a street system based on functional concepts has numerous benefits, including the following:

1. The arterials can be designed to safely accommodate the high traffic volumes and high speeds.
2. Traffic control is simplified.
3. The pavement of designated streets can be designed to carry the high number of repetitions and high wheel loads. Other streets can be designed for a low number of repetitions and light wheel loads. Consequently, total maintenance costs are reduced.

4. Residential areas are not subject to through traffic, which makes them more desirable and safer places to live. Commercial office and retail land uses are concentrated in fewer but larger and better-designed developments. Strip development is reduced.

Other Considerations

The location and spacing of signalized intersections, unsignalized access, and the design of adjacent development must be made within the framework of a functional hierarchy of circulation. The fact that future signal locations must be incorporated into the initial design of streets and highways was recognized by Marks [20, pp. 266–267] in stating:

> Traffic signals are usually considered as a control device installed in response to a specific warrant involving conflicting traffic streams, and constituting a corrective device to resolve a problem at a particular location. However, traffic signals have recently taken on a more comprehensive function. Signals are no longer considered as a purely negative restrictive device, but rather as a positive metering system that regulates the flow of traffic in a predetermined pattern. Sophisticated systems of traffic signal control applied in a sequential pattern according to specific spacing criteria optimize traffic efficiency along an arterial highway. This positive application of signal control is possible when signals are viewed as an integral element of highway design. The highway and its intersections are designed in accordance with traffic signal criteria.
>
> The system of signalization of the arterial should be included in the initial design. Estimates of the relative proportions of through traffic and turning traffic at each major intersection provide the basis for determining the number of through lanes and turn lanes needed. The actual installation of signals may be delayed until traffic volumes mount to a level at which signal control becomes necessary. However, the design of the signal system should be an intrinsic part of the design of the highway with provision made for future installation. The need for early design of the traffic signal system is especially apparent when considering the relationship of access design and control to the locations of future signals.

Signalization is often permitted at short, irregular intervals based upon development decisions that are in conflict with the efficient operation of the future signal system. This ultimately will be detrimental to the arterial and the adjacent development. Identification of locations which will be considered for future signalization, when traffic warrants are met, will influence decisions as to the location, type of activity, and circulation design of development along the arterial.

A private access drive with a public street is an intersection in all respects, the same as that with a public street having the same traffic demand. Functional design criteria distinguish an access as being either a signalized or an unsignalized intersection—no distinction is made between public and private. The provision of unsignalized access to arterial streets will reduce the demand for the same movements at the signalized intersections. However, such access should be located and designed to enhance, not to interfere with, the safe and efficient movement of high volumes of traffic at reasonably high speeds, which is the function of an arterial street.

TRAFFIC LANES

Lane widths may vary from 10 feet to 12 feet. The 12-foot lane widths are most desirable and are generally used on all higher-speed, free-flowing major arterials. An 11-foot lane width is adequate for through lanes, left-turn lanes, and a lane adjacent to a painted median where speeds are 40 mph or less. The 10-foot widths are sometimes used on major collector streets or in highly restricted areas having little or no truck traffic and where the available right-of-way precludes wider lanes.

Lane widths must be selected with judgment. If heavy truck traffic is anticipated, an additional one foot in width is desirable. All the lane-width requirements and intersection design controls should be evaluated when making the lane-width selection. For instance, a wider right-hand lane that provides right turns without adjacent lane encroachment may require a narrower left-turn lane. Local practice and experience regarding lane widths should also be evaluated. Special lane widths for such instances as bike lanes within the roadway require special attention.

At arterial speeds there is substantial danger that a driver will lose control of the vehicle if the curb is struck. Therefore, the gutter should not be considered as part of the traffic lane on arterial streets. Nor should it be considered as part of the traffic lane on major collectors in areas of commercial use or in other locations where high volumes might be expected.

ACHIEVING TRAFFIC SAFETY IN RESIDENTIAL SUBDIVISION DESIGN

Two characteristics distinguish a residential subdivision designed with traffic safety in mind:

1. There are a limited number of access points with the major arterial streets which border the subdivision. These access points are the major collectors serving the subdivision and are commonly spaced at intervals of at least one-quarter mile.

2. The internal street system is discontinuous so as to discourage through traffic from penetrating the subdivision.

These characteristics also make a residential area a more desirable place to live, which preserves property values and helps to stabilize land uses.

Marks [19,20] has demonstrated the superiority of this design, which, in view of the first characteristic given above, has become known as the limited-access division. As indicated in Figure 4-3, the gridiron subdivisions experience nearly eight times the number of accidents as limited-access subdivisions (77.2 as compared to 10.2). The superiority of the limited-access subdivision is further demonstrated by Figure 4-4. Fifty percent of the intersections in the gridiron subdivisions experienced one or more accidents in the five-year period compared to less than 10% in the limited-access subdivisions. Marks also found three-way intersections within the subdivisions to be much safer than four-way intersections. As shown in Figure 4-5, the likelihood of an accident at a three-way intersection is less than 10% per year. Four-way intersections were found to have an accident expectancy of over 27% in limited-access subdivisions and about 56% in gridiron subdivisions.

These data clearly show that superior traffic safety of the three-way configuration for all intersections within a residential subdivision. The four-way intersection should not be used except where traffic movements on two of the approaches result in the intersection's functioning as "opposing three-way intersections" (see Figure 4-6). Jog inter-

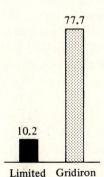

Figure 4-3 Average number of accidents per year. SOURCE: Harold Marks [19].

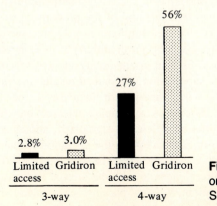

Figure 4-4 Percent of intersections having one or more accidents in a five-year period. SOURCE: Harold Marks [19].

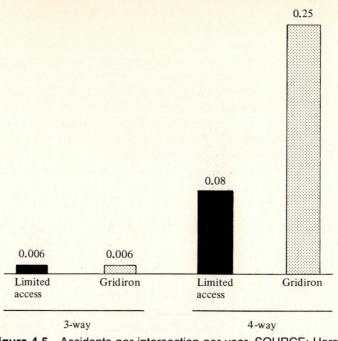

Figure 4-5 Accidents per intersection per year. SOURCE: Harold Marks [19].

sections (Figure 4-7) should be avoided in all cases. However, it must be recognized that there is a relationship between lot depth and the intersection spacing of local streets. For example, if the right-of-way width of a local street is 50 feet, a minimum lot depth of 150 feet is necessary in order to avoid a jog. This minimum lot depth is the minimum distance between rear right-of-way lines (125 feet) plus one-half of the right-of-way width (25 feet). If a shallower lot depth is to be used, a street system such as illustrated in Figure 4-6 should be used.

Residential Development Adjacent to Arterial Streets

Lot arrangement adjacent to an arterial street should use the cul-de-sac or "back-up" lot configurations (see Figure 4-8). As illustrated in Figure 4-9, off-setting three-way intersections can be achieved by using different patterns on opposite sides of the major collector. This will avoid the creation of a four-way intersection on the collector in close proximity to its intersection with the arterial. (See page 90)

The log patterns illustrated in Figure 4-10 (p. 91) should be avoided in all new subdivisions. On existing arterials, the elimination of an existing intersection will create the side-on pattern (see Figure 4-11, p. 92). This is an excellent technique for improving the movement function of existing streets and for providing existing gridiron subdivisions with some of the desirable characteristics of the limited-access subdivision. Abandonment of the right-of-way and deeding of the property to the adjacent lots can be effective in generating support for the elimination of the intersections.

The frontage-road design should not be used in residential subdivision design for the following reasons. First, it orients the residences toward the arterial rather than the other residences in the subdivision. Second, it results in a full-width street which serves properties on one side only. This, in turn, increases the per-lot cost of development. Last, and most important, it creates a complex intersection area with numerous conflicts. The intersection can not be efficiently signalized, and even moderate frontage-road volumes result in serious interference with the operation of the arterial.

The alley design should also be avoided in residential subdivision design, since it also orients the residences toward the arterial and away from the remainder of the subdivision. Furthermore, visitors' parking is a problem, since there should be no parking on an arterial, and the typical alley is of insufficient width for parking.

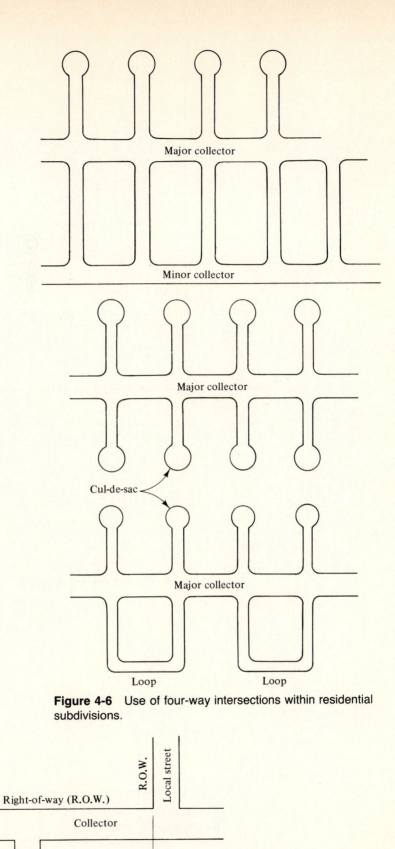

Figure 4-6 Use of four-way intersections within residential subdivisions.

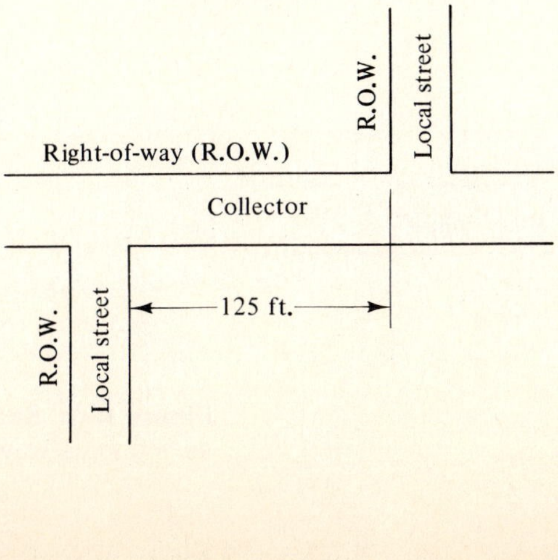

Figure 4-7 Spacing required to avoid a "jog" intersection.

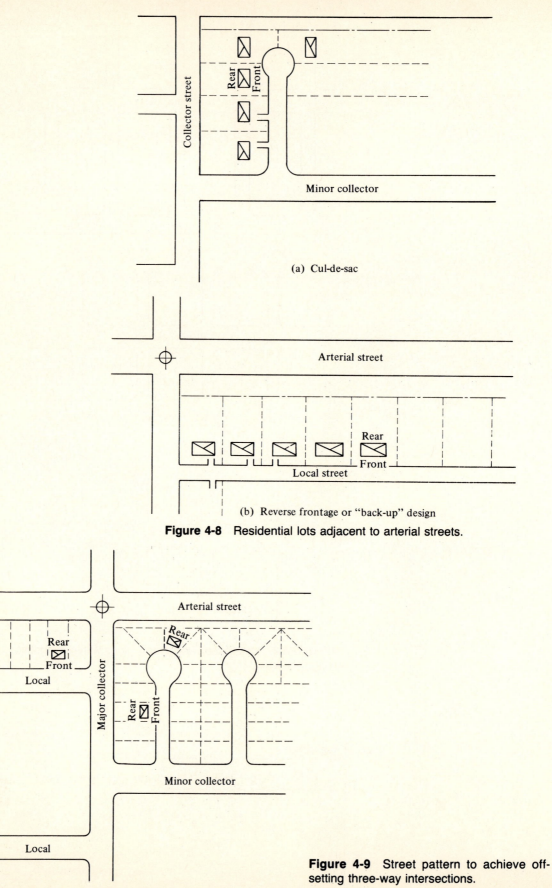

(a) Cul-de-sac

(b) Reverse frontage or "back-up" design

Figure 4-8 Residential lots adjacent to arterial streets.

Figure 4-9 Street pattern to achieve off-setting three-way intersections.

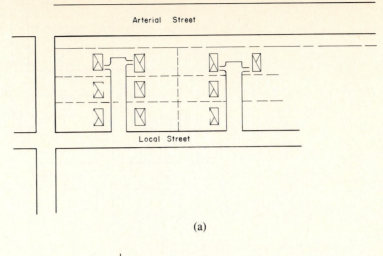

(a)

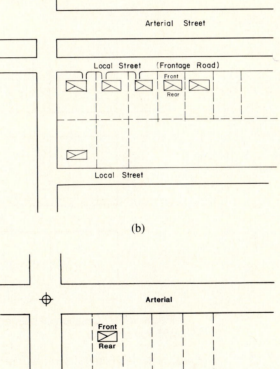

(b)

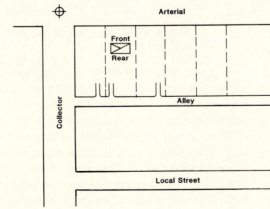

(c)

Figure 4-10 Residential lot arrangements that should not be used: (a) side-on, (b) frontage road, (c) alley.

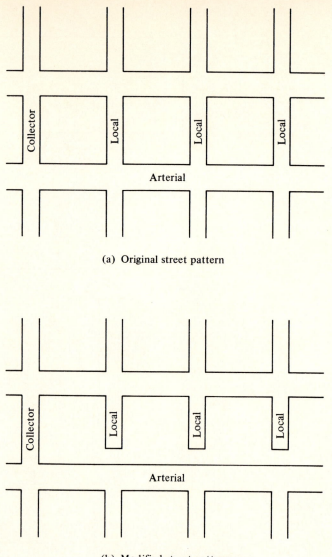

(a) Original street pattern

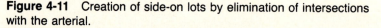

(b) Modified street pattern

Figure 4-11 Creation of side-on lots by elimination of intersections with the arterial.

Local residential streets serve the function of access; volumes should be very low and speeds should be slow. Therefore, the maximum length of cul-de-sacs and other local streets should be limited in terms of both length in feet and the number of dwelling units served. Suggested maximums are 25 dwelling units and 750 feet for cul-de-sacs and 50 to 75 dwellings and 1,300 feet for other local streets.

The radius of the cul-de-sac bulb should allow a fire truck and solid waste truck to complete the turn-around process in one continuous movement when no cars are parked at the curb. This requires a radius of at least 45 feet (preferably 50 feet) to the back of the curb. The radius shown on the subdivision plat must be an additional 10 or 15 feet, depending upon the space in back of the curb used for utilities.

Corner lots should be required to take access to the lesser street (i.e., to the local instead of the collector or to the minor collector rather than the major collector). Access should be at the greatest possible distance from the intersection in order to achieve the maximum possible corner clearance. Both of these requirements should be specified in ordinance and stated on the final plat.

Suggested standards for urban streets are summarized in Table 4-3.

TABLE 4–3

Summary of Minimum Standards for a Street System Based on Functional Design Criteria

	Major Arterial (at-grade)		Minor Arterial		Major Collector[a]		Streets in Residential Areas[b]			
									Local Street	
	6-lane	4-lane	5-lane	4-lane	5-lane	4-lane	Major Collector	Minor Collector	Loop[c]	Cul-de-sac
Paved section, back-to-back of curb (ft.)	—	—	80	47–51	59	45	41	37	29	29
Number of lanes	6	4	5	4	4	4	2	2		n.a.
Lane width (ft.)	11–12	11–12	11–12	11–12	10–11	11	12	10		n.a.
Median width (ft.)	25–30	16	14	n.a.	12	not applicable				
Right-turn lane	channelized or continuous		continuous	channelized or continuous	not applicable					
Left-turn lane(s)	double at signals	single	continuous 2-way left	n.a.	continuous 2-way left	not applicable				
Right-of-way (ft.):										
Recommended	140	110	100	80	90	80	70	65	60	60
Absolute	120	95	80	75	75	75	70	60	50	50
Operating speed (mph)	45	45	40	40	35–40	35–40	35	30	25	25
Minimum radius (ft.)	1,200	1,200	1,000	1,000	700	700	500	350	175	175
Signal spacing (ft.)	1/4 mile				not applicable					
Corner clearance:										
Upstream approach (ft.)	450	450	400	350	200	200	150	most distant location[d]		
Downstream (ft.)	350	350	300	300	200	200	150	most distant location[d]		
Unsignalized access spacing (ft.)	350		300	300	200	200	150–200	lot frontage		
Parking	prohibited						permitted			
Sidewalk	separate ROW		both sides at ROW line		both sides		desirable, both sides			
Continuity	throughout urbanized area		3 miles		1.5 miles		1 mile	0.5 mile	1,400 ft.	750 ft.
Max. no. dwellings served	not applicable						1,000	400	50[e]	24[e]

[a]Multiresidential, retail, office, industrial, institutional, and all uses other than single-family and duplex residential.

[b]Single-family or duplex residential.

[c]Two-ways out (e.g., other than cul-de-sac).

[d]Access to corner lots shall be to the lesser street and located at the property line most distant from the intersection.

[e]Maximum number of dwellings is a more critical criterion than street length.

93

INTERSECTION CAPACITY

There are three basic situations in which the capacity of an intersection needs to be calculated. Dependent upon the type of traffic control, these are:

1. A new intersection which will be created by an access drive of a proposed development and where the estimated site traffic will constitute a substantial proportion of the total intersection volume. The basic capacity analysis should address the following: Will a proposed design, or alternative design, provide capacity which will be (a) considerably greater than demand, (b) somewhat greater than demand, (c) approximately the same as demand, or (d) less than estimated demand?

2. An existing intersection which is located in the developing fringe and, hence, is presently experiencing traffic demand which is substantially less than that which will result when the area is ultimately developed. Under these conditions the existing movements at the intersection do not provide an identification of the future critical movements. The principal problem is to evaluate the increment of capacity that will be absorbed by the proposed development and the increment of unused capacity that will remain.

3. An existing intersection which is presently near or at capacity (volume capacity ratio ≥ 0.85) and where some increment of traffic will be added by the proposed development. In this case the problem is to evaluate alternatives for increasing the capacity and to determine if it is adequate to accommodate the proposed development.

The third situation (an existing intersection is at or near capacity) is the only one in which detailed capacity analysis using the operational analysis presented in Chapter 9 of the 1985 Highway Capacity Manual (1985 HCM) [16] is warranted. The projected turn movements from a traffic assignment are not of sufficient reliability to justify the effort and expense of using the operational analysis. The use of microcomputer models does not improve the accuracy or precision of the individual projected movements. Therefore, in the first two situations, the planning analysis method in Chapter 9 of the 1985 HCM, or some other simplified procedure, should be employed. At the very most, the Level of Service (LOS) should be estimated in very general terms only, using a range of likely cycle lengths and curves such as shown in Figure 4-12.

Signalized Intersections

Optimal and uniform signal spacing is essential if efficient progression and appropriate speeds for arterial streets are to be achieved (see p. 97). Urban arterial streets should operate at 40 to 45 mph in off-peak periods. At these times of the day, cycle lengths of 60 to 70 seconds are commonly required. As illustrated in Figure 4-13 (b), signalized intersection spacing of about one-third mile is necessary if efficient platoon movement is to be achieved. In peak periods, arterial street speeds should be in the 30 to 35 mph range and cycle lengths of 80 to 100 seconds common. Reasonable efficiency in progression requires that signalized intersections be situated at uniform intervals of at least one-third mile — preferably one-half mile where high volumes will necessitate cycle lengths of 100 seconds or longer. Such long uniform spacing of signalized intersections will provide flexibility in the selection of cycle lengths and timing plans that can accommodate a range of traffic volumes and traffic conditions. On minor arterials, spacings of one-fourth mile should be maintained. Reduced flexibility and traffic flow efficiency can be accepted since minor arterials are lower in the functional classification of streets.

Land holding patterns commonly result in a one-fourth mile interval as the practical uniform spacing. In order to achieve desirable operating speeds at this spacing, progression efficiency (progression band width divided by cycle length) must be sacrificed. In order to encourage urban development patterns the urban comprehensive plan should identify the desirable signal spacing to be developed. Implementation should be

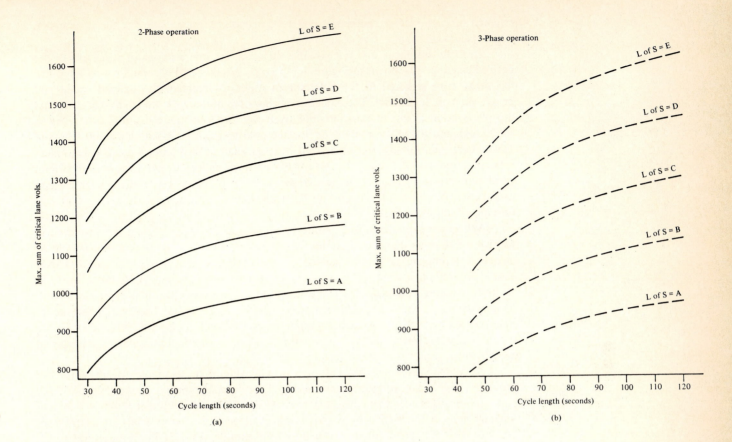

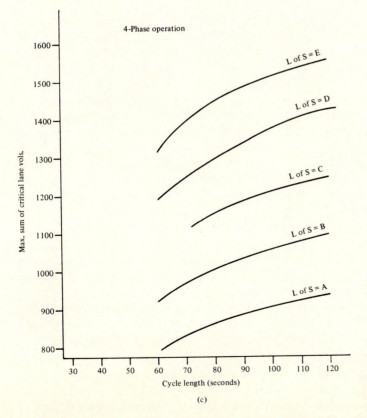

Figure 4-12 Level-of-service by cycle length and sum of critical lane volumes. SOURCE: Roger P. Roess [23].

pursued through clearly stated and widely distributed written policy of the responsible municipal, county, and state government.

In many instances it is not possible to locate the intersections of collectors at the desired spacing. As shown in Figure 4-14 (a), p. 98, this will necessitate a reduction in the green time devoted to the collector in order to maintain the desired speed and progression on the arterial. The reduction is about 1% of the cycle length for each 1% that the intersection is out of position. For example, suppose that the uniform spacing is 1,600 feet and a collector must be located 300 feet out of position (1,900 feet and 1,300 feet from the adjacent signalized intersections) as in Figure 4-14 (b). The intersection is about 19% (300 ÷ 1,600) off the uniform interval. Therefore, the maximum green plus yellow that can be devoted to the collector is about 31%. If the available green time is insufficient for the traffic on the collector, the intersection should be flared to provide additional capacity.

Whenever signalization of public or private access to an arterial is considered at some location other than a desired interval, the effect on speed and progression should be analyzed. Complete programs such as PASSER II, PASSER II-84, and MAXBAND should be used only when the existing volume is close to capacity—V/C ratios ≥ 0.85. At lower existing volumes, the graphical procedure, or one of the simple microcomputer models of this procedure, should be used to obtain the progression band width and speed. The assumption is that at some point along an arterial, the intersection with one or more other arterials will necessitate a 50–50 split of the cycle length. The impact of a proposed signal can then be easily evaluated.

Adequate median width and right-of-way should be available to allow for the provision of left- and right-turn bays at signalized intersections on arterial streets. If not part of the original construction, the median should be of sufficient width for double left-turn lanes at the intersections of two major arterials. Such turn lanes are essential in order to limit the speed differential between the turning vehicles and through traffic.

Signalization of Private Access

Some developments such as regional shopping centers and large industrial plants have extensive frontage on one or more arterial streets. In such cases, signalized access can be provided which conforms to a selected long, uniform signalized intersection spacing.

Large commercial and industrial projects which have been developed in recent years have a well-defined hierarchy of on-site circulation. Private access with an arterial is functionally a major collector, secondary arterial, or primary arterial, depending upon the size of the development and the design of the internal circulation system. The leg of the intersection serving such developments should be designed with the same geometric features as any other major intersection with similar traffic movements (Figure 4-15, p. 99). In addition to being located in conformance to the desired uniform signal spacing, the principal access drives to a regional shopping center should have the following characteristics: (1) free right-turn lanes, both in and out, (2) double left-turn lanes, preferably both in and out, (3) through lanes if required, (4) a median of 6 to 8 feet in width in which a sign is highly visible and properly located to inform approaching drivers of the location at which the ingress maneuver is to be made, and (5) a throat length of at least 250 feet. Intersections serving developments generating lower traffic demand will require lesser cross sections and throat lengths but should have design characteristics at least equal to those of a major collector–arterial intersection.

Median and marginal access should be located at sufficient distance from an upstream or downstream intersection so that access maneuvers do not interfere with operation of the signalized intersection. This upstream corner clearance on arterial streets is a function of the traffic speed as well as queue lengths.

Unsignalized Capacity

The capacity of an unsignalized access location is a function of the distribution of gaps in the traffic stream and the distribution of gaps acceptable to drivers.

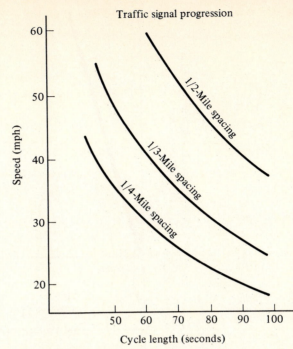

Traffic signal progression

(a) Signal spacing necessary for combinations of cycle length and speed.
SOURCE: Harold Marks [20].

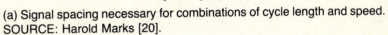
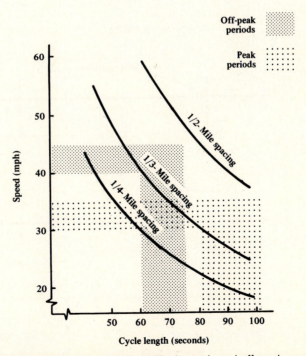

(b) Signal spacing needed for flexibility in peak and off-peak operations.

Figure 4-13   Speed of traffic progression as a function of cycle length and signal spacing.

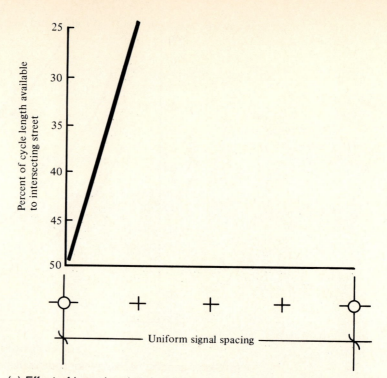

(a) Effect of irregular signal spacing on the percent of cycle length available to an intersecting approach. SOURCE: adapted from Harold Marks [20].

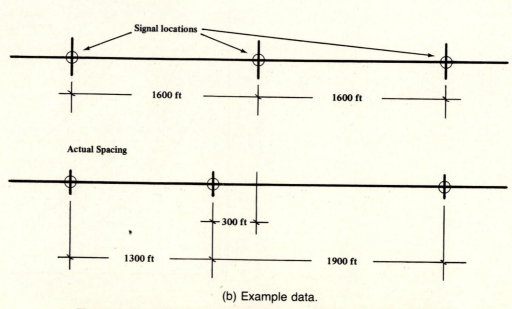

(b) Example data.

Figure 4-14 Reduction in percentage of cycle length devoted to maintain major street progression when a minor street intersection does not conform to the uniform spacing interval.

Figure 4-15 Signalized private access. Access to regional shopping center should conform to the established long, uniform signal spacing. The access should be designed as a primary arterial street intersection including right- and left-turn lanes. In the case of the above photo (Wheaton Plaza Shopping Center), the straight-through volume is very small, so a double left-turn exit was not needed. Incorporating the sign into the access design helps drivers easily and clearly locate the access point at a considerable distance. The median should be at least 150 feet long and a minimum of eight feet wide (at the point where the sign is located).

A driver's acceptable gap increases as the speed of the traffic stream being entered, or crossed, increases; it also increases as the number of lanes which must be crossed increases. If all drivers had the same, or very nearly the same, gap acceptance for the same conditions, the calculation on unsignalized capacity would be much more straightforward. Unfortunately, different drivers differ substantially as to the size of gap they find acceptable. Chapter 10 of the 1985 HCM [16] presents a procedure that analyzes the capacity of an intersection controlled by either a STOP or YIELD sign. The procedure assumes that the major street and its uncontrolled movements are not affected by minor street movements.

The procedure does not consider the reduction in capacity caused by movements to and from other nearby access. When adjacent driveways are situated close together, the overlapping maneuver areas conflict and reduce total capacity. Hence, where there are numerous, close spaced driveways, the total volume of ingress and egress traffic that can actually be accommodated will be less than the calculated capacity. In situations where a high percentage of the volume is on the outside lane of the arterial, the actual capacity will be substantially less than that calculated.

Operational Area at Signalized Intersections

The distances required for a vehicle to maneuver from a through-traffic lane and come to a stop at the end of a right-turn or left-turn lane are given in Table 4-4. As these distances indicate, and observation at major intersections confirms, the intersection maneuver area extends a considerable distance upstream from the physical intersection as defined by crosswalk location (see Figure 4-16). Furthermore, the drivers' maneuver area extends some distance downstream from the crosswalk location because of the need to establish guidance and tracking, often having to pass through areas in which there are no lane lines. This is especially true following a left or right turn.

TABLE 4-4

Minimum Distances for Right- or Left-Turn Maneuver

Street Speed (mph)	Minimum distance for driveway entry (feet)			
	Desirable Conditions[a]		Limiting Conditions[b]	
	Deceleration	Total	Deceleration	Total
35	280	410	240	310
40	360	510	310	390
45	425	590	370	450

SOURCE: Vergil G. Stover [27].

[a]2.0-second perception-reaction time; 7 fps^2 maximum deceleration, 3.5 fps^2 deceleration while moving laterally; lateral movement at 3 fps^2; 10 mph speed differential.

[b]1.0-second perception-reaction time; 9 fps^2 maximum deceleration, 4.5 fps^2 deceleration while moving laterally; lateral movement at 4 fps^2; 15 mph speed differential.

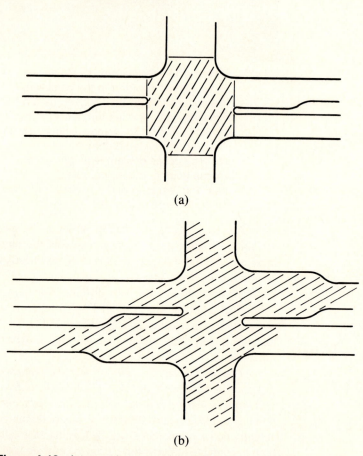

(a)

(b)

Figure 4-16   Intersection area: (a) defined by crosswalk, (b) defined by maneuver area.

Intersection Flaring

The addition of right-turn and/or left-turn bays on one or more approaches of an intersection often is necessary in order to accommodate the additional traffic which will be generated by proposed development. Various intersection configurations, together with typical capacity changes and cost data, are illustrated in Figure 4-17 (pp. 101–3). The cost data are representative values prepared by the City of Dallas. Right-of-way costs, of course, will vary widely from location to location—especially where the existing right-of-way is insufficient and the adjacent property is developed.

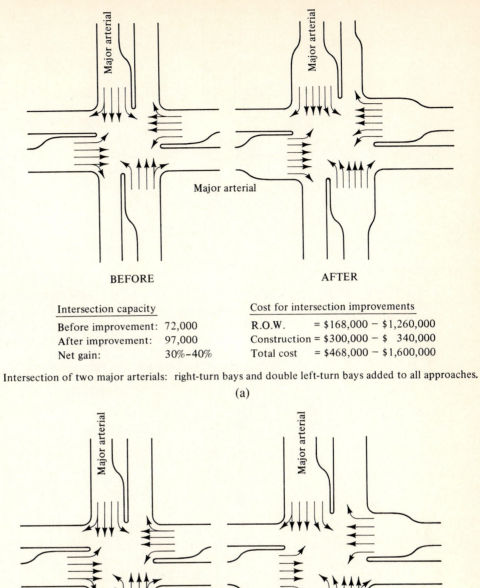

BEFORE   AFTER

Intersection capacity		Cost for intersection improvements	
Before improvement:	72,000	R.O.W.	= $168,000 − $1,260,000
After improvement:	97,000	Construction	= $300,000 − $ 340,000
Net gain:	30%–40%	Total cost	= $468,000 − $1,600,000

Intersection of two major arterials: right-turn bays and double left-turn bays added to all approaches.

(a)

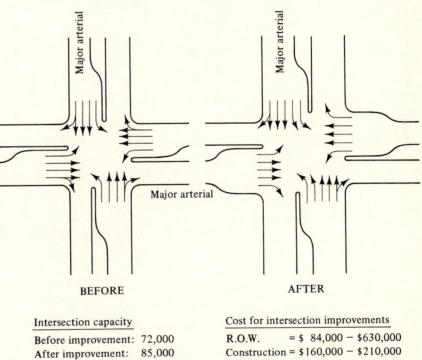

BEFORE   AFTER

Intersection capacity		Cost for intersection improvements	
Before improvement:	72,000	R.O.W.	= $ 84,000 − $630,000
After improvement:	85,000	Construction	= $160,000 − $210,000
Net gain:	15%–20%	Total cost	= $244,000 − $840,000

Intersection of two major arterials: right-turn bays and double left-turn bays added to adjacent approaches.

(b)

Figure 4-17 Typical capacity increases by intersection flaring.
SOURCE: Adapted from the Department of Transportation, City of Dallas [7].

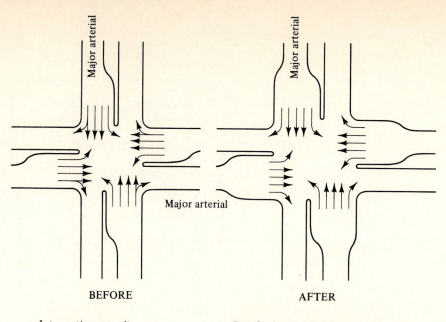

BEFORE   AFTER

Intersection capacity   Cost for intersection improvements

Before improvement: 72,000   R.O.W. = $ 84,000 − $632,000
After improvement: 81,000   Construction = $160,000 − $180,000
Net gain: 10%–15% Total cost = $244,000 − $812,000

Intersection of two major arterials: right-turn bays added to all approaches.

(c)

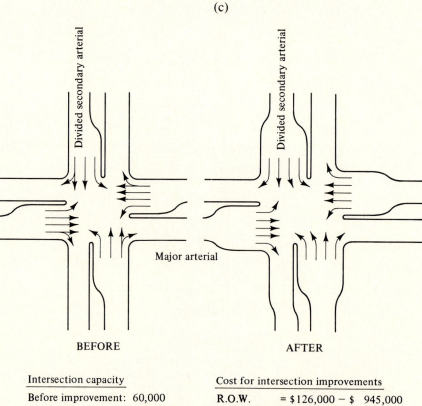

BEFORE   AFTER

Intersection capacity   Cost for intersection improvements

Before improvement: 60,000   R.O.W. = $126,000 − $ 945,000
After improvement: 72,000   Construction = $230,000 − $ 260,000
Net gain: 15%–25% Total cost = $356,000 − $1,025,000

Intersection of a major arterial with a divided secondary arterial: double left-turns added to the secondary street and right-turn bays added to all approaches.

(d)

Figure 4-17 (continued)

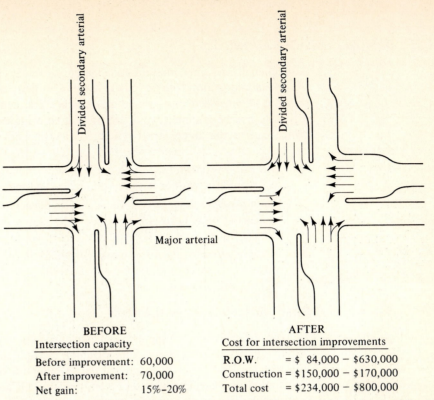

BEFORE	AFTER
Intersection capacity	Cost for intersection improvements

Before improvement:	60,000		R.O.W.	= $ 84,000 − $630,000
After improvement:	70,000		Construction	= $150,000 − $170,000
Net gain:	15%–20%		Total cost	= $234,000 − $800,000

Intersection of major arterial and a divided secondary arterial: double left-turn bays added to the secondary arterial and right-turn lanes added to the major arterial.

(e)

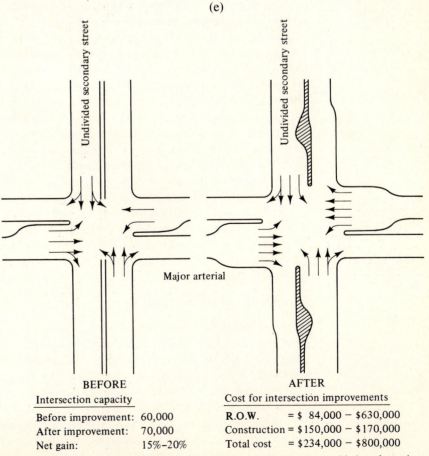

BEFORE	AFTER
Intersection capacity	Cost for intersection improvements

Before improvement:	60,000		R.O.W.	= $ 84,000 − $630,000
After improvement:	70,000		Construction	= $150,000 − $170,000
Net gain:	15%–20%		Total cost	= $234,000 − $800,000

Intersection of major arterial and undivided secondary street: right-turn bays added to the major arterial and left-turn bays added to the secondary street.

(f)

Figure 4-17 (continued)

ACCESS DESIGN CONSIDERATIONS

A functionally designed transportation system recognizes that a private driveway, in fact, creates an intersection with the public street. Conflicts, and the potential for congestion, occur at all intersections—public and private. The detrimental effect of a residential driveway will be minimal, while a heavily used commercial driveway can operate as a critical intersection in the street system. Basic principles of access control include:

Separate the conflict areas. Reduce the number of driveways or increase the spacing between driveways or between driveways and intersections.

Limit the types of conflicts. Reduce the frequency of conflicts or reduce the area of conflict at some or all driveways on the highway by limiting or preventing certain kinds of maneuvers.

Remove turning vehicles or queues from the through lanes. Reduce both the frequency and severity of conflicts by providing separate paths and storage areas for turning vehicles and queues.

Direct Access to Arterial Streets

The concept of functional hierarchy of movement and street system components is becoming increasingly important in the planning, design, and operation of street and highway systems. The policy of functional design/criteria adopted in 1984 by the American Association of State Highway and Transportation Officials (AASHTO) represents an extremely significant change from previous policy and from the outdated practice of using volume-based design criteria. When a generator is of sufficient size to generate traffic equal to the capacity of a freeway ramp, it is appropriate to construct a freeway ramp for access to that generator, provided that (1) the ramp is sufficiently far from any other ramp to permit good signing and geometric design (this normally means at least one mile as an absolute minimum), and (2) the downstream internal-circulation system is designed to have sufficient capacity so that traffic does not back up onto the freeway.

Similarly, a major generator may justify a signalized intersection as access to an arterial street. Such access should be allowed only where (1) the intersection conforms to the long and uniform signal spacing necessary to achieve a high level of progression on the arterial, (2) the downstream internal circulation is designed with sufficient capacity so that backup onto the through traffic lane does not occur, (3) the intersection is designed with a free right-turn lane of sufficient length to limit the speed differential in the outside arterial through traffic lane to 10 mph or less, and (4) the egress drive is designed with sufficient throat width and throat length to ensure high egress capacity.

Moderate-sized traffic generators warrant direct access to a collector street which, in turn, has access to the arterial via a signalized intersection. Other medial and marginal access can be provided between signalized locations without seriously interfering with the arterial's function of movement if such access is carefully located and designed and involves moderate volumes.

Control of Speed Differential

Traffic engineers have long recognized that the elimination of unexpected events and the separation of decision points simplifies the driving task. Since access control reduces the variety and spacing of events to which the driver must respond, it should result in improved traffic operations and reduced accident experience. Various research efforts have explored the general relationships between accidents and medial and marginal access control [e.g., Ref. 2, 4, 5, 6, 10, 14, 15, 17, 21, 24, 25, and 26].

Solomon's research [24, 25] established a relationship between speed differential and accidents. He reported data demonstrating that the chances of being involved in an accident are minimized when the vehicle is traveling at about the average speed of traffic for both night and daytime conditions. Subsequent research by Cirillo, Dietz, and Beatty [5] produced similar results.

As shown in Figure 4-18, the chance of being involved in an accident is minimal when a vehicle is traveling at or slightly under the average speed of traffic and increases at speeds above and below the average speed. The upper graph shows the connection between speed differential and two-car, rear-end accidents. Whereas about 65% of the cars involved in rear-end accidents were traveling at a difference in speed of over 10 mph, only approximately 35% of the other cars (not involved in rear-end accidents) were traveling at speeds which differed by more than 10 mph.

The lower graph clearly shows that the accident involvement rate increases substantially when a vehicle travels much faster or slower than the average speed of traffic. While

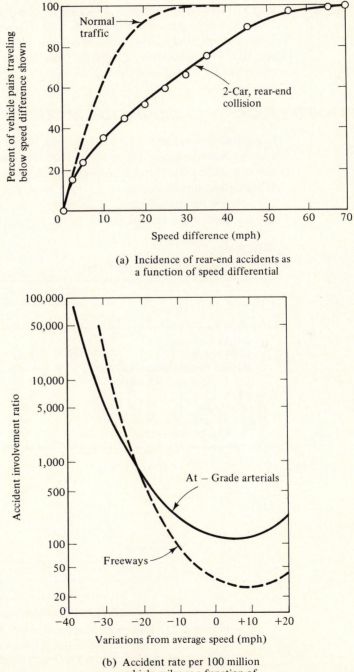

(a) Incidence of rear-end accidents as a function of speed differential

(b) Accident rate per 100 million vehicle-miles as a function of speed differential

Figure 4-18 Relationship between speed differential and accidents.
SOURCE: David Solomon [24].

the actual involvement rates may vary between rural and urban locations, the relative rates presented in Table 4-5 may be expected to be much more transferable. In this form, the data indicate that a vehicle traveling on an at-grade arterial at a speed 10 mph slower than the speed of the normal traffic stream is 180 times (20,000/110) more likely to be involved in an accident than a vehicle traveling at the same speed as the other vehicles in the traffic stream. A vehicle traveling 15 mph slower than the traffic stream has 90 times (20,000/220) the chance of being involved in an accident as a vehicle traveling 10 mph slower. While the relative ranges may be in considerable error, for any specific section of street or freeway, they clearly show that increased speed differentials result in substantially increased accident potential. Thus, designs which produce small speed differentials (less than 10 or 15 mph) should be major criteria for the functional design of arterials.

As will be presented in Chapter 5, all reasonable curb-return radii and throat-width combinations result in low-speed turn maneuvers and, hence, high speed differentials on arterial streets. Therefore, a right-turn bay (Figure 4-19) or a continuous right-turn lane (Figure 4-20) should be provided.

GUIDELINES FOR THE LOCATION OF UNSIGNALIZED ACCESS

Unsignalized direct access to arterial streets can be provided without seriously interfering with the movement function so long as careful attention is given to the location, spacing, movements permitted, and the design of such access. The same criteria should be applied to public and private access.

Poorly designed access, or unrestricted access (Figure 4-21), results in functional obsolescence of the arterial as well as the private development.

TABLE 4-5

Relative Accident-Involvement Rates

	Speed Differential (mph)				
	0	−10	−20	−30	−35
At-grade arterials:					
Accident rate	110	220	720	5,000	20,000
Ratio, 0-mph differential	1	2	6.5	45	180
10-mph differential		1	3.3	23	90
Freeways:					
Accident rate	30	100	600	2,000	
Ratio, 0-mph differential	1	3.3	20	67	
10-mph differential		1	6	20	

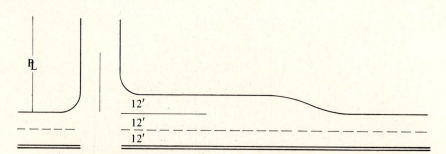

Figure 4-19 Right-turn bay. Provision of a right-turn deceleration lane will reduce the speed differential between turning vehicles and through traffic. It will also decrease the length of time during which the turning vehicle is causing severe turbulence in the traffic stream.
Consequently, rear-end and side-swipe collisions between following cars are reduced.

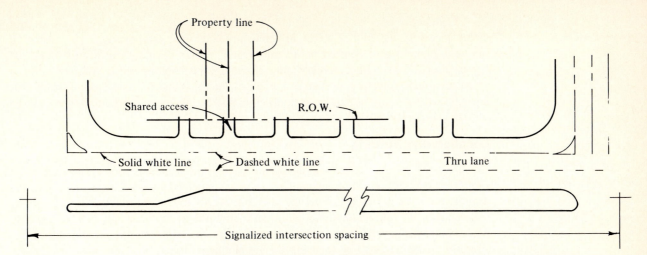

Figure 4-20 Continuous right-turn lane. A right-turn lane might be installed to serve two or more access points or for the entire distance between signalized intersections. In the latter case, channelizing islands at the signalized intersections will establish the beginning and end of the continuous lane and right turns will be "forced" at the downstream signalized intersection. Vehicles can and will enter (ingress traffic) and leave (egress traffic) the lane at random locations. This results in numerous, overlapping conflict areas. Consequently, the operation can be expected to become hazardous when two or more access points have high volumes.

Figure 4-21 Example of unrestricted access. Unrestricted access commonly leads to a severe deterioration in the level-of-service and the ultimate need to construct bypasses for primary intercity arterial highways. In some cases the original bypass has had to be, in turn, bypassed. This photo is of a section on an intercity highway along which "strip development" occurred. The photo was taken a few weeks after the opening of the new bypass.

Contrary to popular belief, the use of frontage roads is not a good technique to limit direct access to an arterial street in urban or developing urban areas. As shown in Figure 4-22, 64 major conflict points are created. When development occurs along the frontage roads, especially commercial development, the resulting traffic volumes result in congestion and accident potential as a result of the low-capacity, overlapping maneuver areas, close proximity of numerous conflict points, and the need for the driver to observe a large and poorly defined area.

Location and Spacing

No direct-access drive to an arterial should be located within the operational area of a signalized intersection. Short spacing between unsignalized access drives compounds the driving task by requiring the driver to watch for ingress and egress traffic at several points simultaneously while maintaining lateral and longitudinal control of the vehicle together with monitoring several vehicles ahead, behind, and in adjacent lanes. Longer spacings simplify the driving task by reducing the amount of information which must be simultaneously acquired, processed, and reacted to and increasing the time between medial and marginal conflict points.

Table 4-6 presents the access-drive spacing that is needed to eliminate overlap of the conflict areas created by a vehicle making a right turn from a driveway and entering the through traffic stream. Thus, it represents the minimum driveway spacing which allows the driver of a through vehicle to monitor one driveway at a time, rather than two or more simultaneously. As indicated by footnotes (b) and (c) to Table 4-6, notice that very high speed differentials will result even at relatively low speeds. Therefore, they should be interpreted as the minimum spacing at which adjacent access drives begin to function as independent intersections.

Major and Buckley [18] have indicated that, from the standpoint of delay to vehicles entering the traffic stream and the ability of the traffic stream to absorb vehicles exiting from driveways, numerous driveways at close spacings result in delay and cause conflicts which increase the traffic hazard. On the other hand, driveways spaced at distances greater than 1.5 times the acceleration distance will reduce delay to vehicles entering the traffic stream and will improve the traffic-absorption characteristics of the traffic stream. Mini-

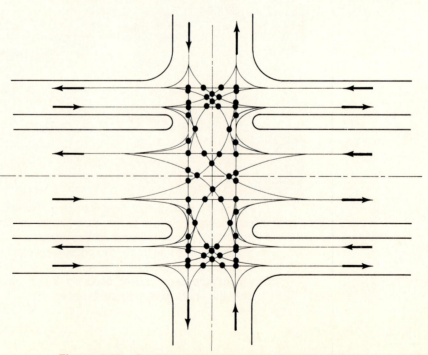

Figure 4-22 Conflict points with parallel frontage road.

TABLE 4-6

Minimum Distance to Reduce Collision Potential Due to Right-Turn Conflict Overlap

Speed (mph)	Minimum Spacing (feet)[a]		
	Author[b]		Glennon, et al.[e]
	Preferable[c]	Limiting[d]	
30	185	100	125
35	245	160	150
40	300	210	185
45	350	300	230

SOURCE: Vergil G. Stover [27].

[a]Spacing allows drivers in the through-traffic stream to consider one access drive at a time. It requires that a through vehicle decelerate in order to avoid a collision when a vehicle enters the through-traffic lane.

[b]Measured center to center of access drives.

[c]A vehicle entering the traffic stream from a driveway completes the 90-degree right turn and accelerates from a stop at 2.0 fps^2. The vehicle in the outside through-traffic lane does not change lanes and decelerates at 6.0 fps^2 after a 2.0-second perception–reaction time. No clearance is provided between the through vehicle and the vehicle entering from the driveway. The implied speed differentials between the driveway vehicle and the through traffic stream are:

Arterial speed, mph	30	35	40	45
Speed differential, mph	20	24	28	32

[d]The driveway vehicle completes the 90-degree right turn and accelerates at an average of 3.1 fps^2. The through vehicle decelerates at an average of 6.0 fps^2 after a one-second perception–reaction time. No clearance is provided between the vehicles. The implied speed differentials are

Arterial speed, mph	30	35	40	45
Speed differential, mph	14	19	24	29

The lower speed differentials for the "limiting" case result from the higher assumed acceleration rate of the driveway vehicle.

[e]Measured near curb to near curb. Assumes: 8.5 fps^2 by the through vehicle; driveway vehicle accelerates at an average of 2.1 fps^2 for a 30-mph speed and an average of 1.7 fps^2 for all higher speeds.

TABLE 4-7

Driveway Spacing Based on AASHTO Acceleration Distances from Stop

Operating Speed (mph)	Spacing (feet)
25	360
30	585
35	825
40	1,140
45	1,575

mum spacings based on AASHTO acceleration distances for passenger cars on level grades are given in Table 4-7.

Influence of Progression on the Choice of Direct-Access Location

The existence of signal systems in urban street networks creates traffic streams which are organized into platoons of vehicles. Platoon flow is substantially different from a random pattern, because intermittent groups of vehicles arrive, followed by substantial gaps between groups (or platoons) in which flow is light.

Therefore, the time–space diagram for platoon flow on the arterial street should be analyzed when considering the location of unsignalized access (public or private). For purposes of example, consider the time–space diagram illustrated in Figure 4-23. The signalized intersections are spaced at quarter-mile intervals. A single alternate system would provide progression in both directions at 30 mph.

Even on arterials with strongly platooned flow, not all flow occurs within platoons. As vehicles enter and/or leave the major street from a variety of sources, such as un-

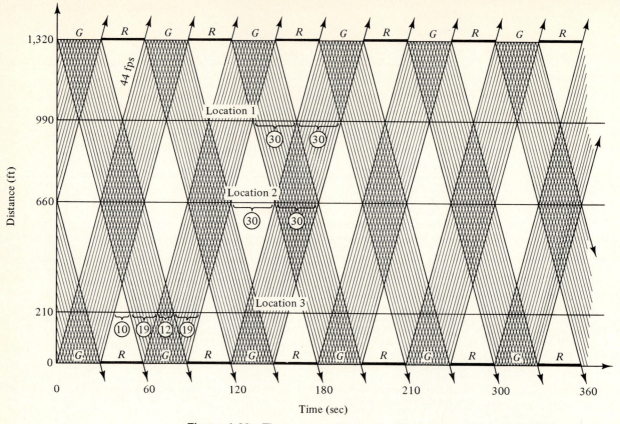

Figure 4-23 Time–space diagram for illustrative problem. SOURCE: Transportation Research Board [16].

signalized intersections, driveways, parking lanes, right-turn-on-red, etc., some volume between platoons occurs. Field studies should be conducted to identify the approximate percentage of total major street volume which occurs within platoons.

Depending on the location of an unsignalized direct-access drive, an egressing vehicle would have different opportunities to make a left turn. For example, if the access were located midway between the signalized intersections (location 2), the platoons from both directions would pass the access drive at the same time. Consequently, gaps between platoons would occur simultaneously. A vehicle at this location would have opportunities to complete a left-turn or crossing maneuver. The capacity for such maneuvers will depend upon the volume of traffic entering the arterial at other direct-access drives and right-turn-on-red at the signalized locations. These arrivals will be approximately random, and the procedures for estimating unsignalized-intersection capacity can be applied.

At locations closer to one of the adjacent signalized locations the simultaneous gap between platoons from both directions decreases. Hence, the capacity for left turns and/or crossing movements will decrease. At a distance of 990 feet from one intersection and 330 feet from the other (location 1), a platoon will block the left-turn and crossing maneuver all the time—first from the left and then from the right. Therefore, without a median of sufficient width to shadow the vehicle, the capacity of the left-turn egress maneuver is zero. At other locations, some capacity for left-turn egress maneuvers will be available. However, even if platooning is extremely good, vehicles entering the arterial from intersecting streets and private access drives will reduce the left-turn capacity.

REFERENCES

1. American Association of State Highway and Transportation Officials, *A Policy on Geometric Design of Highways and Streets,* 1984.

2. Azzeh, J. A., Thorson, B. A., Valenta, J. J., Glennon, J. C., and Wilton, C. J., "Evaluation of Techniques for the Control of Direct Access to Arterial Highways," *Report No. FHWA-RD-76-85,* Federal Highway Administration, August 1975.

3. Bochure, Brian S., "Regulation of Driveway Access to Arterial Streets," Presented at ITE 48th Annual Meeting, Atlanta, Georgia, August 6–10, 1978.

4   Box, Paul C., *Traffic Control and Roadway Elements — Their Relationship to Highway Safety,* Chapter 5, "Driveways," Highways Users Federation for Safety and Mobility, 1970.

5. Cirillo, J. A., et al., "Interstate System Accident Research Study I, Volume 1 — Comparison of Accident Experience on the Interstate and Non-Interstate Highways," *Report of the Bureau of Public Roads,* October 1970.

6. Cirillo, J. A., et al., "Interstate System Accident Research Study II — Interim Report II," *Bureau of Public Roads,* August 1968.

7. Department of Transportation, City of Dallas, correspondence with authors.

8. City of Lakewood, Colorado, *Transportation Engineering Design Standards,* 1985.

9. Colorado Department of Highways, The State Highway Access Code, as revised July 15, 1982, State of Colorado, Department of Highways.

10 Cribbins, P. D., "Correlation of Accident Rates with Geometric Design Components of Various Types of Highways," *Final Report on Project ERD-110-0,* North Carolina State University.

11. "Design Criteria for Left Turn Channelization," *ITE Journal,* Institute of Transportation Engineering, February 1981.

12. Emmerson, J., "A Note on Speed–Road Curvature Relationships," *Traffic Engineering and Control,* November 1970.

13. Emmerson, J., "Speeds of Cars on Sharp Horizontal Curves," *Traffic Engineering and Control,* July 1969.

14. Glennon, J. C., Valenta, J. J., Thorson, B. A., Azzeh, J. A., and Wilton, C. J., "Technical Guidelines for the Control of Direct Access to Arterial Highways, Volume 1: General Framework for Implementing Access Control Techniques," *Report No. FHWA-RD-76-86;* "Volume II: Detailed Description of Access Control Techniques, *Report No. FHWA-RD-76-87;* Federal Highway Administration, August 1975.

15. Heimbach, Clinton L., Cribbins, Paul D., and Chang, Myung-Soon, "The Effect of Reduced Traffic Lane Width on Traffic Operations and Safety for Urban Undivided Arterials in North Carolina," *Final Report, Project ERSD-110-78-1,* Highway Research Program, North Carolina State University, July 1979.

16. "Highway Capacity Manual," *Special Report 209,* Transportation Research Board, 1985.

17. Horn, J. W., Cribbins, P. D., Blackburn, J. D., and Vick, C. E., Jr., "Effects of Commercial Roadside Development of Traffic Flow in North Carolina," *HRB Bulletin 303,* pp. 76–93, 1961.

18. Major, I. T., and Buckley, D. J., "Entry to a Traffic Stream," *Proceedings of the Australian Road Research Board,* pp. 206–228, 1962.

19. Marks, Harold, "Subdividing for Traffic Safety: Engineering Aspects," Paper presented at the Western Section, Institute of Transportation Engineers, undated.

20. Marks, Harold, *Traffic Circulation Planning for Communities,* Gruen Associates under commission from the Motor Vehicle Manufacturers Association, April 1974.

21. McGuirk, William F., "Evaluation of Factors Influencing Driveway Accidents," *Report of the Joint Highway Research Project,* Purdue University, May 1973.

22. Richards, Stephen H., "Guidelines for Driveway Design and Operation," *Research Report 5182-2,* Volume 2, Technical Report, Volume 3, Guidelines, Texas Transportation Institute, April 1980 and unpublished data, 1979.

23. Roess, Roger P., " Addendum to Chapter 6, Critical Movement Analysis, Highway Capacity Analysis," Course Notes, Polytechnic Institute of New York.

24. Solomon, David, "Accidents on Main Rural Highways Related to Speed, Driver, and Vehicle," *Bureau of Public Roads,* July 1964.

25. Solomon, David, "Highway Safety Myths," Highway and Traffic Safety: A Problem of Definition, *North Carolina Symposium on Highway Safety,* Volume II, Spring 1970.

26. Stover, Vergil G., Adkins, William G., and Goodknight, John G., "Guidelines for Medial and Marginal Access on Major Roadways," *NCHRP Report 93,* National Cooperative Highway Research Program, 1970.

27. Stover, Vergil G., "Guidelines for Spacing of Unsignalized Access to Urban Arterial Streets," *Technical Bulletin No. 81-1,* Texas Engineering Experiment Station, January 1981.

28. Stover, Vergil G., Tignor, Samuel C., and Rosenbaum, Merton J., "Synthesis of Safety Research Related to Traffic Control and Roadway Elements," Chapter 4, "Access Control and Driveways," *Technology Sharing Report FHWA-TS-82-232,* December 1982.

29. The Traffic Institute, Northwestern University, Short Course Notes.

30. The Traffic Institute, "Intersections-At-Grade," Northwestern University, 1984.

5

Intersection Design

DESIGN CONSIDERATIONS

The quality of traffic flow and the capacity of an urban arterial are commonly limited by its intersection with another major arterial, where all movements (left, through, and right) normally must be accommodated. Consequently, sufficient right-of-way should be provided at these locations to allow for special turning lanes (right and/or left) in addition to the through traffic lanes. Where sufficient right-of-way is not available, its acquisition should be made a specific precondition to proposed development that would impact the intersection(s).

This chapter discusses considerations involved in the design of at-grade intersections, including access drives and those intersections which are part of the on-site circulation system. Various human, physical, and economic factors, such as listed in Table 5-1, also need to be considered.

Ten different design vehicles are recognized in the AASHTO criteria [1]. The most commonly used design vehicles are passenger vehicles (P), single-unit trucks (SU), and semitrailer combinations of 40-foot (WB-40) and 50-foot (WB-50) wheelbase. The dimensions and minimum turning paths of these four design vehicles are shown in Figures 5-1 through 5-4. Selection of the appropriate design vehicle depends upon the type of vehicles expected in the intersection. However, allowance should be made for occasional semitrailer combinations in most intersection design, even where very few of these vehicles are expected. Even on facilities expected to be used primarily by passenger vehicles, the SU design vehicle is recommended as the basis for selection of minimum intersection dimensions.

The WB-40 and WB-50 design vehicles should be used where trucks approximating these sizes will be frequently encountered. The turn paths of semitrailer combinations require large paved areas in which it is difficult to obtain good traffic control and guidance for passenger-car drivers. Desirable practice is to use larger-than-minimum radii and

TABLE 5-1

Considerations in the Design of Circulation Systems

Human Factors:
- Driving habits
- Driver expectancy
- Driver decision and reaction times
- Driver ability to make correct decisions
- Conformance to natural path of movement
- Pedestrian characteristics and use

Physical Factors:
- Character and use of abutting property
- Topography
- Geometric features
- Traffic-control devices
- Lighting

Economic Factors:
- Costs of improvements
- Effects on abutting residential or commercial properties
- Accident costs or potential accident costs
- Energy consumption
- Travel time and delays

channelize the intersection using painted islands and traffic buttons to identify the maneuver roadways. Research [24] on the turning trajectories of very large trucks indicates that the design of channelizing islands and turning roadways must be substantially different than for the WB-50.

When dealing with residential and commercial development, an appropriate procedure is to design for the passenger vehicle and then check the design to make sure that trucks can negotiate the access drives and on-site circulation system. This approach will minimize the number of intersections in which the auto driver will tend to become disoriented because of the large intersection area. However, special care must be taken to ensure that delivery trucks can be conveniently maneuvered into unloading docks and service areas. This can easily be done using transparent templates which are of the same scale as the site plan and allowing for appropriate clearance beyond the physical size of the vehicle.

Obviously, where large volumes of trucks are expected, as in some industrial areas, the access and circulation must be designed for such vehicles. With large sites that generate large volumes of trucks as well as autos, it is sometimes practical to locate and design separate access and circulation for trucks and autos.

VERTICAL AND HORIZONTAL ALIGNMENT

The alignment and grade of the intersecting roadways should permit users to discern and perform readily the maneuvers necessary to pass through the intersections safely and with a minimum of interference by other users. Therefore, the alignment at intersections should be as straight and the gradients as flat as practical.

The gradients of intersecting roadways should be as flat as practical on those sections that are to be used for storage space for stopped vehicles. The calculated stopping and accelerating distances for passenger cars on grades of 3% or less differ little from the distances on level surfaces. Grades steeper than 3% require correction of the several design factors to produce conditions equivalent to those on level highways. Most vehicle operators are unable to judge the increase or decrease in stopping or accelerating distance that is necessary because of steep grades. Because of this, normal driver reactions may be in error at a critical time. Accordingly, grades in excess of 3% should be avoided on intersecting roadways. Where conditions make such design unduly expensive, grades

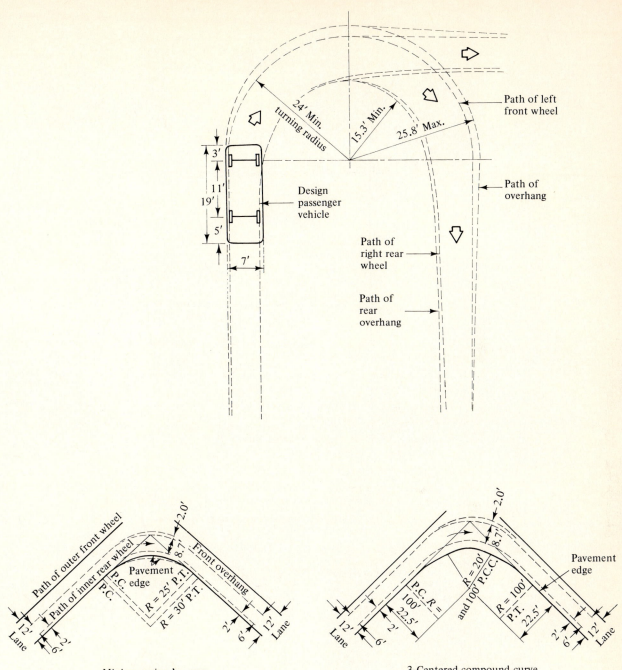

Minimum simple curve
25' or 30' radius

3-Centered compound curve
100'–20'–100' radii, offset 2.5'

Minimum designs for passenger vehicles

Figure 5-1 Minimum turning path for P design vehicle. SOURCE: *A Policy on Geometric Design of Highways and Streets,* Washington, D.C.: The American Association of State Highway and Transportation Officials, copyright 1984. Used by permission.

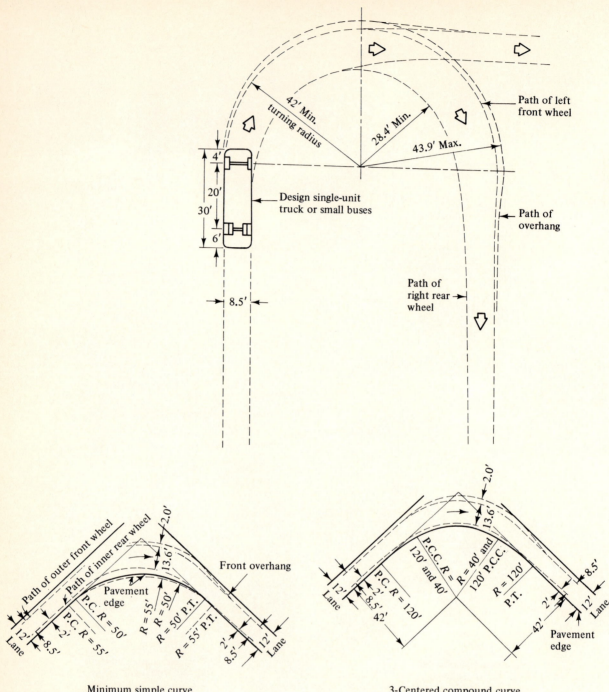

Minimum designs for single-unit trucks and buses

Figure 5-2 Minimum turning path for SU design vehicle. SOURCE: *A Policy on Geometric Design of Highways and Streets,* Washington, D.C.: The American Association of State Highway and Transportation Officials, copyright 1984. Used by permission.

116

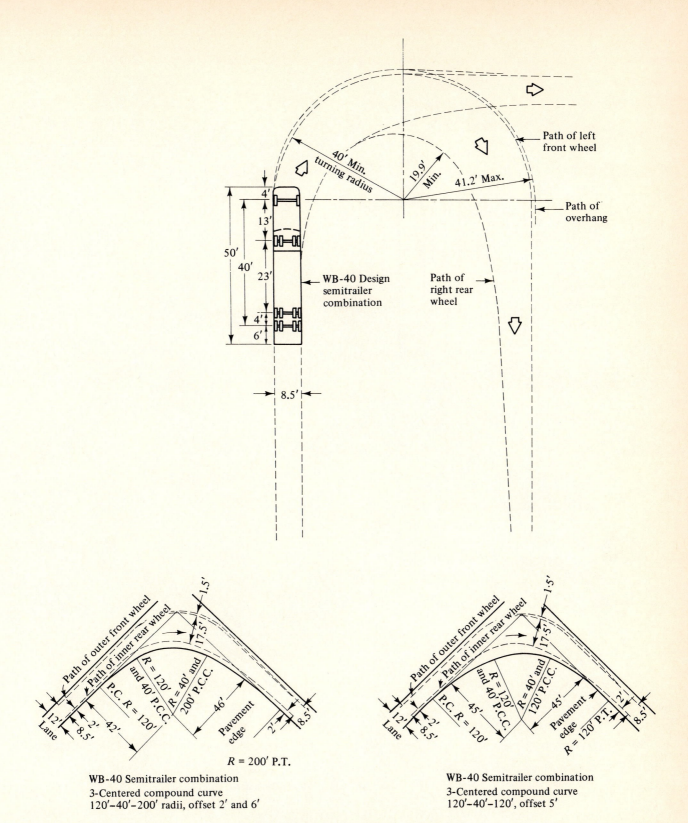

Figure 5-3 Minimum turning path for WB-40 design vehicle.
SOURCE: *A Policy on Geometric Design of Highways and Streets*, Washington, D.C.: The American Association of State Highway and Transportation Officials, copyright 1984. Used by permission.

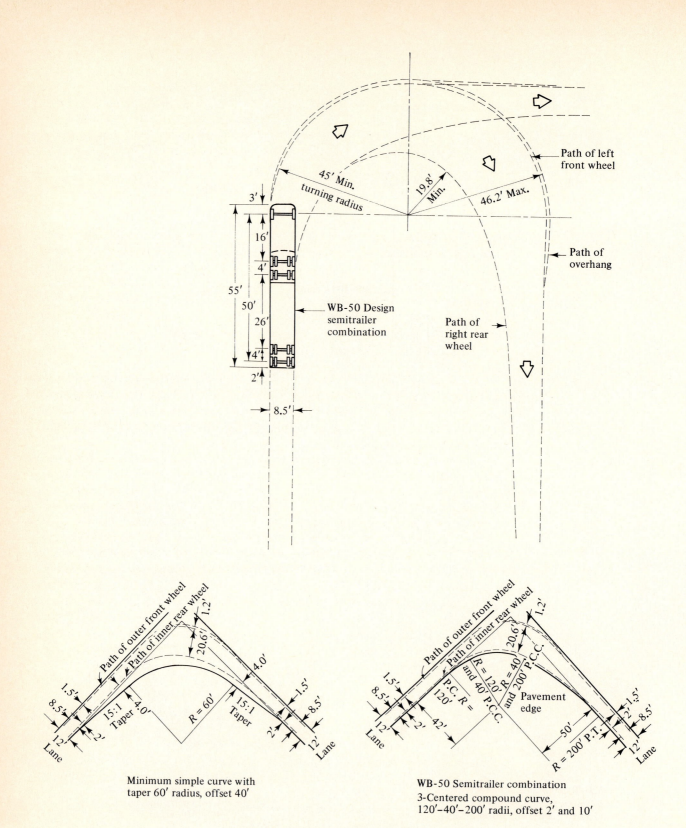

Minimum simple curve with
taper 60′ radius, offset 40′

WB-50 Semitrailer combination
3-Centered compound curve,
120′–40′–200′ radii, offset 2′ and 10′

Minimum designs for semitrailer combinations
(WB-50 design vehicle path)

Figure 5-4 Minimum turning path for WB-50 design vehicle.
SOURCE: *A Policy on Geometric Design of Highways and Streets*,
Washington, D.C.: The American Association of State Highway and
Transportation Officials, copyright 1984. Used by permission.

should not exceed 6%, with a corresponding adjustment in design factors. As a rule, the horizontal and vertical alignments are subject to greater restriction at or near intersecting roads than on the open road. Their combination at or near the intersection must produce traffic lanes that are clearly visible to drivers at all times, understandable for any desired direction of travel, free from sudden appearance of potential hazards, and consistent with the portions of the highway just traveled. The combination of vertical and horizontal curvature must allow adequate sight distance at an intersection. An intersection located downstream from a crest vertical curve followed by a horizontal curve is especially undesirable.

Intersection Angle

Intersecting roadways should cross at, or as close as practical to, a right angle (90°). Angles less than 90° but greater than 60° normally do not seriously interfere with the visibility of auto drivers. Trucks, however, will have a blind spot when the vehicle turns on a large obtuse angle. Furthermore, intersection capacity is reduced about 1% for each one degree of intersection angle less than 90°. Roadways which intersect at other than right angles also have larger intersection areas; this increases the exposure time of vehicles crossing the main traffic flow and may increase the accident potential. Intersections having five or more legs create substantial operational problems and should be avoided in all circumstances — especially on arterial streets.

When two roadways intersect at acute angles, the minor roadway should be re-aligned as illustrated in sketch (a) or (b) of Figure 5-5. However, if the realignment curves require a significant reduction in speed below the normal approach speed, they may prove to be as great a hazard as the acute-angle crossing itself. Warning signs should be provided in advance of such curves.

Another method of realigning a road which intersects at an acute angle is to make a staggered intersection, as shown in sketches (c) and (d) of Figure 5-5. This design regulates crossing vehicles to turn onto the major road and then reenter the minor road. (The terms "major road" and "minor road" are used here to indicate the relative importance of the roadways through the intersection rather than the functional classification of the roads. The designated "minor road" can also be an access drive.) The alignment illustrated in sketch (c) results in a much safer and higher-capacity solution than the alignment in sketch (d). This occurs because vehicles continuing on the minor roadway make a right turn onto the major roadway followed by a left turn which can be "shadowed" in a left-turn bay. The separation between the two intersections should be sufficient to allow vehicles entering the major roadway to safely weave across the through lanes and enter the left-turn bay at the beginning of the taper. Hence, the spacing is a function of speed and expected queue length in the left-turn bay. Suggested minimum distances, exclusive of queue length, are 750 feet where off-peak speeds are 45 mph, 600 feet for 40 mph, and 500 feet for 35 mph. On undivided roadways an isolated left-turn bay must be provided to shadow the turning vehicle.

When the realignment of the minor road is as shown in Figure 5-5(c), the continuity is poor because a crossing vehicle must reenter the minor road by a left turn off the major road. This design arrangement can create storage problems on the major road and should not be used unless the minor highway carries a moderate volume of local traffic, and almost all the traffic turns onto the major highway and does not proceed through the intersection on the minor highway.

When the alignment of the minor road is as shown in Figure 5-5(d), the access continuity is good because a crossing vehicle first turns left onto the major road (a maneuver that can be safely executed by awaiting a gap in the through-traffic stream) and then turns right to reenter the minor road, thus interfering little with through traffic. Where a large portion of the traffic from the minor highway turns onto the major highway, rather than continuing across the major highway, a split-intersection design using two T-intersections may be advantageous regardless of the right or left entry.

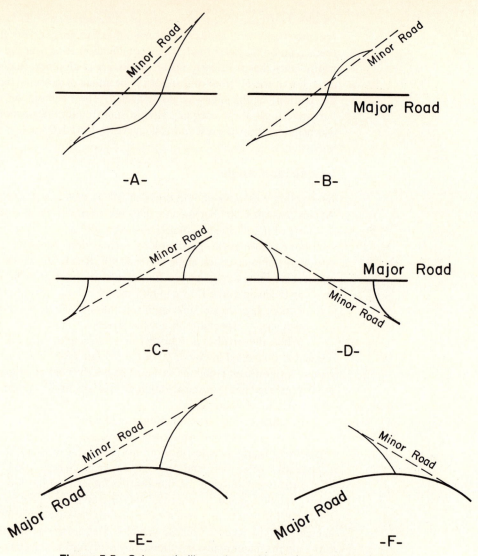

Figure 5-5 Schematic illustrations of intersection realignments.
SOURCE: *A Policy on Geometric Design of Highways and Streets,*
Washington, D.C.: The American Association of State Highway and
Transportation Officials, copyright 1984. Used by permission.

Intersections on sharp curves should be avoided wherever possible because the superelevation and widening of pavements on curves complicate the intersection design.

Where the major road is on a horizontal curve and a subordinate road constitutes an extension of one tangent, realignment of the subordinate road is advantageous, as illustrated in Figure 5-5(e) and (f).

SIGHT DISTANCE AT INTERSECTIONS

The operator of a vehicle approaching an at-grade intersection (including driveways) should have an unobstructed view of the entire intersection and sufficient lengths of the intersecting highway to permit control of the vehicle to avoid collisions. When traffic at the intersection is controlled by signals or signs, the unobstructed views may be limited to the area of control. The sight distance considered safe under various assumptions of physical conditions and driver behavior is directly related to vehicle speeds and to the resultant distances traversed during perception and reaction time and braking.

Sight Triangle

There must be an unobstructed sight distance in both directions on all approaches at an intersection. The sight triangles must be free of obstructions which might interfere with the driver's ability to see other vehicles approaching on the cross-street. At each intersection, assumptions are made about the physical layout and the actions of the vehicle operators on both intersecting roads. For each case, the space–time–velocity relationship indicates the sight triangle that must be free of obstructions.

Any object within the sight triangle high enough above the elevation of the adjacent roadway to constitute a sight obstruction should be removed or lowered, including buildings, cut slopes, hedges, trees, bushes, and tall crops. This also requires the elimination of parking within the sight triangle.

After a vehicle has stopped at an intersection, the driver must have sufficient sight distance to make a safe departure through the intersection area. The intersection design should provide adequate sight distances for all vehicular maneuvers allowed at the intersection. These maneuvers include crossing the intersecting roadway, performing a left turn into the intersecting roadway, or performing a right turn onto the intersecting roadway.

The required sight distance is different for each of the four types of controls that apply to at-grade intersections:

1. *No control.*
2. *Yield control*, where vehicles on the minor intersecting roadway must yield to vehicles on the major intersecting roadway.
3. *Stop control* — at two-way stop signs where traffic on the minor roadway must stop prior to entering the major roadway and at four-way stop signs where all movements on both streets must stop.
4. *Signal control.*

No Control.   When there is no traffic device at an intersection, desirable practice is to provide sufficient sight distance so that a driver may observe a vehicle on another approach in time to bring his or her vehicle to a stop before entering the intersection. The AASHTO policy [1] assumes a 2.5-second perception–reaction time and an average coefficient of friction which varies with speed. The equation used by AASHTO for the stopping distance is as follows:

$$d = 1.47Vt + \frac{V^2}{30f}$$

where:

d = stopping sight distance in feet
V = the approach speed in miles per hour
t = the perception–reaction time (commonly 2.5 seconds)
f = the coefficient of friction between tires and roadway surface

The sight triangle and stopping distances for various speeds are given in Figure 5-6. It should be realized that the AASHTO design criteria reflect the coefficients of friction that encompass the pavement surfaces and likely field conditions that might be encountered. The selection of the design values is based on wet-surface skid tests and represents the lower levels of coefficients of friction that may be expected to be physically available — not necessarily values which the vehicle operator is willing to use. They imply that deceleration rates in the range of 9.7 to 12.9 feet per second per second (fps²) will be utilized by most drivers. While data are limited on deceleration rates which vehicle operators are willing to use under different conditions, generally acceptable rates would seem to be less than 9 fps². Experience with rail transit deceleration suggests that a deceleration rate of 6 to 7 fps² is objectionable to many individuals.

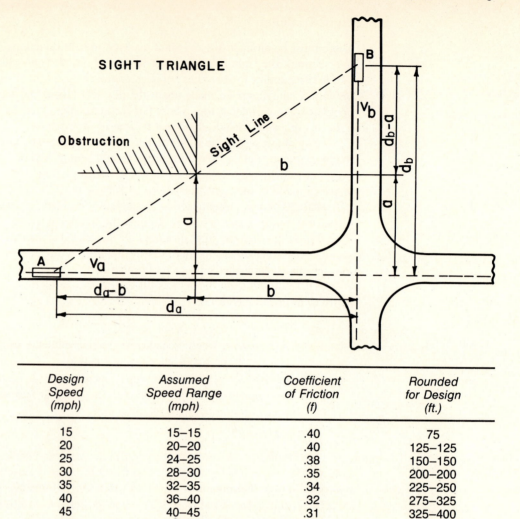

Design Speed (mph)	Assumed Speed Range (mph)	Coefficient of Friction (f)	Rounded for Design (ft.)
15	15–15	.40	75
20	20–20	.40	125–125
25	24–25	.38	150–150
30	28–30	.35	200–200
35	32–35	.34	225–250
40	36–40	.32	275–325
45	40–45	.31	325–400
50	44–50	.30	400–475

SOURCE: American Association of State Highway and Transportation Officials [1].

Figure 5-6 Sight triangle and minimum stopping sight distances. For no control. Also, see Table 5-4 for discussion of conditions. SOURCE: *A Policy on Geometric Design of Highways and Streets,* Washington, D.C.: The American Association of State Highway and Transportation Officials, copyright 1984. Used by permission.

Yield. Posting of a YIELD sign requires the driver on that approach to reduce speed and be prepared to stop if a vehicle is approaching from the left or right. The required line of sight is established by the stopping distance for the vehicle on the YIELD approach and the distance traveled at the design speed by a vehicle on the through street. A reduced approach speed of 15 mph is commonly used for the YIELD approach for urban conditions and 20 to 25 mph for rural conditions.

Two-Way Stop. Where traffic on the minor road of an intersection is controlled by stop signs, the driver of the vehicle on the minor road must have sufficient sight distance for a safe departure from the stopped position. The three basic maneuvers which can occur at the average intersection are described below:

Case A. A through movement across the intersecting roadway, clearing traffic approaching from both the left and the right.

Case B.   A left turn into the crossing roadway, first clearing traffic approaching from the left and then entering the traffic stream approaching from the right.

Case C.   A right turn onto the intersecting roadway, entering the traffic stream approaching from the left.

Case A, Through Movement: Where the principal roadway is undivided, or divided with a narrow median that is not of sufficient width to store ("shadow") the crossing vehicle, the departure maneuver must be made as a single operation. Where the major roadway is divided and has a wide median (wide enough to safely store the design vehicle whether it be a P, SU, WB-40, or WB-50 vehicle), the departure maneuver is considered as two operations.

The sight distance for a crossing maneuver is based on the time it takes for the stopped vehicle to clear the intersection and the distance that a vehicle will travel along the major road at its design speed in that amount of time (see Figure 5-7). This distance may be calculated from the following equation:

$$d = 1.47V(J + t_a)$$

where:

d = sight distance along the major highway from the intersection, feet,

V = design speed on the major highway, mph,

J = sum of the perception time and the time required to actuate the clutch or actuate an automatic shift, assumed to be 2.0 seconds,

t_a = time, in seconds, required to accelerate and traverse the distance S to clear the major highway pavement. The front bumper of the vehicle is assumed to be 10 feet behind the curbline of the street to be crossed.

Case B, Left Turn: Figure 5-8 gives the required sight distance for an automobile to turn left from a two-way stop. Curve B-1 is the required distance with respect to a vehicle approaching from the left. Curves B-2a and b are the sight distances with respect to a vehicle approaching from the left.

Curve B-2a assumes no reduction in speed by the through vehicle approaching from the right. Curve B-2b is the sight distance required for the stopped vehicle to make the left turn and accelerate to the average running speed of the major roadway without being overtaken by a vehicle approaching from the right and reducing speed to the average running speed. At low traffic volumes, average running speeds are assumed to be approximately 90% of the design speed. Therefore the AASHTO curves imply that the turning vehicle will create a speed differential of about 5 mph in the traffic stream. Sight distances which would result in a speed differential of about 10 mph and 15 mph are given in Table 5-2 (p. 126). In the case of undivided highways or divided highways with narrow medians (the median width is less than the length of the design vehicle) the sight distance must be sufficient to allow crossing or entry maneuvers to be performed simultaneously as one operation.

For divided highways with wide medians (the median is wider than the length of the design vehicle), the maneuvers can be performed as two operations. The stopped vehicle must first have a proper sight distance to depart from a stopped position and cross traffic approaching from the left. The crossing vehicle may then stop in the median prior to performing the second operation. This operation requires the necessary sight distance for vehicles approaching on the right to allow the crossing vehicle to depart from the median, to turn left into the cross road, and to accelerate without being overtaken by vehicles approaching from the right.

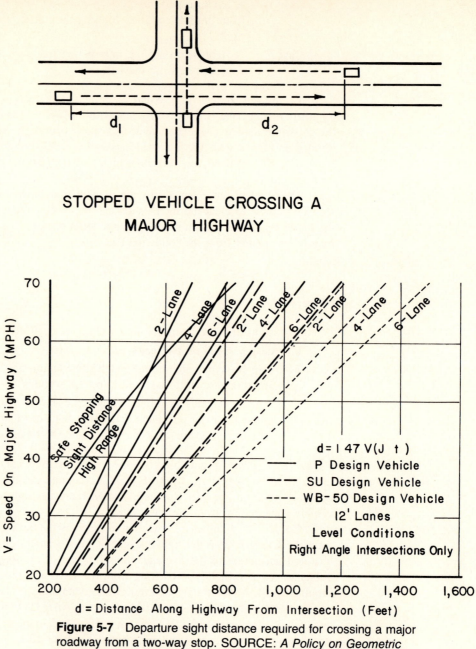

STOPPED VEHICLE CROSSING A MAJOR HIGHWAY

Figure 5-7 Departure sight distance required for crossing a major roadway from a two-way stop. SOURCE: *A Policy on Geometric Design of Highways and Streets,* Washington, D.C.: The American Association of State Highway and Transportation Officials, copyright 1984. Used by permission.

Case C, Right Turn: The sight distance required for a right-turn maneuver by a P-vehicle from a stopped position is given by Figure 5-8. Curve Ca is for the condition where the right-turning vehicle accelerates to the speed of the major roadway without being overtaken by a vehicle approaching from the left. Curve Cb assumes that the right-turning vehicle accelerates to the average running speed of the major roadway and that the vehicle approaching from the left decelerates to the average running speed.

Signal Control. Sight distances at signal-controlled intersections should be the same as those provided for stop control. The reasons for providing such sight distances include (1) violations of the signal, (2) right turn on red, (3) signal malfunction, and (4) flashing red/yellow mode.

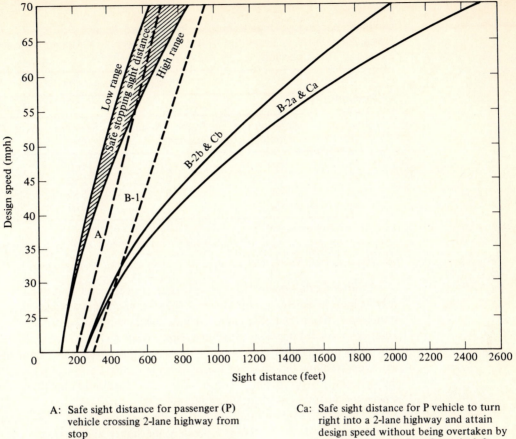

A: Safe sight distance for passenger (P) vehicle crossing 2-lane highway from stop

B-1: Safe sight distance for P vehicle turning left into 2-lane highway across P vehicle approaching from left

B-2a: Safe sight distance for P vehicle to turn left into 2-lane highway and attain design speed without being overtaken by vehicle approaching from the right and maintaining design speed

B-2b: Safe sight distance for P vehicle to turn left into 2-lane highway and attain average running speed without being overtaken by vehicle approaching from the right reducing speed from design speed to average running speed

Ca: Safe sight distance for P vehicle to turn right into a 2-lane highway and attain design speed without being overtaken by a P vehicle approaching from the left traveling at design speed

Cb: Safe sight distance for P vehicle to turn right into 2-lane highway and attain average running speed without being overtaken by vehicle approaching from the left and reducing from design speed to average running speed

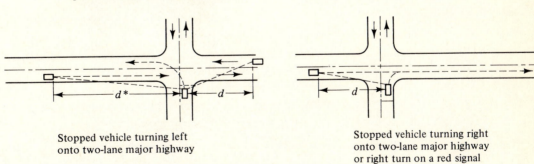

Stopped vehicle turning left onto two-lane major highway

Stopped vehicle turning right onto two-lane major highway or right turn on a red signal

d* = Sight distance

Figure 5-8 Departure sight approaches required for left and right turns to a major roadway from a two-way stop. SOURCE: *A Policy on Geometric Design of Highways and Streets,* Washington, D.C.: The American Association of State Highway and Transportation Officials, copyright 1984. Used by permission.

TABLE 5-2

Minimum Spacing of Driveways and Unsignalized Access Points Necessary to Allow an Egressing Vehicle to Enter the Traffic Stream without Creating a Speed Differential in Excess of That Specified

Through-Traffic Speed (mph)	Speed Differential[a]			
	10 mph		15 mph	
	Spacing (feet)	In Traffic Stream (seconds)	Spacing (feet)	In Traffic Stream (seconds)
30	210	9.5	160	7.1
35	300	11.9	240	9.4
40	420	14.2	350	11.9
45	550	16.7	470	14.2

SOURCE: Vergil G. Stover [23].

[a] The difference between normal traffic speed and the reduced speed caused by a vehicle entering traffic from a driveway. For example: with a 10-mph differential, a vehicle entering traffic from a driveway would cause an upstream vehicle(s) in the through-traffic lane to decrease speed from a normal 40 mph to 30 mph.

Other Considerations.　A basic requirement for all controlled intersections is that drivers must be able to see the control device far enough in advance to perform the action it indicates. When the traffic control device cannot be seen soon enough, advance warning signs are needed. Longer sight distances are needed at skewed intersections and on grades.

Where left turns are permitted from the major roadway, sight distance must be sufficient to allow the driver of the left-turning vehicle to judge whether or not a gap in the opposing traffic stream is sufficient to safely make the turn. The required sight distances for an automobile are given in Table 5-3.

The AASHTO minimum stopping sight distances [1] are based upon passenger-car operation. Trucks, as a whole, especially the larger and heavier units, require longer stopping distances and longer sight distances than passenger vehicles do. However, the truck operator is able to see the vertical features of the obstruction substantially farther because of the higher position of the seat in the vehicle. Separate stopping sight distances for trucks and passenger cars, therefore, are not included in the highway design standards.

TABLE 5-3

Sight Distance Required for a Passenger Car to Complete a Left Turn from a Major Roadway

Operating Speed (mph)	Safe sight distance (feet)		
	2-lane	4-lane	6-lane
20	240	260	280
30	360	390	420
40	470	520	560
50	590	650	700

SOURCE: The Traffic Institute, Northwestern University [26].

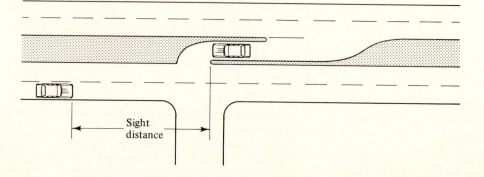

TABLE 5-4

Minimum Stopping Sight Distance—Passenger Car on Wet Surface and Level Pavement

| Speed (mph) | Perception–Reaction | | Breaking Distance (ft.) [a] | Stopping Sight Distance, Rounded (ft.) [b] |
	Time (sec.)	Distance (ft.)		
20	2.5	73	33	125
25		92	55	150
30		110	86	200
35		128	120	250
40		147	167	325
45		165	218	400
50	2.5	183	278	475

Effect of Grade on Stopping Sight Distance—Wet Conditions [b]

| Design Speed (mph) | Increase for Downgrades | | | Assumed Speed for Condition (mph) | Decrease for Upgrades | | |
| | Correction in Stopping Distance (ft.) | | | | Correction in Stopping Distance (ft.) | | |
	3%	6%	9%		3%	6%	9%
30	10	20	30	28	—	10	20
40	20	40	70	36	10	20	30
50	30	70	—	44	20	30	—

[a] The AASHTO breaking distances are based upon an assumed utilized coefficient of friction. These distances imply that a driver can and will use very high average deceleration rates as follows:

speed (mph):	20	25	30	35	40	45	50
deceleration (ft/sec^2):	13.1	12.3	11.3	11.0	10.4	10.0	9.7

Inasmuch as drivers commonly use a lower deceleration rate at the beginning of braking and higher rates near the end, the implied maximum deceleration rates are considerably higher. Deceleration rates above 5 or 6 ft/sec^2 are uncomfortable. Items slide off the seat at about 8 ft/sec^2, and most drivers will have great difficulty controlling the vehicle at maximum deceleration rates above 10 ft/sec^2. Calculated braking distances for an average deceleration of 7 ft/sec^2 and total stopping distances are as follows:

speed (mph):	20	25	30	35	40	45	50
braking distance (ft.):	58	90	130	176	230	292	360
total stopping distance, rounded (ft.):	130	200	240	310	380	460	550

[b] See American Association of State Highway and Transportation Officials [1, pp. 137–144].

There is one situation that should be treated with caution, in which every effort should be made to provide stopping sight distances greater than the minimum design value. When horizontal sight restrictions occur on downgrades, particularly at the ends of long downgrades, the greater height of the eye of the truck operator is of little value, even when the horizontal sight obstruction is a cut slope, and even when (on long downgrades) truck speeds may closely approach or exceed those of passenger cars. Although the average truck operator tends to be more experienced than the average passenger-car operator and quicker to recognize hazards, it is best under such conditions to supply a stopping sight distance that meets or exceeds the values in Table 5-4.

TURNING ROADWAYS

The turn movements will be easier when the pavement edge is designed with spirals or compound curves. The natural path of a turning vehicle is actually a spiral. Spiral designs for 20- and 30-mph design turn speeds are shown in Figure 5-9. Minimum designs for three-center compound curves are given in Table 5-5; example designs for a 90° turn are shown in Figure 5-10. The minimum radii for unsuperelevated turning roadways are given in Table 5-6.

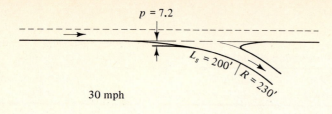

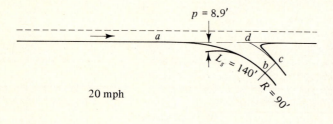

Figure 5-9 Spiral transition curve for turning roadway. SOURCE: *A Policy on Geometric Design of Highways and Streets,* Washington, D.C.: The American Association of State Highway and Transportation Officials, copyright 1984. Used by permission.

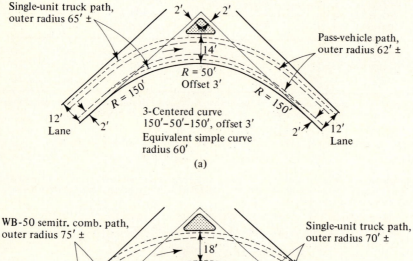

Single-unit truck path, outer radius 65' ±

Pass-vehicle path, outer radius 62' ±

14'

R = 50'
Offset 3'

R = 150'

R = 150'

12'
Lane

2'

2'

12'
Lane

3-Centered curve
150'–50'–150', offset 3'
Equivalent simple curve
radius 60'

(a)

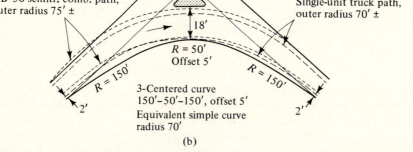

WB-50 semitr. comb. path, outer radius 75' ±

Single-unit truck path, outer radius 70' ±

18'

R = 50'
Offset 5'

R = 150'

R = 150'

2'

2'

3-Centered curve
150'–50'–150', offset 5'
Equivalent simple curve
radius 70'

(b)

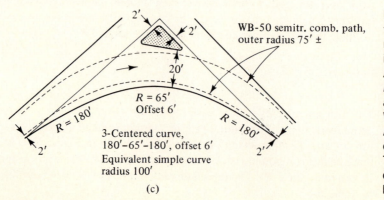

2'

2'

20'

WB-50 semitr. comb. path, outer radius 75' ±

R = 65'
Offset 6'

R = 180'

R = 180'

2'

2'

3-Centered curve,
180'–65'–180', offset 6'
Equivalent simple curve
radius 100'

(c)

Figure 5-10 Designs for turning roadways ninety degrees intersection. SOURCE: *A Policy on Geometric Design of Highways and Streets,* Washington, D.C.: The American Association of State Highway and Transportation Officials, copyright 1984. Used by permission.

TABLE 5-5

Minimum Designs for Turning Roadways

Angle of Turn (degrees)	Design Classification*	Three-Centered Radii (ft.)	Compound Curve Offset (ft.)	Width of Lane (ft.)	Approximate Island Size (sq. ft.)
75	A	150-75-150	3.5	14	60
	B	150-75-150	5.0	18	50
	C	180-90-180	3.5	20	50
90†	A	150-50-150	3.0	14	50
	B	150-50-150	5.0	18	80
	C	180-65-180	6.0	20	125
105	A	120-40-120	2.0	15	70
	B	100-35-100	5.0	22	50
	C	180-45-180	8.0	30	60
120	A	100-30-100	2.5	16	120
	B	100-30-100	5.0	24	90
	C	180-40-180	8.5	34	220

SOURCE: American Association State Highway and Transportation Officials [1].

Notes: Asymmetric three-centered compound curves and straight tapers with a simple curve can also be used without significantly altering the width of pavement or corner island size.

Painted island delineation is recommended for islands less than 75 ft² in size.

*Design classification:
A—Primarily passenger vehicles; permits occasional single-unit truck to turn with restricted clearances.
B—Provides adequately for SU; permits occasional WB-50 to turn with slight encroachment on adjacent traffic lanes.
C—Provides fully for WB-50.
†Illustrated in Figure 5-10.

TABLE 5-6

Minimum Radii for Intersection Curves

Design (turning) speed, V (mph)	10	15	20	25	30	35	40
Side friction factor, f	0.38	0.32	0.27	0.23	0.20	0.18	0.16
Assumed superelevation, e	0.00	—	—	—	—	—	0.00
Total e + f	0.38	0.32	0.27	0.23	0.20	0.18	0.16
Calculated minimum radius, R, feet[a]	18	47	92	154	231	314	426
Suggested minimum radius, feet, for design[b]	25	50	90	150	230	310	430

[a] $R = (V^2)/15(e + f)$

[b] The speed–radii relationships are in reasonable agreement with results reported by Emmerson.

Emmerson [9] reported that speeds decrease substantially on radii less than about 300 feet. The observed mean speed of 18 mph and 85th percentile speed of 20 mph observed on a 70-foot curve suggests that the AASHTO speed–radii criteria presented in the above are reasonable for design for radii of about 50 to 90 feet.

Emmerson [10] developed the following equation for speeds on short-radius curves:

$$v = 74(1 - e^{-0.017r})$$

Where:
v = average speed in kph
r = radius in meters, measured at the centerline
e = 2.718

This equation has the desirable characteristic that speed is zero when the radius is zero. The equation produces reasonable agreement with the AASHTO equation.

R	Emmerson's Equation	AASHTO
25 ft.	6 mph	10 mph
50 ft.	11 mph	14 mph
90 ft.	17 mph	18 mph
150 ft.	25 mph	23 mph

CHANNELIZATION

Potential conflicts among vehicles and between vehicles and pedestrians may be reduced through channelization of traffic movements. The traffic may be channeled to separate and direct traffic movements into specific and clearly defined vehicle paths. Channelization may be used for one or more of the following purposes:

1. *To separate conflicts* caused by the overlapping of maneuver areas. This separation makes it possible to present the driver with only one important decision at a time.

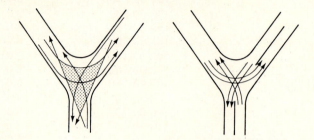

2. *To control the angle of conflict* and reduce relative speeds in merging, diverging, weaving, and crossing maneuvers. The potential severity of conflict may be decreased substantially by reducing the angle between the vehicle paths.

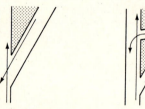

3. *To reduce excessive pavement areas* caused by skewed and flared intersection arrangements. Large areas of open pavement may confuse drivers and cause erratic and improper maneuvers.

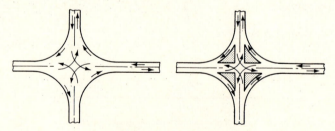

4. *To control speed* by bending or funneling movements to support stop-sign controls or reduce speed differentials prior to merging, weaving, or crossing maneuvers.

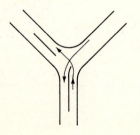

5. *To protect pedestrians* by providing a safe refuge between traffic streams.

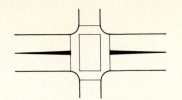

6. *To protect and store turning and crossing vehicles* by enabling them to slow or stop out of the path of other traffic flows. This is sometimes called "shadowing."

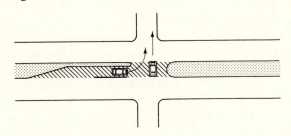

7. *To block prohibited movements* by making it impossible or inconvenient to perform illegal, improper, or unsafe maneuvers.

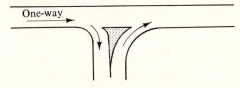

8. *To segregate traffic movements* with different requirements in terms of speed, direction, and right-of-way control.

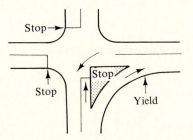

9. *To locate and protect traffic-control devices* such as signs and signals where the most desirable location for these devices is within the intersection area.

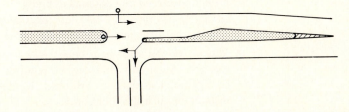

Channelization design does not lend itself to standardization. Traffic volumes, pedestrian patterns, and physical conditions vary, requiring individual treatment of each intersection. AASHTO policy [1] presents guides for various elements of the design, but the combination of elements within a specific design is an engineering art. Good designs should adhere to the following principles:

1. The proper traffic channels should appear natural and convenient to drivers and pedestrians. There should be no choice of vehicle paths leading to the same destination. The number of islands should be held to a practical minimum to avoid confusion.

2. Islands should be large enough to be effective. Islands that are too small are ineffective as a method of guidance and often present problems in maintenance. The area of an island should be at least 75 square feet. Accordingly, triangular islands should not be less than about 12 feet on a side, after the rounding of corners. Elongated or divisional islands should be at least 4 feet wide and 12 to 20 feet long.

3. Channelization should be visible. It should not be introduced where sight distance is limited. When an island must be located near a high point in the roadway profile or near the beginning of a horizontal curve, the approach end of the island should be extended so that it will be clearly visible to approaching drivers.

4. The major traffic flows should be favored.

5. Conflicts should be separated so that drivers and pedestrians may deal with only one conflict and make only one decision at a time.

6. Islands should be designed for the design speed of the road. The approach end treatment and delineation should be carefully designed to be consistent with the speed characteristics of the roadway design.

The operational objectives of channelization are to:

- Direct traffic movements
- Assure orderly movement
- Increase capacity
- Improve safety
- Maximize effective traffic control and communication with the driver

Channelizing Islands

Islands can be grouped into the following functional classes. Some islands serve more than one function:

- *Directional islands* to control and direct traffic movement and to guide the motorist into the proper path.
- *Divisional islands* to separate opposing traffic flows, to alert the driver to the crossroad ahead, or to regulate traffic through the intersection. These islands are often introduced on undivided highways at intersections and are particularly advantageous in controlling left turns at skewed intersections and in preventing wrong-way turns into right-turning traffic lanes.
- *Refuge islands* at or near crosswalks to aid or protect pedestrians crossing the roadway. Such an island may be required for pedestrians in intersections where complex signal phasings are used. Refuge islands may also serve as areas for installation of traffic-control devices.

Delineation and approach end treatment are critical to good channelization design. Four types of island designs are employed:

1. Raised islands with barrier curb
2. Raised islands with mountable curb

3. Flush, or slightly raised, islands delineated by pavement markings, buttons, "jiggle bars," and contrasting surfaces

4. Unpaved areas where the island is formed by the edge of pavement and often supplemented by delineators

Islands must be of sufficient size and design to command attention. The smallest curbed island that normally should be considered is one that has an area of approximately 50 square feet for urban streets and 75 square feet for rural intersections. However, 100 square feet is preferable for both. Accordingly, triangular islands should not be less than about 12 feet and preferably 15 feet on a side after the rounding of corners. Elongated or divisional islands should be no less than 4 feet wide and 20 to 25 feet long. In general, introducing curbed divisional islands at isolated intersections on high-speed highways is undesirable unless special attention is directed to providing high visibility for the islands. Curbed divisional islands introduced at isolated intersections on high-speed highways should be at least 100 feet and preferably several hundred feet in length. When they cannot be long, they may be preceded by visibly roughened pavement, jiggle bars, or markings. When situated in the vicinity of a high point in the roadway profile or at or near the beginning of a horizontal curve, the approach end of the curbed island should be extended to be clearly visible to approaching drivers.

Islands should be delineated or outlined by a variety of treatments, depending on their size, location, and function as well as the type of area in which the intersection is located (i.e., rural versus urban).

The raised island with mountable curb should be used in preference to the barrier curb to minimize the chance that the driver will lose control if a vehicle hits the curb. Where the size of the island permits, landscaping should be used to facilitate identification and delineation. Landscaping materials need to be carefully selected which require little maintenance, and they should be placed so that sight distance will not be obstructed.

Small curbed islands may be mounded, but where pavement cross slopes are outward, large islands should be depressed to avoid draining across the pavement. This is especially desirable where alternate freezing and thawing of stored snow may occur.

Delineation of small curbed islands relies primarily on the size of the curb. Large curbed islands may be sufficiently delineated by color and texture, contrast of vegetative cover, mounded earth, shrubs, guard posts, signs, or any combination of these. Curbed islands should be offset from the edge of the through-traffic lanes by at least 2 feet. The leading edge of large islands is commonly offset a greater distance, as illustrated in Figure 5-11.

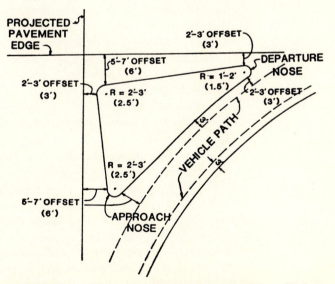

Figure 5-11 Island offset from edge of through-traffic lane.

In order to more easily define the various elements of channelization, the following set of definitions have been established:

1. *Approach taper (AT)* is from the point where all approaching traffic begins a lateral shift to the right, to the beginning of the bay taper.

2. *Bay taper (BT)* is from the left edge of the adjacent through-traffic lane to the beginning of the full-width left-turn storage lane.

3. *Storage length (SL)* is the distance from the end of the bay taper to the intersection nose or stop line.

4. *Intersection nose (IN)* is the distance from the end of the storage bay to the near edge of cross-route exit lanes for the left-turning vehicle. This cross-route exit reference is normally the center line of an unchannelized two-way street or the far edge of the median on a channelized street.

5. *Departure taper (DT)* is from the point where through traffic beyond the intersection begins a lateral shift to the left, to the point where the through lane is adjacent and parallel to the center line.

6. *Full shadowed lane* is when the approach taper laterally shifts on approaching vehicles the full distance to the right of the separate turn lane before the bay taper begins.

7. *Partial shadowed lane* is when the bay taper begins before the approach taper is complete. The combining of the approach and bay taper decreases the length of improvement.

Figure 5-12 illustrates the various elements of left-turn channelization.

With respect to the various tapers, the ITE Committee [15] recommended the following criteria:

Approach taper: The rate of lateral transition of a vehicle approaching a channelized intersection should be the same whether the channelization is achieved by a painted or a curved section. The difference in the two methods should be the location of the point of beginning. If the section is developed with painted lines, the approach taper should begin at the point of departure from the roadway centerline. If the section is developed by introducing a curbed median, the edge of the approach nose of the median should be offset a minimum of 2 feet to the left of the roadway centerline. The location would be the point of beginning of the approach taper. If pavement widening is to be all on one side of the centerline, a painted approach area should be introduced in advance of the barrier nose.

The taper should have a tangent alignment, but its derivation with respect to length varies depending on whether the storage lane is fully or partially shadowed. If the lane is fully shadowed, it is recommended that the length to width ratio be $V^2/60$ per unit of offset, where V is speed in miles per hour. If the lane is partially shadowed, the length should be the speed (V) in miles per hour times the width (W). The width and the length have the same longitudinal units (feet or meters). The minimum ratio for either full or partial shadow should be 10:1.

Bay taper: The bay taper is an element of channelization with the greatest dissimilarity of use throughout the nation. The use of reverse curves or a straight taper is almost evenly split, but the methods used to determine length vary greatly.

The recommended design is a straight taper whose length is derived by a length-to-width ratio of $V/2.5$ per unit of offset (lane width of the storage lane). This ratio closely conforms to taper length recommended in AASHTO publications for one-third of a second per foot of lateral shift. If local restrictions necessitate a shorter design and the use of partially shadowed storage lane, the taper should end opposite the end of the approach taper and be projected backward until it intersects the approach taper. Short curves or minor rounding (maximum 25 feet in length) can be

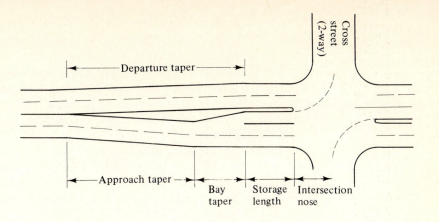

(a) Full shadowed lane

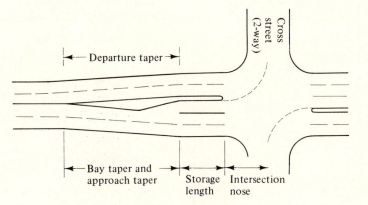

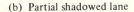

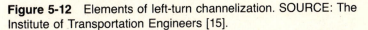

(b) Partial shadowed lane

Figure 5-12 Elements of left-turn channelization. SOURCE: The Institute of Transportation Engineers [15].

used at the points of beginning and ending, but a discernible angle should be noticeable to the approaching driver. This "break-away" angle communicates to the driver, in the same manner as the angle for an exit lane from a freeway, that a special-purpose lane is being introduced to the traveled way.

Departure taper: The departure taper should begin opposite the beginning of the storage lane. The location of the end of the taper depends upon whether the channelization is painted or constructed with a curbed median. If it is a painted channelization, the departure taper should terminate at the point of beginning of the approach taper.

If channelization includes a curbed median, the edge of pavement taper should continue past the approach nose in a straight line until it intersects the edge of pavement of the typical roadway section.

Medial Channelization and Left-Turn Storage

The concept of a functional hierarchy of circulation suggests that deceleration lanes should be provided at all transition areas (intersections). Cities, counties, and states are becoming increasingly vulnerable to liability suits where inadequate left-turn lane storage exists.

Therefore, where turn lanes were not part of the original construction, local and state jurisdictions should develop criteria and programs for the construction of these roadway elements. Such criteria for left-turn deceleration lanes are given in Figure 5-13.

The right-of-way for all new major arterial streets should be sufficient to accommodate double left-turn bays at major intersections. Such a median width will be adequate to store (shadow) passenger cars making left-turns from direct-access drives and crossing maneuvers as well as facilitate the design of median openings to accommodate specific designated movements.

On existing arterials, additional right-of-way should be obtained before or when development occurs. In areas where the adjacent properties are already developed, it requires patience and consistent policy enforcement as redevelopment or expansion occurs.

Median access openings should be spaced and designed so that the speed differential between a left-turning vehicle and other vehicles in the traffic stream is limited — preferably to 10 mph. Minimum and desirable spacings are given in Table 5-7.

It is essential that sufficient left-turn storage be provided to store all left-turn arrivals, a high percentage of the time. It is recommended that the design have at least a 95% probability of storing all left-turn arrivals during the peak hour.

The required storage for any selected probability of storing all vehicles can be determined using the queueing analysis presented in Chapter 7. Various tables and charts, such as the nomographs shown in Figure 5-14 for signalized intersections and Figure 5-15

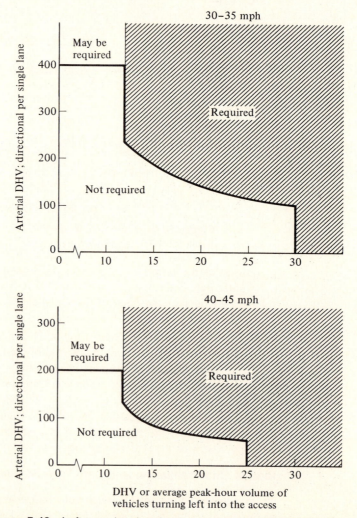

Figure 5-13 Left-turn deceleration-lane warrants. SOURCES: State of Colorado [7] and City of Lakewood, Colorado [16].

TABLE 5-7

Minimum Spacing Between Median Openings

Speed (mph)	Minimum Spacing (feet)	
	Absolute[a]	Desirable[b]
30	190	370
35	240	460
40	300	530
45	360	670
50	430	780
55	510	910

SOURCE: Vergil G. Stover, William G. Adkins, and John C. Goodknight [22, p. 19].

[a] 8.0 ft/sec² average deceleration rate and 10 mph deceleration in through-traffic lane.

[b] 6.5 ft/sec² average deceleration rate and no deceleration in through-traffic lane.

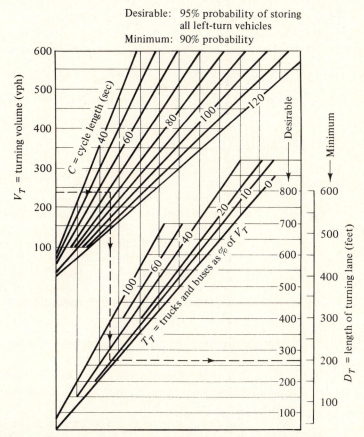

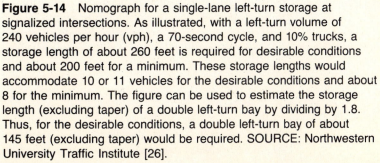

Figure 5-14 Nomograph for a single-lane left-turn storage at signalized intersections. As illustrated, with a left-turn volume of 240 vehicles per hour (vph), a 70-second cycle, and 10% trucks, a storage length of about 260 feet is required for desirable conditions and about 200 feet for a minimum. These storage lengths would accommodate 10 or 11 vehicles for the desirable conditions and about 8 for the minimum. The figure can be used to estimate the storage length (excluding taper) of a double left-turn bay by dividing by 1.8. Thus, for the desirable conditions, a double left-turn bay of about 145 feet (excluding taper) would be required. SOURCE: Northwestern University Traffic Institute [26].

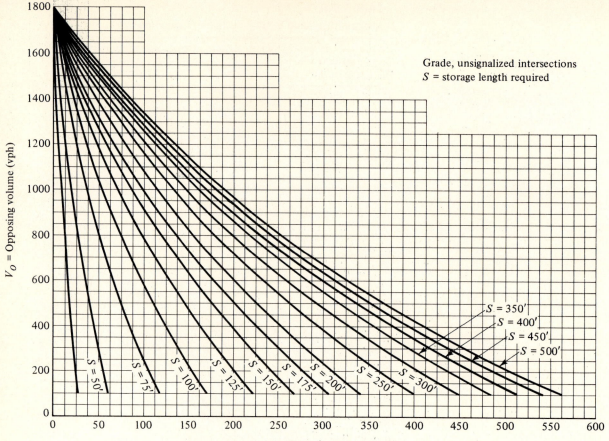

Figure 5-15 Nomograph for left-turn storage at nonsignalized intersections. The nomograph is used by reading horizontally from the opposing traffic volume, V_O, on the vertical axis and reading vertically from the left-turn volume, V_L, on the horizontal axis and locating the minimum storage length, S, at the point where the horizontal and vertical lines cross. For example, 100 left-turning vehicles per hour, V_L, with an opposing through volume, V_O, of 950 vph, will require a minimum storage length of about 150 feet. SOURCE: M. D. Hamelink [12].

for unsignalized intersections, have been developed for estimating the left-turn storage required.

It is emphasized that the deceleration distance (see Table 5-8) must be added to the storage length to obtain the total length of turn bay, including the taper as illustrated by the example in Table 5-9.

The above procedures are applicable to the analysis of expected turn-bay requirements based on estimated future traffic conditions. Where existing traffic conditions are to be evaluated, actual traffic counts should be used. Changing traffic volumes and/or patterns frequently require lengthening of the left-turn storage at major intersections. This may necessitate the elimination of left-turns at nearby intersections of minor public street or private access points.

CORNER CLEARANCE

Corner clearance is the distance from a signalized intersection to the nearest access (public or private) upstream or downstream from it. From a traffic operations point of view, the near curb lines constitute the corner clearance (see Figure 5-16). However,

TABLE 5-8

Deceleration Distances

Speed (mph)	Deceleration Distance (feet) (rounded for design)	
	Desirable[a]	Minimum[b]
30	200	150
35	275	250
40	350	300
45	425	375

[a] Assumes 2.5 seconds perception–reaction time, 7 fps² maximum deceleration, and 10 mph speed differential.

[b] Assumes 1.0 second perception–reaction time, 9 fps² maximum deceleration, and 15 mph speed differential.

TABLE 5-9

Example Calculation of Left-Turn Bay

	Peak	Off-Peak
Expected left-turn volume, vph	200	100
Cycle length, sec.	120	60
Arterial speed, mph	35	45
Trucks, %	<1	5
Single-lane left turn:		
Desirable storage, feet, Figure 5-14	325	100
Deceleration, feet[a], Table 5-8	250	425
	575	525
Double left turn:		
Desirable storage, feet	180	55
Deceleration, feet[b]	250	425
	430	480

[a] Includes standard 120-foot taper for single left turn.

[b] Includes standard 180-foot taper for double left turn.

corner-clearance requirements are most appropriately specified in ordinance as the distance from the right-of-way line to the near edge of a private access drive or curb of public street. Medial opening corner clearance is measured as illustrated in Figure 5-17.

No access (medial or marginal) should be permitted to an arterial street within the approach area of a signalized intersection [1, p. 888].

Minimum corner clearance on the approach of a signalized intersection should allow for the following conditions:

1. Right-turn ingress and egress movements do not interfere with right turns at the downstream signalized intersection.

2. Left-turn ingress and/or egress movements to and from the unsignalized access do not interfere with left turns at the signalized intersection. Interference will occur when an ingress or egress maneuver occurs within the approach length where turning vehicles are maneuvering from the through traffic lane to the left-turn or right-turn lane. This condition will prevail during off-peak hours. During arterial peak traffic periods, interference occurs when the ingress or egress vehicles attempt to turn across the queue of vehicles waiting to make a left or right turn at the signalized intersection (see Figure 5-18).

3. A through or turning vehicle will clear the intersection before having to be concerned with a downstream intersection (see Figure 5-19).

Corner clearance downstream from an intersection should be sufficient to allow a driver to enter the street without interfering with a vehicle approaching from an up-

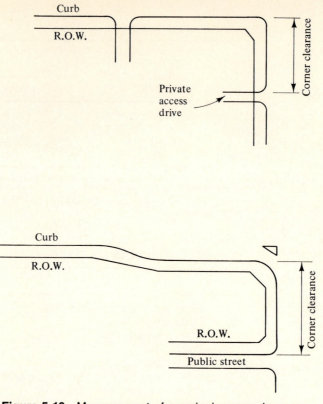

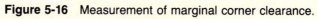

Figure 5-16 Measurement of marginal corner clearance.

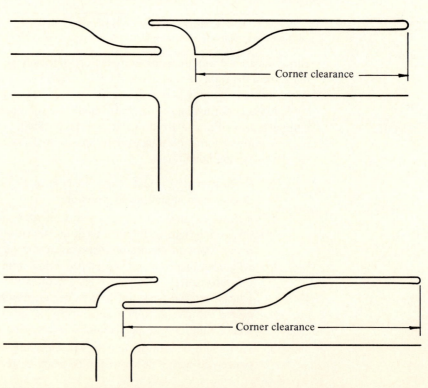

Figure 5-17 Measurement of medial corner clearance.

Figure 5-18 Left-turn queue storage at a major intersection.

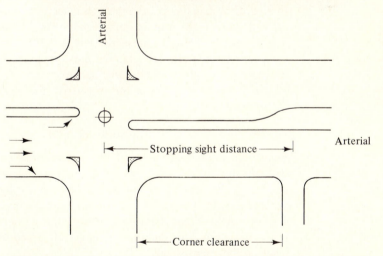

Figure 5-19 Departure corner clearance for a through movement.

stream intersection (Condition #1, Figure 5-20). At a minimum, the corner clearance must be adequate to allow a vehicle approaching from an upstream intersection to stop in the event a vehicle at the downstream intersection pulls out into the street (Condition #2, Figure 5-20).

Drivers should not be presented with downstream problems until the vehicle has cleared the intersection (i.e., when the driver has properly positioned the vehicle in the selected traffic lane). For the purpose of establishing minimum corner-clearance require-

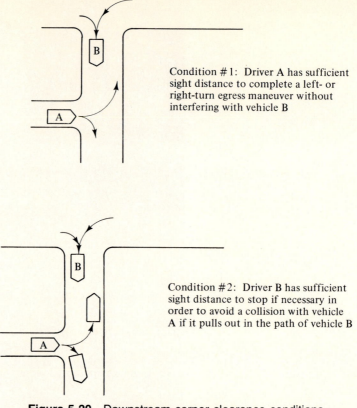

Condition #1: Driver A has sufficient sight distance to complete a left- or right-turn egress maneuver without interfering with vehicle B

Condition #2: Driver B has sufficient sight distance to stop if necessary in order to avoid a collision with vehicle A if it pulls out in the path of vehicle B

Figure 5-20 Downstream corner-clearance conditions.

ments, the vehicle is assumed to have cleared the intersection when the rear bumper clears the crosswalk or, in absence of a marked crosswalk, when it crosses an imaginary line perpendicular to the tangent at the end of the curb return radius. The turn maneuvers are more critical than the straight-through maneuver, since the vehicle guidance task is more difficult and the driver of a turning vehicle does not have a clear view of any downstream access. At channelized intersections with YIELD control and at right-turn-on-red, the right-turn driver's primary attention must be given to observing the straight-through and left-turn lanes. For the left turn maneuver, the driver is fully occupied with vehicle guidance (steering). Minimums based on the right-turn maneuver are illustrated in Figure 5-21.

Corner Clearance on Intersecting Streets

Small corner clearance will result in a high probability that an access drive to a minor street will be blocked by vehicles stopped at the intersection (see Figure 5-22). Although blockage of the egress movement may be bad for business, it does not present a traffic problem. However, blockage of an ingress maneuver presents a serious operational problem. When there are numerous turns from the major street to the minor street, traffic backup may extend into the intersection and seriously interfere with traffic movement on the major street.

Table 5-10 gives the probability of blockage when the minor street approach to the major street is STOP controlled. Table 5-11 (p. 145) gives similar information when the intersection is under signal control. As traffic flow in the lane adjacent to the driveway approaches the capacity of the intersection, the probability that the intersection will be blocked increases rapidly for very limited corner clearances. An example for the use of Table 5-10 is illustrated in Figure 5-23; Table 5-11 is used in a comparable maneuver.

Suggested minimum dimensions for design are given in Figure 5-24 (p. 145). Note that these dimensions are for a 30 mph operating speed (average speed); for 40- to 45-mph arterial streets, these values should be doubled.

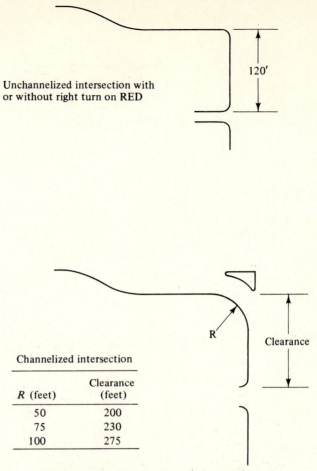

Figure 5-21 Downstream corner clearances.

TABLE 5-10

Probability of Driveway Blocking Upstream from Stop-Controlled Intersections

Volume in Lane Adjacent to Driveway (vph)	Intersection Service Rate (vph)	Percent Probability That Driveway is Blocked (Corner Clearance as Number of Autos*)						
		1	2	3	4	5	6	7
50	100	50	25	13	6	3	2	1
	200	25	6	2				
	300	17	3	1				
	400	13	2					
	500	10	1					
100	200	50	25	13	6	3	2	1
	300	33	11	4	1			
	400	25	6	2				
	500	20	4	1				
	600	17	3	1				
150	200	75	56	42	32	24	18	13
	300	50	25	13	6	3	2	1
	400	38	10	5	2	1		
	500	30	9	3	1			
	600	25	6	2				

SOURCE: Vergil G. Stover, William G. Adkins, and John C. Goodknight [22].

*The space required by each auto is approximately 25 feet (7.5 meters) including the space between autos; therefore, three autos translates to approximately 75 feet (24 meters) for corner clearance.

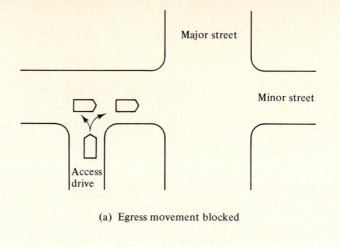

(a) Egress movement blocked

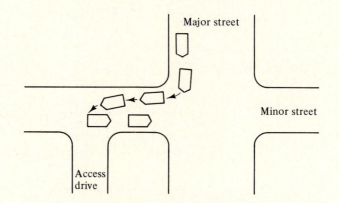

(b) Ingress movement blocked

Figure 5-22 Blocking of near-corner access.

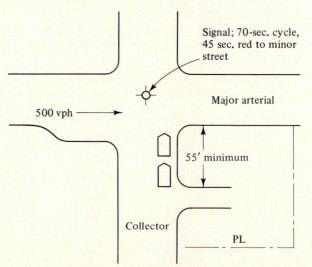

Figure 5-23 Example of inadequate corner clearance. *Example analysis:* The corner clearance of 55 feet is sufficient for no more than two cars (approximately 25 feet per car, including distance from stop line to first vehicle and space between vehicles). Interpolating from Table 5-10, there is over a 90% probability of blockage (89% at 400 vph and 98% at 600 vph; therefore, 500 vph is approximately 93%).

TABLE 5-11

Percent of Cycles During Which Driveway in Close Proximity to a Signalized Intersection Will Be Blocked

Flow in Lane Adjacent to Driveway (vph)	Duration of Red Phase (sec)	Percentage of Cycles During Which Blocking Occurs (Corner Clearance in Number of Autos)									
		1	2	3	4	5	6	7	8	9	10
200	15	20	5	1							
	25	40	16	5							
	35	58	31	13	5	2					
	45	71	46	24	11	4	1				
400	15	50	23	9	3	1					
	25	77	53	30	15	6	2	1			
	35	90	75	55	35	20	10	5	2	1	
	45	96	88	74	56	38	24	13	7	3	2
600	15	71	46	24	11	4	1				
	25	92	79	60	40	24	13	6	3	1	
	35	98	93	83	69	53	37	23	14	7	4
	45	100	98	94	87	76	62	48	34	22	14
800	15	85	65	43	24	12	5	2	1		
	25	98	92	81	65	49	32	20	11	6	3
	35	100	98	95	89	79	66	52	38	26	16
	45	100	100	99	97	93	87	78	67	54	42

SOURCE: Vergil G. Stover, William G. Adkins, and John C. Goodknight [21].

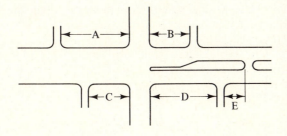

Minimum Corner Clearances*

Item	Functional Classification of Road		
	Arterial	Collector	Local
A	230	175	50
B	115	85	50
C	230	175	50
D	230	175	50
E	75	0	0

(a) Signalized intersection control

Minimum Corner Clearances*

Item	Functional Classification of Road		
	Arterial	Collector	Local
F	115	75	50
G	115	85	50
H	85	85	50
J	115	75	50
K	75	0	0

(b) Stop-sign intersection control

Figure 5-24 Minimum corner clearances for urban conditions. In recognition of the difference in volumes and level-of-service requirements for various roadway classes, separate values are suggested for different functional classifications. SOURCE: Adapted from The Traffic Institute, Northwestern University [26].

*The dimensions assume a 30 mph operating speed. For rural and other high-speed roads, clearances of the order of two times as great should be used.

THE INGRESS MANEUVER AT UNSIGNALIZED ACCESS

The speed at which a vehicle is able to leave the through lane on an arterial or other classification of roadway and safely enter a driveway has a significant effect on the safety and operational efficiency of the specific roadway. The geometric factors affecting the driver's path and speed when entering or leaving a driveway are a combination of driveway width and curb return radius.

Figure 5-25 shows the trajectory of the right front wheel of passenger cars making a right turn into a driveway having a 10-foot return radius and a 30-foot width. The solid line labeled "mean" is the average position of the right front wheel during the maneuver. The dashed line labeled "+1" is one standard deviation above the mean. Approximately 85% of the vehicles were to the right of this vehicle path. The "+2" line is the mean plus two standard deviations; over 97% of the trajectories are to the right of this line. In interpreting the figure, remember that the vehicle (approximately $6\frac{1}{2}$ feet wide) would be to the left of any given trajectory of the right front wheel. Therefore, the drivers of vehicles at the mean plus two standard deviations are using the entire throat width on the ingress maneuver. Similar figures, at a smaller scale, are given in Figure 5-26 for a variety of other combinations of throat width and curb return radii.

The presence of a vehicle stopped in the drive while waiting for a gap in the traffic stream will restrict the throat width available to the vehicle entering the driveway. Consequently, the trajectories of right-turning vehicles will be less dispersed (see Figure 5-27).

Review of these data reveals the following general conclusions:

- At driveways with a curb return radius of 20 feet or more, the paths of vehicles turning right into the driveways tended to parallel the entry curbline, and drivers tended to remain on the entry side, regardless of driveway width, when no exiting vehicle was present.

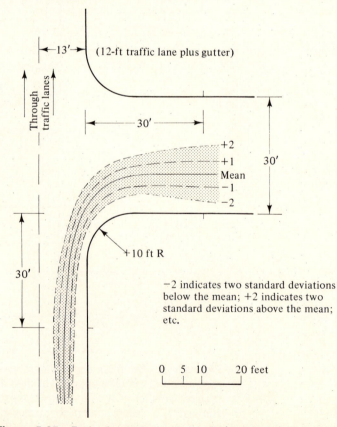

Figure 5-25 Path of right front wheel. SOURCE: Vergil G. Stover [23].

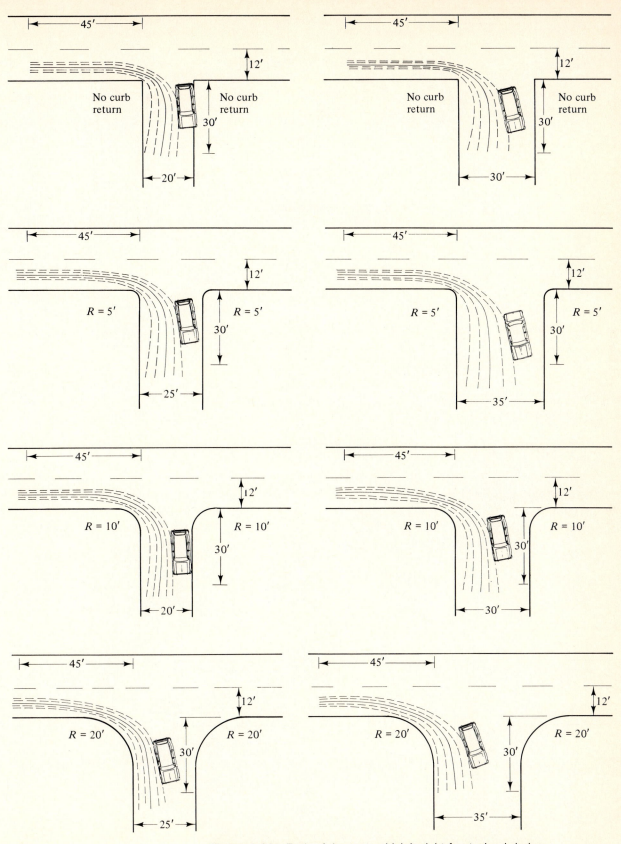

Figure 5-26 Path of the test vehicle's right front wheel during right-turn entry maneuvers when no exiting vehicle is present. SOURCE: Stephen H. Richards [19].

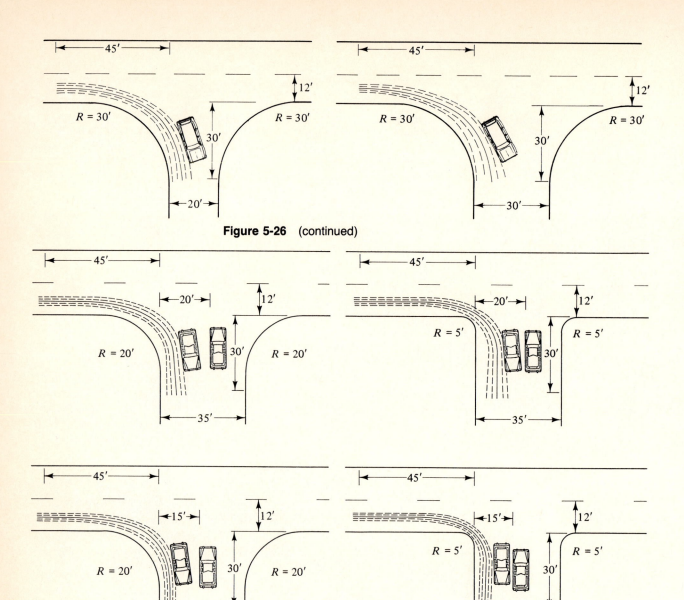

Figure 5-26 (continued)

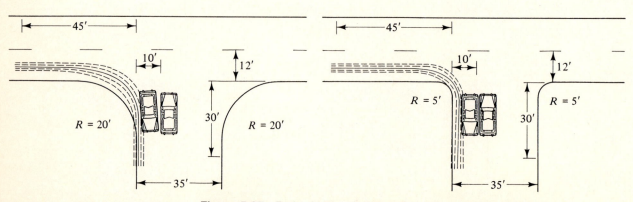

Figure 5-27 Path of test vehicle's front wheel during right-turn entry maneuvers when an exiting vehicle is present. SOURCE: Stephen H. Richards [19].

- At driveways with a curb return radius of 10 feet or less, drivers tended to make a wide turn using all of the available throat width to compensate for the relatively small curb return radius. Once in these driveways, drivers immediately steered back toward the entry curbline to reposition the vehicle on the proper (entry) side of the driveway.

- The exit curb radius had very little influence on the exit speed and acceleration of right-turn exiting traffic. This finding indicates that, at some driveways, the use of unequal curb return radii (large entry radius and small exit radius) may be acceptable.

As shown in Figure 5-28, the speed of the vehicle while maneuvering through the driveway opening decreases as the available throat width and/or curb return radius decreases. The presence of an exiting vehicle stopped in the throat has a greater effect on the speed and path of the right front wheel than explained by the reduction in the available throat width only. This undoubtedly results from the driver's desire (requirement) to maintain a greater clearance between his or her vehicle and a stopped vehicle than an edge of the driveway.

Nevertheless, a simple review of Figure 5-28 clearly indicates that the speed of a vehicle entering a driveway is very slow for all reasonable combinations of throat width and curb return radii. Even excessive radii (30 feet) and throat width (35 feet) produce entry speeds of only 12 to 13 miles per hour. Consequently, a vehicle making a driveway maneuver is decelerating a considerable distance upstream from the driveway (see Figure 5-29). As a result, for off-peak arterial speeds of 40 to 45 mph, a speed differential of 10 mph or more occurs at least 250 feet upstream from the driveway. This fact probably results in an underreporting of accidents resulting from driveway traffic.

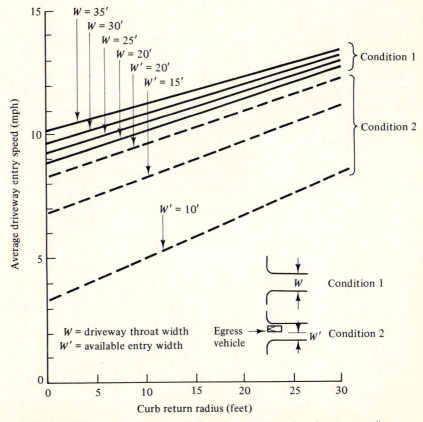

Figure 5-28 The influence of driveway width and curb return radius on second lane driveway entry speed. SOURCE: Stephen H. Richards [19].

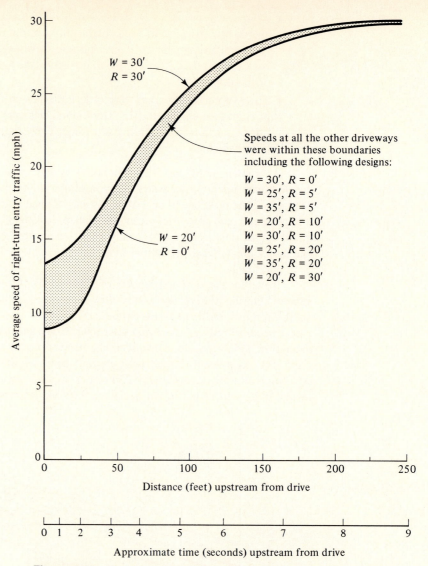

Figure 5-29 Speed profiles for various combinations of driveway throat width and curb return radii. SOURCE: adapted from Vergil G. Stover [23].

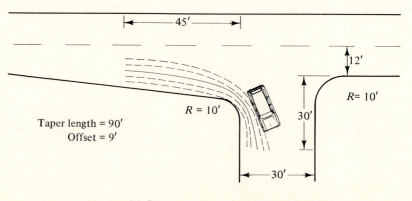

(a) Direct taper approach treatment

Figure 5-30 Path of the test vehicle's right front wheel during right-turn entry maneuvers.

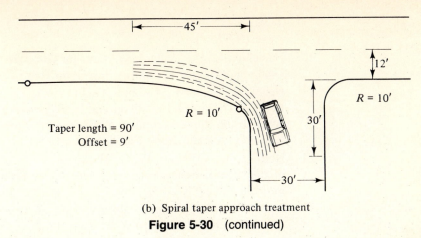

(b) Spiral taper approach treatment
Figure 5-30 (continued)

The research also found that use of a taper on the upstream side of the driveway does not significantly influence the speed of the vehicle making the driveway maneuver. However, the dispersion of the path of the right front wheel in the driveway throat is reduced (Figure 5-30), and the taper results in a reduction in exposure time (the time which the turning vehicle is blocking the through traffic lane).

REFERENCES

1. American Association of the State Highway and Transportation Officials, *A Policy on Geometric Design of Highways and Streets,* 1984.

2. Azzeh, J. A., Thorson, B. A., Valenta, J. J., Glennon, J. C., and Wilton, J. C., "Evaluation of Techniques for the Control of Direct Access to Arterial Highways" *Report No. FHWA-RD-76-85,* Federal Highway Administration, August 1975.

3. Bochner, Brian S., "Regulation of Driveway Access to Arterial Streets," Presented to ITE 48th Annual Meeting, Atlanta, Georgia, August 6–10, 1978.

4. Box, Paul C., "Traffic Control and Roadway Elements—Their Relationship to Highway Safety," Chapter 5, "Driveways," Highways Users Federation for Safety and Mobility, 1970.

5. Cirillo, J. A., et al., "Interstate System Accident Research Study I, Volume 1, Comparison of Accident Experience on the Interstate and Non-Interstate Highways," *Report of the Bureau of Public Roads,* October 1970.

6. Cirillo, J. A., et al., "Interstate System Accident Research Study II, Interim Report II, *Bureau of Public Roads,* August 1968.

7. Colorado, State of, Department of Highways, *The State Highway Code,* as revised, August 15, 1985.

8. Cribbins, P. D., "Correlation of Accident Rates with Geometric Design Components of Various Types of Highways," *Final Report on Project ERD-110-0,* North Carolina State University.

9. Emmerson, J., "Speeds of Car on Sharp Horizontal Curves," *Traffic Engineering and Control,* July 1969.

10. Emmerson, J., "A Note on Speed–Road Curvature Relationships," *Traffic Engineering and Control,* November 1970.

11. Glennon, J. C., Valenta, J. J., Thorson, B. A., Azzeh, J. A., and Wilton, C. J., "Technical Guidelines for the Control of Direct Access to Arterial Highways, Volume I: General Framework for Implementing Access Control Techniques," *Report No. FHWA-RD-76-86;* "Volume II: Detailed Description of Access Control

Techniques," *Report No. FHWA-RD-76-87,* Federal Highway Administration, August 1975.

12. Hamelink, M. D., "Volume Warrants for Left-Turn Storage Lanes at Unsignalized Grade Intersections," *Highway Research Record 211,* 1967.

13. Heimback, Clinton L., Cribbins, Paul D., and Chang, Myung-Soon, "The Effect of Reduced Traffic Land Width on Traffic Operations and Safety for Urban Undivided Arterials in North Carolina," Final Report, Project ERSD-110-78-1, Highway Research Program, North Carolina State University, July 1979.

14. Horn, J. W., Cribbins, P. D., Blackburn, J. D., and Vick, C. E., Jr., "Effects of Commercial Roadside Development on Traffic Flow in North Carolina," *HRB Bulletin 303,* pp. 76–93, 1961.

15. Institute of Transportation Engineers, Committee 5-S, "Design Criteria for Left-Turn Channelization," *ITE Journal,* February 1981.

16. Lakewood, City of, Colorado, *Transportation Engineering Design Standards,* 1985.

17. Major, I. T., and Buckley, D. J., "Entry to a Traffic Stream," *Proceedings of the Australian Road Research Board,* pp. 206–228, 1962.

18. McGuirk, William F., "Evaluation of Factors Influencing Driveway Accidents," *Report of the Joint Highway Research Project,* Purdue University, May 1973.

19. Richards, Stephen H., "Guidelines for Driveway Design and Operation," Research Report 5182-2, Volume 2, Technical Report, Volume 3, Guidelines, *Texas Transportation Institute,* April 1980, and unpublished data, 1979.

20. Solomon, David, "Accidents on Main Rural Highways Related to Speed, Driver, and Vehicle," *Bureau of Public Roads,* July 1964.

21. Solomon, David, "Highway Safety Myths," Highway and Traffic Safety: A Problem of Definition, *North Carolina Symposium on Highway Safety,* Volume II, Spring 1970.

22. Stover, Vergil G., Adkins, William G., and Goodknight, John G., "Guidelines to Medial and Marginal Access on Major Roadways," *NCHRP Report 93,* National Cooperative Highway Research Program, 1970.

23. Stover, Vergil G., "Guidelines for Spacing of Unsignalized Access to Urban Arterial Streets," *Technical Bulletin No. 81-1,* Texas Engineering Experiment Station, January 1981.

24. Stover, Vergil G., Tignor, Samuel C., and Rosenbaum, Merton J., "Synthesis of Safety Research Related to Traffic Control and Roadway Elements," Chapter 4, Access Control and Driveways, *Technology Sharing Report FHWA-TS-82-232,* December 1982.

25. Texas Transportation Institute, research in progress, 1987.

26. The Traffic Institute, Northwestern University, "Intersection-At-Grade," Course Notes, 1984.

6

Access and Site Circulation

ELEMENTS OF SITE DESIGN

Site design involves the following three major elements:

- Access location and design
- Site circulation and parking
- Building "footprint" and location

Good site design is achieved when all three elements are integrated. It is recommended that the site-design process begin with an identification of the street frontage to which access is most acceptable, given the functional classification of the street and the functional design of nearby intersections. Sketch plans showing the alternatives for the on-site circulation system should then be developed to identify the general area in which the building(s) might be located. The design should then be evolved by the process discussed in Chapter 2 and illustrated in Figure 6-1. Analysis of the access capacity may demonstrate that the access needs to be redesigned, that the project needs to be scaled back to reduce the traffic generation, that the project could be enlarged, that the nature of the activities in the proposed development should be changed so that the peak traffic generation is shifted to some other time period, or that a combination of the above should be considered.

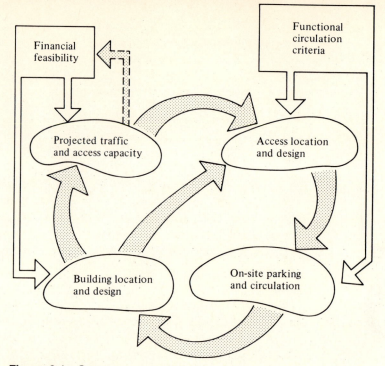

Figure 6-1 Systems approach to site design. (Same as Figure 2-2, repeated for convenience.)

Effect of Project Size

It becomes easier to develop good access and site designs when the size of the development is large, at least 80 acres. The substantial arterial street frontage typically allows locating access points to conform to a long uniform signal spacing (one-fourth mile or more). The frontage also facilitates the provision of speed-change lanes and channelization for a double left-turn lane for ingress and egress. The large size of the site also provides for flexibility in building location as well as adequate throat length for major access drives. Consequently, the access drives can be designed to provide very high capacities and minimal negative impact on the arterial street(s).

With sites of much less than 80 acres, it is unlikely that the frontage will allow locating a signalized intersection (access drive) to conform to a uniform signal spacing of at least one-fourth mile. With corner sites of less than 10 acres, it becomes difficult to provide right-turn lanes and left-turn channelization. Therefore, an activity center, comprised of several smaller individual developments which are independently designed, can be expected to result in the following:

- The total traffic generated by the combined development may equal or exceed that of a single project of the same total area.
- The limited frontage and depth of the individual projects preclude the design of high-capacity access drives.
- The proximity of the access drives serving the several separate development results in interference and a lower total ingress/egress capacity than access drives of improved design and at a longer spacing.
- The level of land access seriously interferes with the movement function that an arterial should provide. The turbulence created in the traffic stream results in low-capacity, high-accident experience. The location becomes less desirable vis-a-vis other locations having better circulation and access design.

DESIGN GUIDELINES FOR ACCESS DRIVES

In theory, a very large number of combinations of horizontal geometry elements could be used. In practice, a small number of different designs should be adopted in order to present the driver with design consistency.

Throat width should be restrictive enough to discourage erratic maneuvers, control the location and angle of conflict points, and limit ingress and egress to the number of lanes of operation intended. Suggested combinations of radii and throat width for 90 degree driveways are presented in Table 6-1 for low-volume two-way driveways. Table 6-2 gives suggested combinations for one-way operations. The minimum throat widths should be used only with a maximum curb return radius. It is suggested that simple designs employing these dimensions be restricted to use for direct-access drives to collector streets.

Access designs suggested for use on arterial streets are illustrated in Figures 6-2 and 6-3. For high-volume driveways, divisional islands might be used to prevent egress traffic from encroaching upon the side of the drive used by ingress traffic. This ensures that the ingress traffic has the necessary maneuver space. However, the island must not present a hazard. This can be accomplished by using one of the following designs:

1. Curbed island using the AASHTO four-inch, nonbarrier curb or similar design with a median at least 6 feet wide, preferably 8 or 10 feet wide. The median island should be landscaped to provide a high degree of visibility. The island is also the preferred location for a sign to identify the development and aid the driver in locating the access point. Appropriate attention, of course, must be given to the design and positioning of the sign to ensure that sight distance is not interfered with.

2. A contrasting surface raised slightly above the driveway surface. The surface of the median should be no more than two inches higher than the drive. Use of paving brick for the median provides an attractive contrast. The minimum width should not be less than 2 feet and preferably 4 feet.

An island should be used whenever any combination of egress and ingress lanes is three or more. On low-volume access points having one ingress and one egress lane, a solid yellow paint stripe is preferable to an island.

TABLE 6-1
Recommended Width and Curb Return for Low-Volume Two-Way Access Drives

Land Use	Throat Width (feet)			Curb Return Radius (feet)		
	Desirable	Maximum	Minimum	Desirable	Maximum	Minimum
Apartment and commercial	30	35	25	20	25	15
Industrial	35	40	30	30	50	20

TABLE 6-2
Recommended Width and Curb Return for Low-Volume One-Way Access Drives

Land Use	Throat Width (feet)			Curb Radius (feet)		
	Desirable Entry/Exit	Maximum	Minimum	Desirable	Maximum	Minimum
Apartment and commercial	18 16	20	15	20	25	15
Industrial	20 20	25	15	30	50	20

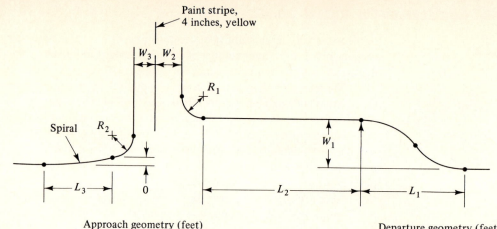

Approach geometry (feet)							Departure geometry (feet)			
Arterial speed (mph)	L_1	$L_2{}^a$		$W_1{}^b$	$W_2{}^c$	R_1	$W_3{}^c$	R_2	L_3	0
							all speeds			
45 desirable[d]	120	250					14	20	10	5
limiting[e]	100	130		12	16	20	16	15	15	5
40 desirable	120	190	f	12	18	15	16	20	0	0
limiting	90	100		12	20	10				
35 desirable	90	120								
limiting	60	60								

[a] Maneuver distance only; does not include storage for more than one vehicle.

[b] Excluding curb and gutter.

[c] Stripe to back of curb.

[d] 10 mph speed differential, 7 fps^2 average maximum deceleration.

[e] 15 mph speed differential, 9 fps^2 average maximum deceleration.

[f] Any set of $L_1 L_2$ values may be used with any set of $W_1 W_2 R_1$ values.

Figure 6-2   Suggested design for undivided driveway access to arterial streets. SOURCE: Vergil G. Stover [2].

Where the driveway spacing is less than that necessary to accommodate a right-turn deceleration lane (Figure 6-4) and still have substantial lengths of curb between successive driveways, a continuous right-turn lane should be considered (Figure 6-5). Any continuous right-turn lane should terminate at signalized intersections. The termination should be accomplished by a channelizing island which forces all traffic in the lane to turn right at the intersection.

Whenever a channelizing island is used at the terminus of a right-turn bay or lane, the inside curb return radius should be a minimum of 75 feet. This will provide an island of sufficient size to allow for landscaping and enhanced visibility. The absolute minimum radius necessary to provide for an island of minimum legal size is 50 feet.

Designs to Restrict Certain Movements

In some instances, it is desirable to prohibit certain movements through the use of channelizing islands (Figure 6-6). Signing and pavement markings are not effective in eliminating prohibited movements. The geometry must physically define and block the movements which are prohibited. Use of a channelizing island which prohibits left turns in and out (Figure 6-6) is suggested on arterials without a median and on one-way streets.

The installation of supplementary one-way drives reduces the number of turning vehicles at a T-intersection on a divided arterial having a barrier median (Figure 6-7). The supplementary drives might be installed to serve egress or ingress maneuvers or both.

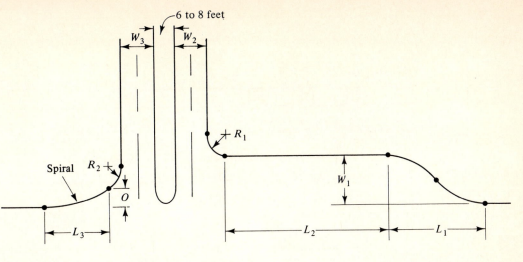

	Approach Geometry (feet)					Departure Geometry (feet)			
Arterial Speed (mph)	L_1	L_2	$W_1{}^a$	$W_2{}^b$	R_1	$W_3{}^d$	R_2	L_3	0
45	120	250 ⎫	12	30	20	28	20	10	5
40	120	200 ⎬ c 12	12	32	15	30	15	15	5
35	90	120 ⎭	12	34	10	30	25	0	0

^{a} Excluding gutter.

^{b} Back-to-back of curb's total width, entrance width, W_2, divided by solid white line, lane line to back of curb, as follows:

^{c} Any set of $L_1 L_2$ values may be used with any set of $W_1 W_2 R_1$ values.

^{d} Total width back to back of curb; divided solid line as follows:

W_2	Right lane	Left lane
30	16.5	13.5
32	18.5	13.5
34	20.5	13.5

W_3	Right lane	Left lane
28	14.5	13.5
30	16.5	13.5

Figure 6-3 Suggested design for divided-driveway access to arterial streets. SOURCE: Vergil G. Stover [2].

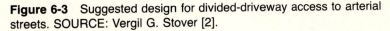
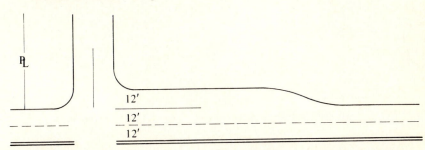

Figure 6-4 Right-turn bay. Provision of a right-turn deceleration lane will reduce the speed differential between turning vehicles and through traffic.

A pair of two-way drives with limited turns (Figure 6-8) might be used in place of a single standard two-way drive or a pair of standard two-way drives. The number of conflict points is reduced, and turning velocity is increased. The median must be of sufficient width (at least 18 feet) to allow construction of median openings designed to confine the movement to that intended and to store the left-turn egressing vehicle.

A raised median treatment provides positive medial access control on multilane, divided arterials. Left turns, crossing movements, and U-turns are prevented except at

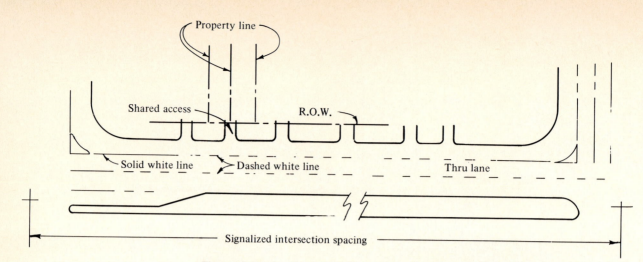

Figure 6-5 Continuous right-turn lane. A right-turn lane might be installed to serve two or more access points between signalized intersections. Vehicles can and will enter and leave the lane at random locations. This results in numerous, overlapping conflict areas. Consequently, the operation can be expected to become hazardous when two or more access points have high volumes.

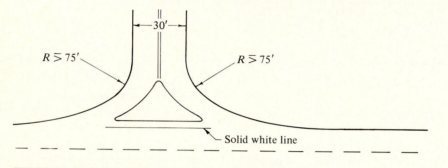

(a) Channelizing island to prohibit left-turn maneuvers

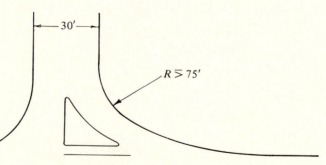

(b) Channelizing island to prohibit left-turn ingress maneuver

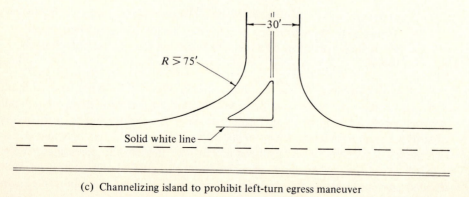

(c) Channelizing island to prohibit left-turn egress maneuver

Figure 6-6
Channelizing islands to prohibit left turns.

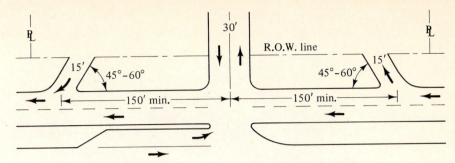

Figure 6-7 Supplementary one-way right-turn driveway.

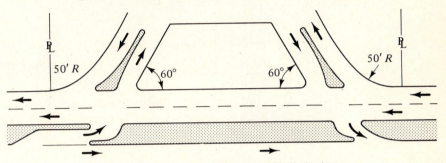

Figure 6-8 Two-way driveways with limited turns.

those locations where median openings are provided. In addition to preventing left turns at minor access points, the divider reduces friction between the opposing traffic streams.

A minimum width of 14 feet (preferably 16 feet) is required for a median with a single left-turn lane. For a double left-turn lane at least 25 feet is desirable. Sketches are shown in Figure 6-9.

Median channelization can be designed for specific movements and prohibiting others, as illustrated in Figures 6-10 through 6-12. In order to provide channelization which effectively prohibits the undesired movements, a median width of at least 18 feet is needed. In order to provide landscaping to make the channelization more visible, as well as aesthetically pleasing, a 25-foot width is necessary.

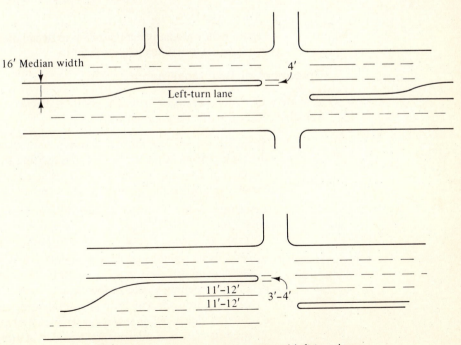

Figure 6-9 Medians with protected left-turn lanes.

Figure 6-10 Median channelization to accommodate left-turn egress movement and prohibit left-turn ingress.

Treatment of Turn Movements

A variety of options exist for reducing conflicts between roadway through traffic and vehicles entering and exiting a driveway.

1. Table 6-3 (p. 162) summarizes various treatments and conditions under which the savings from accident reduction on existing streets can be expected to offset the cost of construction and other costs such as loss of business to establishments fronting on the street, circuity of travel, etc.

2. Left turns should be prohibited to and/or from driveways under the following conditions:
    a. Inadequate corner clearance (prohibit left turns to and from).
    b. Inadequate sight distance (prohibit left turns with inadequate sight distance).
    c. Inadequate driveway spacing (prohibit left turns to and from).
    d. Median opening would be too close to another median opening (prohibition dependent on specific locations of adjacent openings).
    e. Site has signalized driveway on same arterial at which left turns can be made (prohibit left-turn movements provided at signalized driveways).
    f. Other capacity, delay, or safety conditions make specific left turns dangerous.

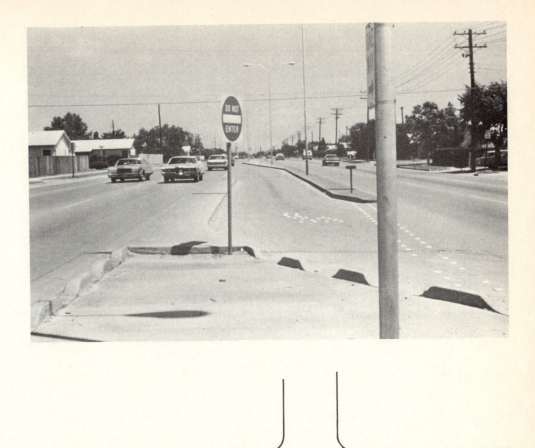

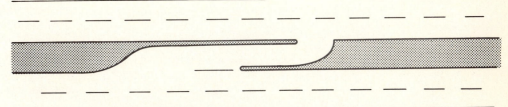

Figure 6-11 Median channelization to accommodate left-turn ingress maneuver and prohibit left-turn egress.

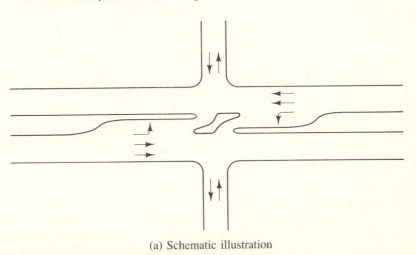

(a) Schematic illustration

Figure 6-12 Median channelization to accommodate left turns from major roadway and prohibit crossing traffic. See page 162 for median detail.

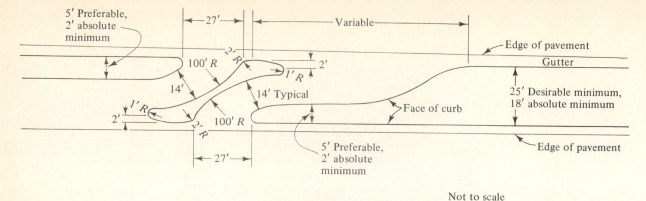

(b) Median detail

Figure 6-12 (continued)

TABLE 6-3

Cost-Effective Techniques to Enhance Capacity and Safety on Existing Roadways

Left turns into driveway	
Provide continuous two-way left-turn lane	> 60 driveways/mile; > 20% left turns during peak hour
Provide alternating left-turn lanes	> 45 driveways/mile; > 15% left turns during peak hour
Provide isolated median and left-turn lanes*	< 30 driveways/mile; > 1,000 vpd driveway traffic, > 1,000 vpd roadway traffic
Right turns into driveway	
Provide continuous right-turn lane	> 60 driveways/mile; > 15,000 vpd roadway traffic with > 20% right turns/mile
Provide supplementary right-turn-only driveways	high-volume driveway; > 300-foot frontage
Provide right-turn deceleration lane*	> 35 mph; > 1,000 right turns/day and > 40 right turns during peak hour; adequate frontage
General	
Provide frontage road*	> 60 driveways/mile; > 20,000 vpd roadway traffic; 40–55 mph
Provide 2 one-way driveways instead of 1 two-way driveway	< 60 driveways/mile; < 35 mph; > 150-foot frontages
Provide right-turn acceleration lane*	> 35 mph; > 75 right turns during peak hour; adequate frontage

SOURCE: Adapted from Glennon et al. [1].

*Adequate geometrics are critical to the satisfactory functioning of these techniques.

3. Left-turn prohibitions are most desirable when physically implemented with median channelization (if a median exists) or driveway channelization. Signing should also be installed as necessary.

4. To a great extent, the width for entering movements will be determined by the turning requirements. Exit width will be determined by peak turning volumes.

ACCESS DRIVES

In order to ensure efficient internal circulation, storage areas at access drives must be designed to allow for adequate capacity. Storage on the driveway should be of sufficient length to keep stopped vehicles from blocking the path of entering vehicles or vehicles traveling along the internal circulation roadways. Failure to provide sufficient storage will result in unsafe and confusing vehicle conflicts as indicated in Figure 6-13.

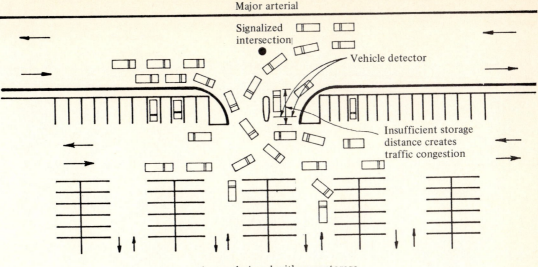

Figure 6-13 Schematic example of insufficient storage. SOURCE: Courtesy of Barton-Aschman Associates, Inc.

Where large developments (greater than 500,000 square feet) are involved, one of the two following basic site layouts should be used in order to develop good access and site-circulation design:

1. Locate the building at least 500 feet back from the street. This will provide a throat length of 250 feet, which is necessary for a high-capacity access drive and adequate parking-bay lengths between the ring road and the building face.

2. Orient the long dimension of linear developments perpendicular to the arterial. This will provide for long signalized access spacing and good on-site circulation.

Figure 6-14 illustrates the essential elements of good design which provides for: (1) long signalized intersection spacing, (2) long throat length between the intersection of the access drive in the arterial and its intersection with the ring road, (3) ample parking between the ring road and the building, and (4) a discontinuous perimeter road.

Figure 6-15(a) illustrates the major site-circulation features of a large medical complex. Signalized intersection spacing is at one-fourth mile. This results in very poor horizontal alignment of the major site circulation on the south end of the complex. Relocating the intersection further to the south would cause interference at the adjacent intersection to the south. Furthermore, the long unobstructed perimeter roadway along the west side is conducive to high speeds and results in high vehicular–pedestrian conflicts. It also results in poor geometry at the intersection of the perimeter and ring road.

The original development consisted of part of the center third of the complex. At that time, the major on-site circulation roadways north and south of the complex were a considerable distance from the structure; parking was provided between these roadways and the structure. As the complex was expanded to the south and the emergency room was relocated, it was necessary to relocate the south roadway. The increase in staff and visitors necessitated a substantial increase in parking. The circulation, as developed, experienced the following problems: (1) It is very difficult to develop signing to direct persons who are not familiar with the complex to the appropriate entrance. (2) The long peripheral roadway (in excess of a quarter of a mile) at the face of the complex is condcive to high volume and high speeds; also, there are numerous conflicts between vehicles entering or leaving the parking lots, dropping off or picking up patients (passengers), and other movement. (3) Access to the emergency room is not as direct as desirable. (4) Truck access (several WB-50s per day) is awkward, and maneuvering into the unloading docks is difficult. (5) Circulation from the visitor's parking area to the building entrances to pick up passengers is inconvenient. (6) The on-site roadway to the south of the building complex has

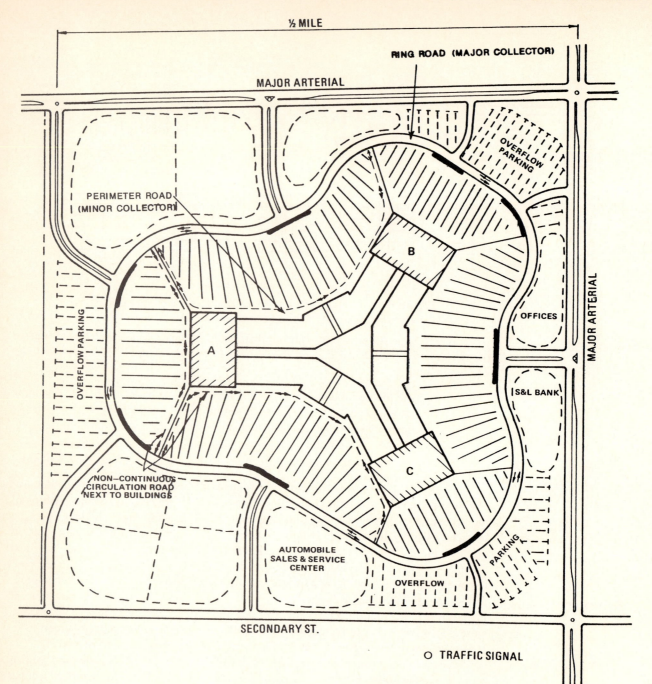

Figure 6-14 Typical features of a large site development. SOURCE: Courtesy of Barton-Aschman Associates, Inc.

intersections on short-radius horizontal curves. (b) Sketch of improved circulatioon that could be achieved if the long dimension were perpendicular to the street.

If the complex had been oriented perpendicular to the arterial, as in Figure 6-15(b), a much better alignment of the ring road and site circulation could have been achieved.

The site has extensive frontage on the arterial street. The major access roadways are suitable for signalization, since they conform to the long, uniform signal spacing on the arterial. Orientation of such a complex perpendicular to the arterial street would facillitate expansion while maintaining a substantial separation for parkiing between the structures and the major on-site circulation roadways. Signing would be greatly simplified. The south access roadway could be signed as the visitor and patient entrance; once on the site,

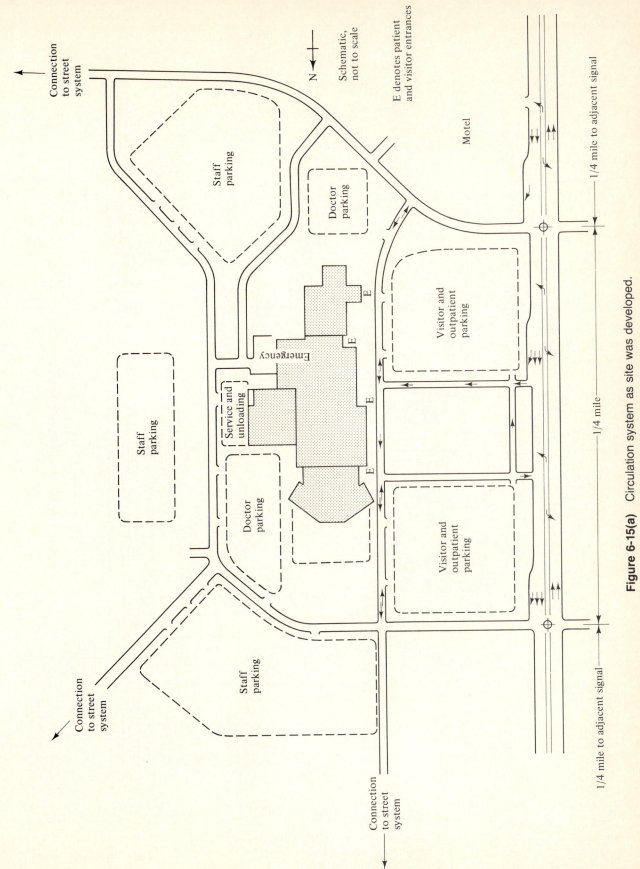

Figure 6-15(a) Circulation system as site was developed.

165

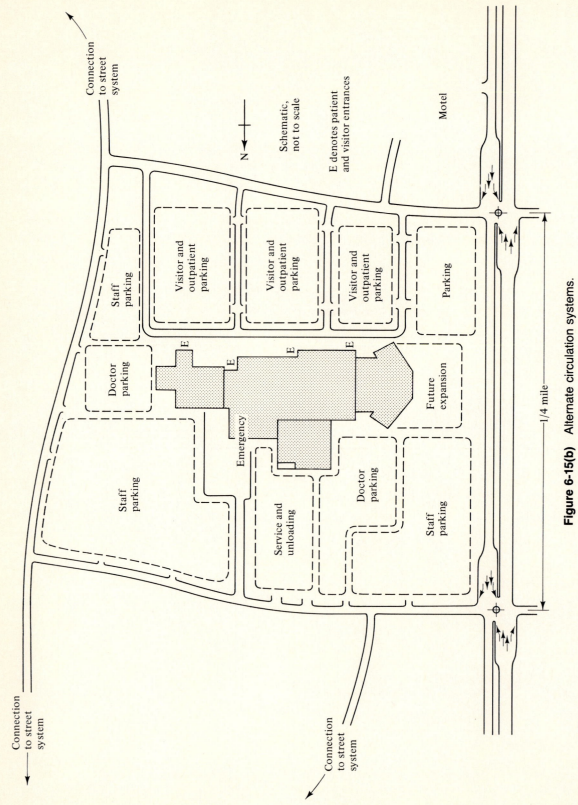

Figure 6-15(b) Alternate circulation systems.

subsequent signing would direct individuals to a specific part of the complex. This would sequence and separate drive decision points and thereby reduce driver confusion. The volume of traffic along the building face on the visitor/patient side would be reduced, together with the potential for higher speeds. As a result, pedestrian–vehicular conflicts would also be reduced. Truck access and unloading could be greatly improved. Finally, vehicular circulation between the north and south sides of the complex would be significantly improved, and less site traffic would use the arterial street.

Maneuvering Area

When the throat length and width of an access drive are inadequate, the capacity of the signalized intersection of an access drive and an arterial will be limited by the conflicts of the intersection of the access drive and the ring road (Figure 6-16) or the weaving area (Figure 6-17). In both cases, the flow rate (vehicles per hour) sustainable by the signalized intersection is greater than the volume that can be delivered to the intersection by the inadequate geometry of the access drive.

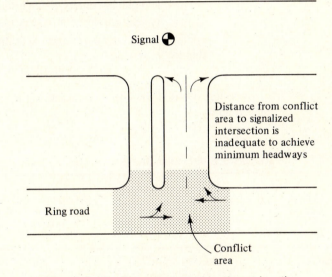

Figure 6-16 Capacity limited by throat length.

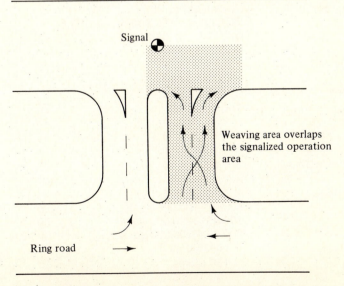

Figure 6-17 Capacity limited by weaving area.

In such cases, the use of signalized-intersection capacity analysis is not appropriate. Instead, the capacity should be evaluated by dividing the green time by the expected average headway of vehicles passing through the signal. This value will be approximately 4.5 seconds when the throat length is less than 150 feet. A more specific value might be obtained by the detailed study of access drives of similar design.

Internal Storage

To determine the necessary length of storage, traffic volumes should be assigned to the applicable lanes and the highest lane volume should be accommodated. The techniques to determine storage lengths for both signalized and nonsignalized intersections are described in Chapter 5.

In the absence of adequate traffic-volume data, engineering judgment should be utilized along with several commonly accepted values:

1. For major regional centers, double left turns and a 250-foot throat length for vehicle storage should be provided.
2. For smaller community centers, a minimum of 120 to 150 feet of storage space should be provided.

More detailed guidelines for throat length and vehicle storage requirements are given in Table 6-4.

TABLE 6-4

Minimum Throat Length and On-Site Vehicular Storage for Delivery Exits

Land Use	Size	Minimum Throat Length (ft.) Collector (ft.)	Arterial (ft.)	Minimum Total Storage (ft.)
Light industrial	< 100,000 sq. ft.	25	50	100
	100,001–500,000 sq. ft.	50	100	600
	> 500,000 sq. ft.	50	200	1,000
Discount store	< 30,000 sq. ft.	25	50	300
	> 30,000 sq. ft.	25	75	600
Shopping center	< 250,000 sq. ft.	25	50	500
	250,001–500,000 sq. ft.	50	75	1,000
	500,001–750,000 sq. ft.	75	200	1,500
	> 750,000 sq. ft.	125	250	2,000
Supermarket	< 20,000 sq. ft.	50	75	300
	> 20,000 sq. ft.	75	125	500
Apartments	< 100 units	25	50	300
	100–200 units	50	75	500
	> 200 units	75	125	750
Quality restaurant	< 15,000 sq. ft.	25	50	100
	> 15,000 sq. ft.	25	75	150
Drive-in restaurant	< 2,000 sq. ft.	25	75	100
	> 2,000 sq. ft.	50	100	200
General office	< 50,000 sq. ft.	25	50	500
	50,001–100,000 sq. ft.	25	75	750
	100,001–200,000 sq. ft.	50	100	1,000
	200,001–500,000 sq. ft.	100	150	1,500
	> 500,000 sq. ft.	125	250	2,000
Motel	< 150 rooms	25	75	150
	> 150 rooms	25	100	200

3. Size and shape (footprint) of the building(s) and location(s) on the site.
4. Amount of public street frontage and the functional class of the street.
5. Distribution of the site traffic at the access points.
6. Predominant movements at the access points.
7. Proximity of freeway interchange on major at-grade intersection(s).
8. Local zoning ordinance constraints.
9. Local access design criteria and standards.

On-Site Intersections

Tee (three-way) intersections should be used for all on-site design in order to minimize conflicts and simplify maneuver areas. On-site intersections should be designed to the same geometric standards as the intersection of comparable classes of public streets. The geometrics should be checked using turning-path design templates to ensure that service vehicles can be accommodated.

Sight distances also should be checked at all on-site intersections and on horizontal curves. Minimum speeds for sight-distance determination should be 20 mph on parking aisles and perimeter roads and 30 mph on ring roads. On very large sites, where long travel distances are possible, a speed of 40 mph or more may be appropriate.

CRITIQUE OF INTERNAL SITE-DESIGN ELEMENTS

Figures 6-18 through 6-54 (pp. 172–84) illustrate selected elements of internal site design and circulation. The text accompanying each photograph or sketch briefly identifies and evaluates a design feature which was handled in a way that contributes to a good or a poor design.

When reviewing a site plan it should be recognized that site-specific considerations will influence a design and that various compromises are required in the development of any site layout. The manner in which a specific element is handled may vary from site to site. Good design results when the compromises reflect the hierarchical nature of circulation systems—an element in a lower functional class should be compromised in preference to one in a higher classification.

REFERENCES

1. Glennon, J. C., Valenta, J. J., Thomson, B. A., and Azzeh, J. A., "Technical Guidelines for the Control of Direct Access to Arterial Highways: Volume II, Detailed Description of Access Control Techniques," *Report No. FHWA-RD-76-87*, Federal Highway Administration, August 1975.

2. Stover, Vergil G., "Guidelines for Spacing of Unsignalized Access to Urban Arterial Streets," *Technical Bulletin No. 81-1*, Texas Engineering Experiment Station, January 1981.

3. Stover, Vergil G., Adkins, William G., and Goodknight, John C., "Guidelines for Medial and Marginal Control on Major Roadways," National Cooperative Highway Research Program, *Report 93*, Highway Research Board, 1970.

4. Stover, Vergil G., "Driveway Design," *Short Course Notes*, Texas Engineering Extension Service, January 1986, presently under revision.

Figure 6-18 Example of poor access design. What's wrong with the access and circulation of this 150,000-square-foot (approximately) shopping center in northeast Lake County, Ohio? The throat length (about 25 feet) is inadequate to separate driver decision points. The 6-inch raised divider separating ingress and egress maneuvers has very limited visual qualities. The asphalt paving of the parking lot extends beyond the right-of-way/property line to the sidewalk, resulting in extremely poor delineation as to where vehicles should and should not be. The installation of four-inch steel posts along the right-of-way line was an attempt to rectify the problem. In order to deter high-speed diagonal movement in the parking lot, 6-inch raised concrete dividers were constructed. Visibility of these barriers on other than bright sunny days is very poor.

Figure 6-19 Inadequate visibility of access drive. This access to a shopping center offers very poor delineation to the driver. The photograph was taken five days after the median and curbs were painted; the tire markings indicate that many drivers have difficulty maneuvering through the access point—especially the ingress maneuver. Tire markings on the backside of the curb clearly indicate that some drivers missed the driveway. The median is too narrow to be clearly visible, as also indicated by tire markings. Throat length is inadequate for the volume of traffic generated.

Figure 6-20 Right-turn channelization island. Use of a 50-foot radius for right-turn channelization as shown in this photograph provides an island which is of maximum size. A 75-foot radius will create a large island which will be much more visible to drivers. It also can be suitably landscaped to make it more esthetically attractive. The intersection shown is one of the access drives to a regional shopping center in Sacramento, California. A similar island is located on the far side of the intersection (view blocked by the VW van). Signalized access is located at quarter-mile intervals. The curb lane is a right-turn deceleration/acceleration lane. There are no intermediate unsignalized access drives.

Figure 6-21 Poor driveway cross section and profile. This access drive exhibits poor cross-section and profile design. The narrow paved median with a 6-inch vertical face is not clearly visible to drivers. The entire median was painted yellow to provide better contrast. Tire marks on the vertical face and on top of the median indicated that several vehicles had hit it within the 6-day period after it was painted. The abrupt change in grade produced a very severe joust, even at speeds less than 10 mph. These and other considerations resulted in the access drive being removed.

Figure 6-22 Poor delineation of access drives. The portland cement concrete sidewalk provides contrast between the asphaltic concrete surfaces of the street and the on-site parking areas. However, the access drives are very poorly delineated and extremely difficult for the driver to identify. The spacing visible between the two drives in the foreground is prevalent along the entire street. The lack of contrast between the access drives and the space between them makes it very difficult to spot a driveway which is more than 150–200 feet away, even on a clear day.

Figure 6-23 Corner-clearance problems. Inadequate corner clearance results in drivers forcing their way through a queue of vehicles. Note the left-side traffic.

Figure 6-24 An early application of an "arterial-type" design for a shopping-center access drive. This photo was taken shortly after the shopping center was opened in the mid-1940s; since then, successive additions have increased the floor area severalfold. It illustrates one of the early applications of a long throat length and multilane cross section. Note the median design which provides for the left-turn egress maneuver. The area directly across the arterial from the center is a cemetery.

Figure 6-25 Inadequate medial features. These 6-inch-high, 6-inch-wide barriers offer extremely poor delineation. Yellow paint makes a very marginal improvement.

Figure 6-26 Inadequate throat length. This photograph is an example of a very poor design which is in common use. The throat is about one car in length. Immediately upon completing the turn maneuver onto the site the driver is presented with a complex maneuver area. The close proximity of the four-way intersection of access drive and the ring road and the intersection of the driveway with the arterial street results in overlapping maneuver areas. This results in low driveway capacity, especially egress capacity, and high accident potential.

Figure 6-27 Better, but not good. An extremely inadequate throat length at this large shopping center resulted in frequent accidents and numerous citizen complaints. The intersection of the peripheral circulation roadway with the access drive was eliminated to increase the throat length. This was accomplished by simply installing a 6-inch-high slab of concrete and painting the surface yellow. The manner in which the retrofit was made is a functionally poor design and esthetically displeasing.

Figure 6-28 Lack of contrast results in poor visibility. This photo was taken shortly after the small office and retail center was opened. The portland cement concrete (pcc) divider does not contrast with the pcc pavement. If not of sufficient width to allow suitable landscaping, such dividers should be omitted.

Figure 6-29 Example of good design for a small shopping center. This 150,000-square-foot shopping center constructed in 1960 shows many of the desirable features of a good design, including adequate throat length (75 feet), a 1½-inch-high median with rounded edges and a contrasting surface to separate ingress and egress traffic, and on-site circulation which minimizes pedestrian–vehicle conflict. The design would be enhanced by provision of a right-turn lane for ingress traffic, widening of the median to allow for placement of the sign in the median and for landscaping to more clearly define the median and outside edges of the drive, and a narrow landscape buffer between the parking surface and the right-of-way line.

Figure 6-30 Inadequate access to a regional shopping center. This main access drive to a regional shopping center (slightly over 1 million feet GLA) is grossly inadequate. The throat length is much too short. Vehicles making left and right turns to exit the center must weave through each other during the green phase. As a result, capacity is far below that for a signalized intersection. Furthermore, the cross section provides for only a single left turn. The second photograph shows the resulting queue of vehicles waiting to leave the shopping center. Traffic counts indicated that the center was generating about one-third of the number of trips that a center of this size generates on an average Saturday.

Figure 6-31 Where are the driveways? Paving over the right-of-way of this major street diminishes the edge of the outside traffic lane and makes it extremely difficult for drivers to identify the driveway locations. The numerous deep grooves in the asphalt surface all along the roadway clearly indicate that many drivers have mistakenly driven over the curb. The double yellow paint stripe shown in the second photograph marks the edge of a driveway.

Figure 6-32 Developer elected not to take access to major street. Developers of this office building elected to take access via the existing street intersecting the major street rather than having direct access. As a result, there is minimum interference with the arterial, and a better site plan was achieved.

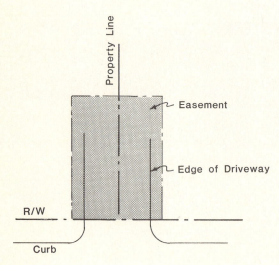

Figure 6-33 Access easement for shared drive. Shared-access easements reduce the frequency of access drives and can be implemented in the subdivision process. This practice will reduce the conflict between adjacent access drives.

Figure 6-34 Examples of poor curb cut construction. Failure to remove the entire curb results in an apron which is of insufficient strength. Placing a 2 × 4 in the flow line as a form prior to pouring the apron adds thickness and strength. It also maintains the flow line in its original position. However, the 2-inch vertical rise results in a very noticeable bump to vehicle occupants. Such a treatment should be avoided on arterial and collector streets.

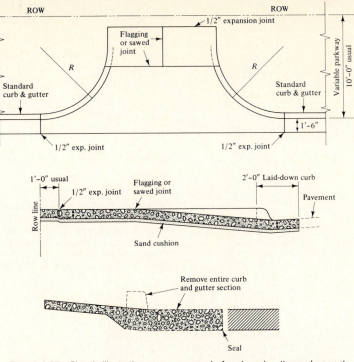

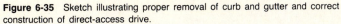

Figure 6-35 Sketch illustrating proper removal of curb and gutter and correct construction of direct-access drive.

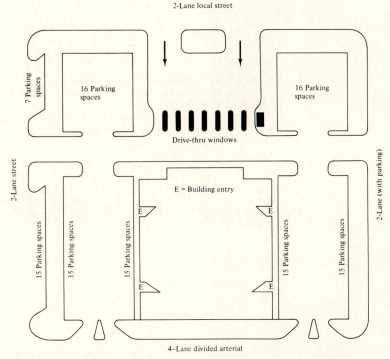

Figure 6-36 Example of poor building location and site circulation. Centering the building on the arterial street frontage of this square-block site (approximately 480 feet × 455 feet) results in poor site circulation. Drivers not finding a parking space on one side use the arterial to reach the other side; this circulation is of a very minor collector type movement. SOURCE: Vergil G. Stover, William G. Adkins, and John C. Goodknight [3].

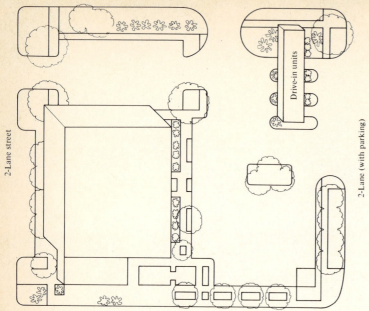

2-Lane local street

2-Lane street

Drive-in units

2-Lane (with parking)

4-Lane divided arterial

Figure 6-37 Example of good building location and site circulation. Location of the building in one corner of the square-block site (approximately 350 feet × 310 feet) allows for efficient circulation and parking design. Drivers can conveniently find a parking space without circulating on the adjacent street system. SOURCE: Vergil G. Stover, William G. Adkins, and John C. Goodknight [3].

Figure 6-38 Long continuous circulation adjacent to building face. The long continuous circulation adjacent to the building face of this regional shopping center produces high volumes and speeds. This results in pedestrian–vehicular conflict problems. The structure in the left center of the photograph is a drive-through bank facility.

Figure 6-39 Poor design compounds pedestrian–vehicular conflicts. Traffic entering and leaving the site must pass through the intersection at the building face. This produces high traffic volumes along the building face, in turn generating pedestrian–vehicular conflicts.

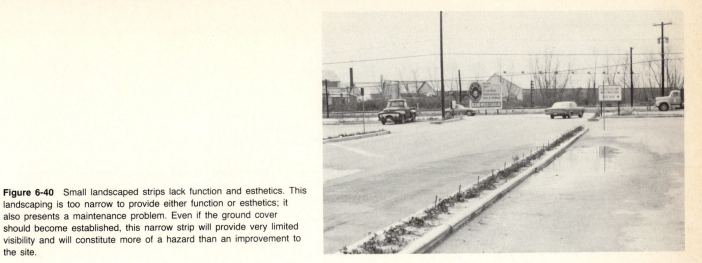

Figure 6-40 Small landscaped strips lack function and esthetics. This landscaping is too narrow to provide either function or esthetics; it also presents a maintenance problem. Even if the ground cover should become established, this narrow strip will provide very limited visibility and will constitute more of a hazard than an improvement to the site.

Figure 6-41 Inadequate on-site radius. Inadequate radius in this on-site circulation system interferes with vehicular movement as well as creating maintenance and esthetic problems.

Figure 6-42 Speed bumps—an admission of poor site planning. The need to use a speed bump is a clear indication of a poor site plan. Speed and volume should be controlled by the design and continuity of the on-site circulation.

Figure 6-43 Pedestrian movement must be considered in the site plan. Pedestrian access to the sidewalk is blocked when a car is parked in the end space.

Figure 6-44 Shopping carts—a site-design detail. Shoppers commonly leave shopping carts in the parking lot. Racks should be conveniently provided in an area where carts are used. Temporary storage should not interfere with the on-site circulation, as it does in this case. Note the left-hand traffic.

Figure 6-45 Inadequate attention to utilities. When the shopping center was first opened (the main building is to the left of the photographs), the poor location of the fire hydrant did not present a serious problem (first photograph). The hydrant was protected by simply installing four 4-inch steel pipes, filled with and set in concrete. The second photo shows the situation after the center was fully developed. Right-turning vehicles occupy the entire width of the two-way circulation roadway. Inspection of the posts indicates that they have been hit so hard as to pull one out of the ground and to lay the other over at an angle of about 45°, even though they were imbedded about 2½ feet into the ground.

Figure 6-46 Poor delineation between street and adjacent development. A high-volume restaurant is located at the intersection of this urban minor arterial and a major intercity highway. The city allowed the property owner to pave to the back of the curb. As a result, delineation between the on-site circulation and the street is lost. A large portion of the restaurant's customers are tourists. A sadistic person might obtain considerable entertainment by watching the expression on the faces of vehicle occupants when they drive off the curb or attempt to locate the access drive. A little maintenance (street sweeping) would help, but not solve, the delineation problem. It could, however, significantly improve tourists' impressions of the city.

Figure 6-47 Innovative service station design. Larger sites provide an opportunity for flexibility in service station design. This Liberty Oil Company station in Mount Vernon, Illinois, is an example. Note the substantial corner clearances.

(a)

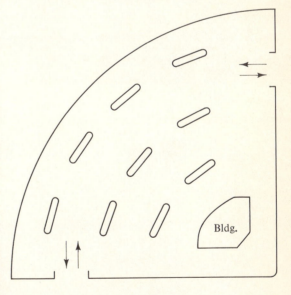

(b)

Figure 6-48 Large sites permit flexibility in design. (a) This large service station site was developed in the traditional design—with the pump islands in the front and two access drives to each street. Note the extensive nonproductively used space to the rear of the station building. (b) The sketch illustrates how a large service station site might be redesigned to increase the corner clearance and increase the number of pump islands.

Figure 6-49 Improper location of a drive-thru window. The corner clearance between the drive-thru window and the intersection of the two streets at this laundry and cleaners is grossly inadequate. An exiting vehicle attempting to enter the signalized intersection will be situated at an angle in the intersection approach, and the rear of the vehicle will encroach upon the other traffic lane. Drivers making left or right turns from the arterial to the collector are presented with a conflict while still making the turn maneuver.

Figure 6-50 Typical design of a regional shopping center. This regional shopping-center design illustrates the separation of the parking area into separate lots. Vehicles use the ring road to get between lots. Thus, pedestrian–vehicular conflicts are minimized. Limiting the length of the peripheral road adjacent to the building helps control vehicular speeds. Note that the parking aisles are oriented at 90° to the building.

Figure 6-51 Site layout typical of a small commercial center. This large discount store is illustrative of the site arrangement for a small commercial center. The throat lengths are adequate for this size of development. Note the intersections of the access drives and the on-site circulation on three-way intersections. Notice, too, that wide landscaped areas are used to help delineate the intersections. However the design (proximity of two of the access drives to the front of the building and 60-degree parking) encourages pedestrian–vehicular conflicts at the building face. High-speed diagonal movements are also a potential hazard.

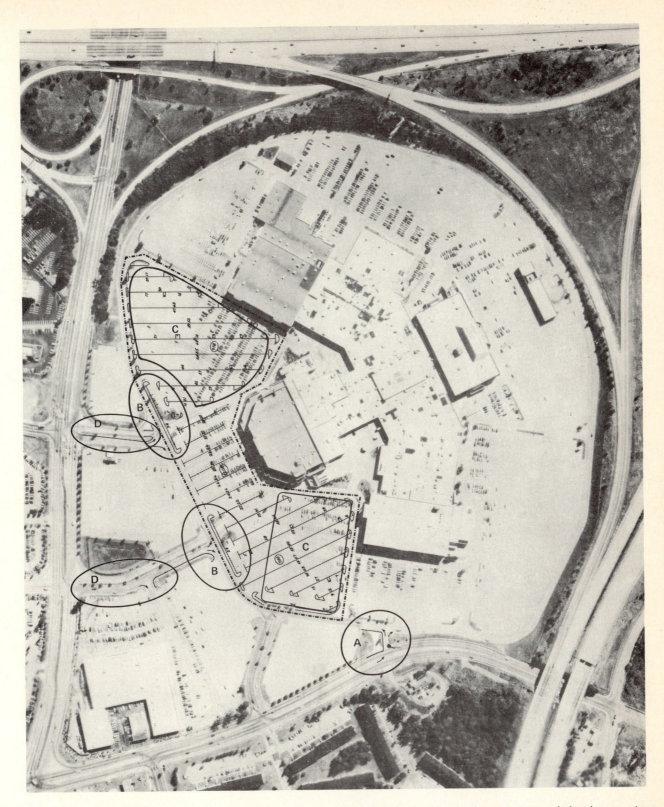

Figure 6-52 Site layout of a regional shopping mall. Critique of site-plan elements: *Location A:* This secondary access was redesigned as an entrance only. This greatly reduces the conflict area as well as the number of conflict points. The change mitigates the problems associated with a short throat length. It also minimizes the effect of the jog resulting from the inadequate "canoe" length. *Location B:* Extension of the "canoe" eliminates the complex four-way intersection area. It also results in more traffic on the ring road and much less traffic along the building face. *Location C:* Rearrangement of the parking rows facilitates vehicular traffic from and to the ring road; vehicular–pedestrian conflicts at the building face are reduced, and pedestrian movement to and from the building is improved. *Location D:* The long multilane access drives provide substantial storage which results in high exit and entrance capacities. *Other comments:* The design of the perimeter road discourages high volumes and high speeds. On-site traffic circulation is encouraged to use the ring road. SOURCE: Courtesy of Barton-Aschman Associates, Inc.

Figure 6-53 Poor access design misleads drivers. The signs at this regional shopping center are located downstream of the exit side of the divided access drive serving a regional shopping center. The signs, but not the access drive, are well lighted at night. The combination of horizontal curvature and sign location confuses many drivers at night. Drivers frequently pass the entrance side of the driveway before they realize it and stop in the outside traffic lane while considering their predicament. Observation indicated that about 40% back up and enter, about 40% enter by going the wrong way on the exit side of the drive, and about 20% continue on to find another entrance.

7

Parking and Service Facilities

PARKING REQUIREMENTS

A study for The Urban Land Institute (ULI) by Barton-Aschman Associates [11], together with data from The Institute of Transportation Engineers [5] and The Traffic Institute, Northwestern University [10], suggests the following parking indices for stand-alone uses:

Office:	3.0 spaces per 1,000 square feet of gross leasable floor area (GLA)
Retail:	5.0 spaces per 1,000 square feet of GLA for shopping centers over 600,000 square feet
	4.5 spaces per 1,000 square feet of GLA for centers having 400,000 to 600,000 square feet
	4.0 spaces per 1,000 square feet of GLA for centers having 25,000 to 400,000 square feet
	3.0 spaces per 1,000 square feet of GLA for convenience grocery stores without gasoline pumps
Industrial:	0.6 spaces per employee
Residential:	2.0 spaces per single-family dwelling unit (DU)
	2.0 spaces per multifamily DU with three or more bedrooms
	1.5 spaces per multifamily DU with one or two bedrooms
	1.0 spaces per multifamily efficiency DU
Restaurants:	20.0 spaces per 1,000 feet GLA
Cinemas:	0.3 space per seat
Hotels:	1.25 spaces per room

The ITE report [5] contains the average as well as the range in peak parking rates (see Figure 7-1). This source will be of increased value as the ITE Standing Committee on Parking continues to acquire additional information for inclusion in this report.

SUMMARY OF PARKING GENERATION RATES

Land Use/Building Type ___Discount Stores___ ITE Land Use Code ___830___

Independent Variable-Occupied Parking Spaces Per ___1000 SFGLA___

	Peak Parking Rates		Standard Deviation	Number of Studies	Average Size of Independent Variable
	Average	Range (Min. to Max.)			
Weekday Parking Rates	3.7	1.3 - 5.4		17	99.3
Saturday Parking Rates	3.5	1.9 - 5.7		15	99.2
Sunday Parking Rates	2.8			1	88.0
Reported Peak Parking Time Period					

Source Numbers _____

ITE Technical Committee 5-BB-Parking Generation

Date: ___Jan. 1985___

ITE Parking Generation Report

Figure 7-1   Example of ITE parking data. SOURCE: Institute of Transportation Engineers [5].

The ULI study by Barton-Aschman Associates found that parking demand was not sensitive to city size or geographic regions. However, site-specific factors such as transit use were found to be more related to parking demand. Furthermore, location-specific factors (such as accessibility relative to competing locations within an urban area market) presumably contribute to the variation in the parking demand at similar activity centers.

Substantial differences occur in the hourly pattern of parking accumulation (Figures 7-2 and 7-3) for different land use activities. The general patterns are listed below:

Office: Peak parking accumulation occurs in midmorning and mid-afternoon; evening (after 7 p.m.) demand is less than 10% of the peak. As shown in Figure 7-2, offices experience extremely low parking demand on Saturday.

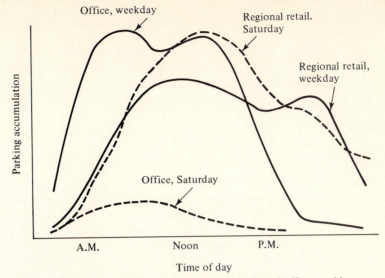

Figure 7-2 Hourly variations in regional retail and office parking demand. SOURCE: Adapted from ULI — The Urban Land Institute [11].

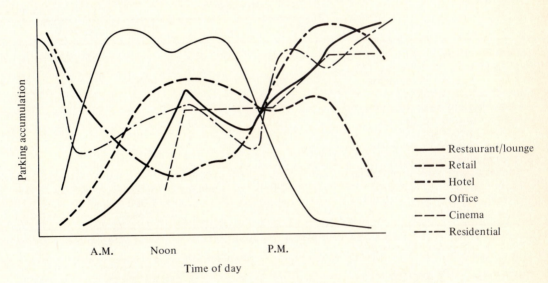

Figure 7-3 Hourly variations in weekday parking accumulations. SOURCE: Adapted from ULI — The Urban Land Institute [11] and The Traffic Institute, Northwestern University [10].

Regional retail: At some centers, the weekday peak occurs at midday and is about 70% of the peak parking that occurs on Saturdays. However, at many regional retail centers the weekday peak parking accumulation occurs between 7:30 and 9:00 p.m. and is 75% to 80% of the peak Saturday accumulation.

Cinemas: The afternoon parking demand is approximately 70% of the peak which occurs on Saturday evening.

Hotels: Peak parking accumulation occurs in the evening with very low demand at midday.

Restaurants: The pronounced midday demand is approximately 70% of the peak parking accumulation which occurs in the evening.

Residential: The peak occurs in the evening, with midday parking accumulation being 60% to 65% of the peak.

The ULI study by Barton-Aschman Associates [11] shows that various land use activities also experience seasonal variation in peak parking demand. The seasonal variation implies a similar variation in traffic generation as well. However, hourly parking accumulation data cannot be used to calculate trip generation or to adjust trip generation rates.

SHARED PARKING

Different land use activities are known to have different peak parking accumulation patterns. When such uses are combined in a mixed-use development, the total number of parking spaces required is less than the summation of the spaces required when the same land use activities exist as stand-alone developments [11]. When such land uses are combined in a single development or are located adjacent to each other, variances in the individual parking requirements should be allowed. As suggested by the example shown in Table 7-1, the percent reduction will depend upon the relative mix of different uses.

TABLE 7-1

Example of Reduction in Total Parking Required by Mixed-Use Development

	Example No. 1			Example No. 2		
	Office	Retail	Total	Office	Retail	Total
Square feet GLA	400,000	1,000,000		200,000	1,200,000	
Parking spaces per 1,000 sq ft GLA	3.0	5.0		3.0	5.0	
Number of spaces, stand-alone	1,200	5,000	6,200	600	6,000	6,600
Shared parking, weekday:						
Percentage of peak accumulation	97%	75%		97%	75%	
Number of parking spaces	1,165	3,750	4,915	582	4,500	4,982
Saving, spaces			1,285			1,618
Saving, percent			20.7%			24.5%
Shared parking, Saturday						
Percentage of peak accumulation	10%	100%		10%	100%	
Number of parking spaces	120	5,000	5,120	60	6,000	6,060
Saving, spaces			1,000			540
Saving, percent			17.4%			8.2%

NOTE: Detailed information for the calculation of the reduction in total parking that can be achieved with mixed development, with examples, is contained in the ULI publication *Shared Parking* [11].

PARKING-LOT LAYOUT

Parking-lot layout involves arrangement of the circulation aisles, parking stalls, islands, and traffic diverters in association to the building footprint and entrances and the access drives to the adjacent public street. Users should find circulation and parking to be safe and convenient in a self-parking lot or garage. Poorly designed lots result in confusion, customer frustration, traffic accidents, damage to parked vehicles, and, ultimately, loss of customers when they have other alternatives.

Orientation of Parking

In large developments the primary parking should be oriented with the parking bays perpendicular to the building face as illustrated in Figure 7-4. This provides for visibility between pedestrians and vehicles and more convenient pedestrian movement between the parking stalls and the building. When the bays are arranged parallel to the building, the pedestrians must walk between the parked cars. This results in greatly reduced visibility between pedestrians and drivers; children walking out from between parked cars create an especially hazardous situation.

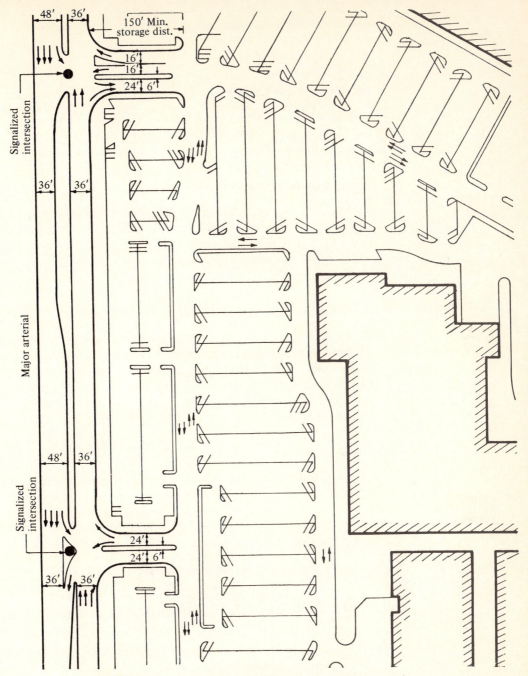

Figure 7-4 Sketch of site plan with desirable access and parking-aisle arrangement. Note that building setback must be at least 400 feet in order to provide adequate throat length and parking aisles of reasonable length.

In neighborhood centers and other small generators the size of the site commonly requires that the parking bays be parallel to the building. Adequate driveway design and on-site circulation can be developed for the traffic volumes generated.

No Parking Immediately Adjacent to Building

Parking adjacent to the building should be prohibited. Exceptions are very small parking lots, lots where parking turnover is very low, or overflow parking where the spaces are not often used. This prohibition provides for unobstructed visibility of pedestrians—

especially small children—moving between the building and parking area. It also provides for rapid access of emergency services. Designation of the curb space immediately adjacent to the building face as a fire lane enables municipal enforcement of the no-parking restriction.

Maximum Aisle Length

Parking aisles should not exceed 300 to 350 feet without a break in circulation. This will aid the customer in conveniently finding a parking space when the lot is approaching capacity. It also will help eliminate high speeds in the aisles.

Prime Customer Parking

Prime customer parking for office and retail activities should be located within short walking distance of the building entrance. Stall and module dimensions should be generous in all heavily used, high-turnover locations. The combination of stall width and aisle width should be sufficient to allow the driver to complete the parking and unparking maneuvers in a single, convenient, smooth turn.

Overflow and Employee Parking

Overflow parking for customers and employee parking usually is located in the more distant areas of parking for commercial retail and office space. In larger regional shopping centers and activity centers, this parking frequently is located outside of the major on-site circulation roadway or ring road. Narrower stalls and modular widths are commonly used for employee parking. Tighter dimensions are also frequently used for overflow customer parking.

Parking Angle

The dimensions and shape of small tracts may result in one parking angle being more efficient than others. Normally, however, the average gross area per space is essentially independent of parking angle, and different angles result in approximately the same number of gross square feet per space. The advantages and disadvantages commonly stated regarding different parking angles are summarized below.

Advantages of 90-Degree Parking

1. Provides greater freedom of vehicular circulation.
2. End islands at the end of parking bays are easier to design and construct.
3. Aisle width facilitates pedestrian movement and passing of stalled vehicles.
4. Minimizes travel distance for drivers seeking a parking space; also minimizes travel distance after unparking.
5. Directional signing is not needed.
6. Shopper traffic is not required to use the circulation roads immediately adjacent to the building; pedestrian–vehicular conflicts at the front are reduced.

The decrease in pedestrian–vehicular conflict is the most significant and compelling reason for the use of the 90-degree parking angle. Much of the customer traffic will reach and leave a parking stall directly from the ring road. Only those who did not find a vacant parking stall when traversing the aisle are required to use the perimeter roadway.

Disadvantages of 90-Degree Parking

1. A 90-degree turn is required to park and unpark.
2. The potential for sideswipe conflicts is greater for two-way aisles than for one-way aisles.

Advantages of Angle Parking

1. When observed, one-way aisles minimize the head-on and sideswipe conflicts.
2. Maneuvering into and out of the parking space is facilitated, and the time required for the maneuver is reduced. Delays to other vehicles are minimized.
3. Rear doors can be opened without interference of an adjacent vehicle. At angles of 30 degrees or less the front door also can be opened without interference.
4. Conflict points are fewer at the intersection of the aisle and circulation (on-site collector) roadways.

Disadvantages of Angle Parking

1. The results include more traffic on the circulation roadway adjacent to the building front and increased pedestrian–vehicular conflicts.
2. Drivers frequently go the wrong way on the one-way aisles. As a result the potential for head-on and sideswipe accidents is increased. The potential for accidents exists at the intersection of the aisle and the perimeter road and the ring road.
3. End islands are larger and more expensive to construct because of the more complex curb-line arrangements.
4. Travel distance and total on-site circulation is increased.
5. Directional signing and markings are required which are visible under all weather conditions.
6. Drivers frequently drive through the parking row in order to avoid using the perimeter roadway.

Parking Design

The characteristics of the parker must be considered in addition to the physical characteristics of the vehicle when deciding on parking-lot dimensions. Wide stalls make it easier to get in and out of a vehicle, and the parking/unparking maneuvers are facilitated by combination of stall width and aisle width.

A large proportion of mid-size and compact autos in the U.S. passenger car fleet are two-door models. When the door is opened to the "first stop," the distance from the side of the car to the outside edge of the door is approximately 32 inches for a compact and 34 inches for a mid-size automobile. This will provide about a two-foot opening between the inside edge of the door and the door post for entering and exiting.

When an automobile door is opened, the design of the hinge mechanism tends to cause the door to swing open to the first stop. Failure to have adequate clearance between parked vehicles results in dents in the side of the adjacent vehicle. Side-molding reduces the frequency of this damage but does not eliminate it.

As indicated in Table 7-2 (p. 192), a mid-sized, two-door U.S. automobile is about 8.7 feet wide when the door is open to the first stop, and the compact two-door is just under 8 feet in width.

Where the parking duration is very short, and especially when packages or other items will be taken out or placed in the passenger compartment, an extra-wide parking space is highly desirable. For example, a 10-foot-wide stall should be standard for convenience grocery stores. On the other hand, where parking durations are long, as in office or industrial developments, an 8-foot-6-inch or even an 8-foot wide stall might be acceptable. Table 7-3 (p. 192) gives suggested stall widths for standard and compact autos for various applications.

Parking-Module Arrangement

Suggested parking-module dimensions for 90-degree parking of standard and mid-size autos are given in Table 7-4. Tables 7-5 and 7-6 are for 60-degree and 45-degree parking, respectively. Dimensions for compact autos are given in Table 7-7. See pp. 193–4.

TABLE 7-2

Typical Dimensions of Automobiles with Door Open to First Stop

Auto Classification	Vehicle Width (feet)		Door Outside Edge to Body (inches)
	Body	Door Open	
Full-size, 4-door	6.7	9.2	30
Mid-size, 2-door	5.8	8.7	34
Compact, 2-door	5.1	7.8	32
Compact, 4-door	5.1	6.9	22
Subcompact, 2-door	5.0	6.8	32

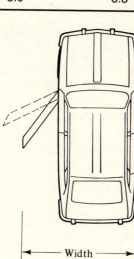

← Width →

TABLE 7-3

Recommended Parking-Stall Widths for Different Applications

Application	Standard Mid-Size (feet)	Compact (feet)
Convenience store, consumer/visitor: short duration, high turnover	10.0	9.0
	9.5	8.5
consumer/visitor: low turnover		
employee, 4 hours	9.0	8.0
employee, all day	8.5	
	8.0	7.5

Often parking designers do not take note of the fact that stall width and module width are related. That is, when a narrower stall width is used, a wider module width must be used to achieve a given convenience in the parking and unparking maneuvers. For example, as illustrated in Figure 7-5 using dimensions suitable for customer parking, the use

TABLE 7-4

Desirable Dimensions for 90-Degree Parking of Standard and Mid-Size Automobiles

Application	S Stall Width (feet)	W Module (Bay) Width (feet)
Customer, high turnover	10.0 9.5	60 61
Customer, low turnover	10.0 9.5 9.0 8.5	59 60 62 63
Employee	9.5 9.0 8.5 8.0	58 60 61.5 63

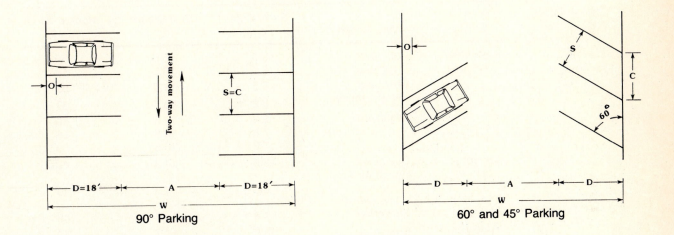

90° Parking

60° and 45° Parking

TABLE 7-5

Desirable Dimensions for 60-Degree Parking of Standard and Mid-Size Automobiles

Application	S Stall Width	C Stall Length	D Stall Depth	O Front Overhang	A Aisle Width	W Module Width
	------------------- Dimensions in feet -------------------					
Customer, high turnover	10.0 9.5	11.5 11.0	15.6	2.6	22.8 23.8	54 55
Customer, low turnover	10.0 9.5 9.0	11.5 11.0 10.4			20.8 21.8 22.8	52 53 54
Employee	9.5 9.0 8.5 8.0	11.0 10.4 9.8 9.2	15.6	2.6	20.8 21.8 22.8 23.8	52 53 54 55

Note: Dimensions are given to the nearest 0.1 ft.

TABLE 7-6

Desirable Dimensions for 45-Degree Parking of Standard and Mid-Size Automobiles

Application	S Stall Width	C Stall Length	D Stall Depth	O Front Overhang	A Aisle Width	W Module Width
	-------------	----------- Dimensions in feet -----------				
Customer, high turnover	10.0	14.1	12.7	2.1	22.6	48
	9.5	13.4			22.6	48
Customer, low turnover	10.0	14.1			21.6	47
	9.5	13.4			22.6	48
	9.0	12.7			23.6	49
Employee	9.5	13.4			21.6	47
	9.0	12.7			22.6	48
	8.5	9.8			23.6	49
	8.0	11.3	12.7	2.1	24.6	50

Note: Dimensions are given to the nearest 0.1 ft.

TABLE 7-7

Desirable Parking Dimensions for Compact Cars

Parking	Application	Stall Width (feet)	Stall Depth (feet)	Module Width (feet)
90-degree, two-way	Customer, high turnover	9.2	16.5	56
		8.5	16.5	58
	Customer, low turnover	8.5	16.5	52
		8.2	16.5	57
	Employee	8.2	16.5	50
		7.8	16.5	56
		7.2	16.5	55
60-degree, one-way	Customer, high turnover	8.5	14.3	49
	Customer, low turnover	8.2	14.3	49
	Employee	7.8	14.3	48
45-degree, one-way	Customer, high turnover	8.5	11.7	42
	Customer, low turnover	8.2	11.7	43
	Employee	7.8	11.7	43

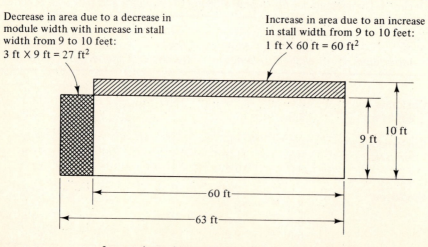

Decrease in area due to a decrease in module width with increase in stall width from 9 to 10 feet:
3 ft × 9 ft = 27 ft²

Increase in area due to an increase in stall width from 9 to 10 feet:
1 ft × 60 ft = 60 ft²

10 ft

9 ft

60 ft

63 ft

Increased area due to module width less decreased area due to stall width: 60 ft² − 27 ft² = 33 ft² or 16.5 ft² per stall

Figure 7-5 Relationship between increase in stall width and module width.

of a 10-foot stall results in an increase of 16.5 square feet per parking space (including aisle) compared to a 9-foot stall. Therefore, where convenience in getting in and out of the car is important, as with short-duration customer parking, consideration should be given to an increase in the stall width rather than an increase in module width in order to facilitate the parking and unparking maneuvers.

Use of the interlocking or herringbone design (Figure 7-6) is discouraged, especially for customer parking. This pattern involves a front-to-side parking arrangement which introduces the potential for front-to-side accidents, which are very likely to involve considerable damage.

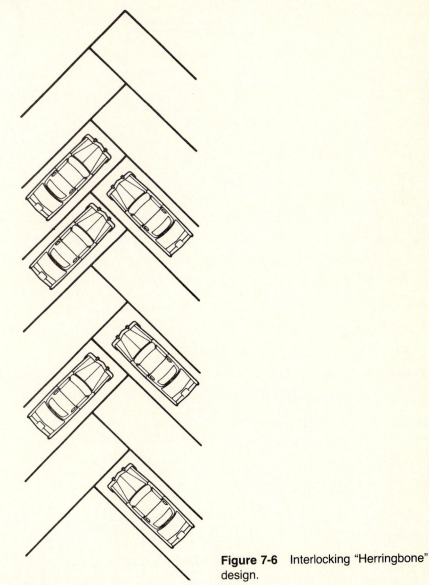

Figure 7-6   Interlocking "Herringbone" design.

Handicapped Spaces.   Parking for the handicapped should be located close to the building entrances. Care should be taken to ensure that there is a barrier-free path between parking spaces and the entrance—wheelchair ramps need to be provided at all curbs.

Municipal ordinance should restrict the use of handicapped spaces to those individuals having the required permit and should specify a fine for improper use by others. The handicapped area should be identified with signing as shown in Figure 7-7 (p. 196). Preferably, a sign should be erected in front of each handicapped space. Dimensions for handicapped parking stalls are shown in Figure 7-8 (p. 196).

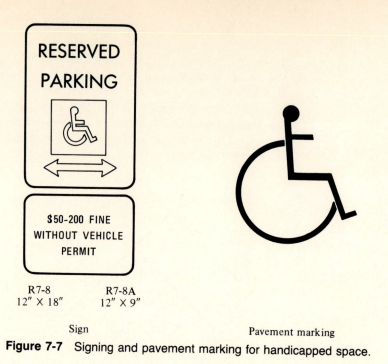

R7-8
12″ × 18″

R7-8A
12″ × 9″

Sign   Pavement marking

Figure 7-7 Signing and pavement marking for handicapped space.

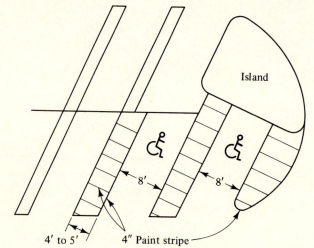

Island

8′   8′

4′ to 5′   4″ Paint stripe

(a) 60-Degree parking

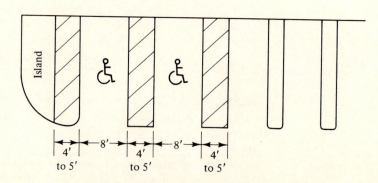

Island

8′   8′

4′
to 5′   4′
to 5′   4′
to 5′

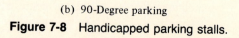

(b) 90-Degree parking

Figure 7-8 Handicapped parking stalls.

Mixing Standard and Small Cars

The increased number of small or compact cars has led to the design of some parking lots and garages with areas specifically designed for such vehicles. However, the proportion of small cars varies between different parts of the country, and the local market should be evaluated to determine the appropriate mix of small and standard spaces to be used for a special exception (or variance) from a given zoning ordinance.

In order to take advantage of the smaller space required by the compact car, the following design options may be used:

1. Design to allow conversion at a later date.
2. Use of two different designs (stall width and module size).
3. Use of one stall size with reduced width.

Design to Allow Conversion. The conversion alternative allows for the greatest flexibility. It is particularly applicable where there is a low percentage of compact cars at present. Design of the parking module for standard cars at 60- to 65-degree parking angle (one-way aisle) allows for conversion to a 75- to 90-degree angle (two-way aisle) with compact cars.

This option recognizes that while the width of the two-door compact with the door open is somewhat less than that of the standard auto, the vehicle length and turning radius are substantially less. Conversion is a relatively simple matter of restriping the stalls.

Different-Size Stalls. The use of two different designs can be achieved by two methods: (1) use of a narrower stall for small cars with the same module (wall-to-wall) width or (2) use of module designs with different stall widths and wall-to-wall dimensions for small and compact autos.

The first has been used where the module was designed for 90-degree parking of standard automobiles. This commonly results in excessive aisle widths and inadequate stall widths. Redesign of the parking lot using stall and module widths which are appropriate for small cars requires extensive reconstruction, since all existing curbed islands and landscaping within the lot must be removed.

The second method does not lend itself to modification as the mix of small and large vehicles changes. The zoning ordinance of many cities limits the maximum percentage of small-car stalls. As conditions change, these ordinances will eventually be changed. Furthermore, it is difficult to force the use of the spaces except in long-term employee parking lots. Small cars will be parked in the standard spaces if the location is more convenient to the customer. Similarly, drivers of standard cars will park in the compact stalls if the space is more convenient to the driver's ultimate destination or when the lot approaches capacity.

Single Stall Size. The use of a single design for both standard and small cars avoids the control problem. Drivers of standard vehicles will find it inconvenient to make the parking/unparking maneuver, and the door-opening space will be rather tight when standard autos are parked in adjacent stalls.

Parking Stall and Lot Delineation

Parking stalls should be marked with a hairpin striping pattern when the standard stall width is 8.5 feet or more — 7.0 feet for compact cars (see Figure 7-9, p. 198). This greatly reduces the tendency to park vehicles at an angle and/or to encroach upon an adjacent parking stall. Therefore, a much more uniform spacing is achieved between parked cars, doors can be opened without bumping the adjacent vehicle, and it is easier to exit and enter the vehicle. A 4-inch-wide line should be used for hairpin as well as single-line striping to mark parking stalls.

When cars are parked at 90 degrees to a sidewalk as shown in Figure 7-10, a 2.5-foot minimum-width overhang area should be provided. Where sidewalks are present, this will

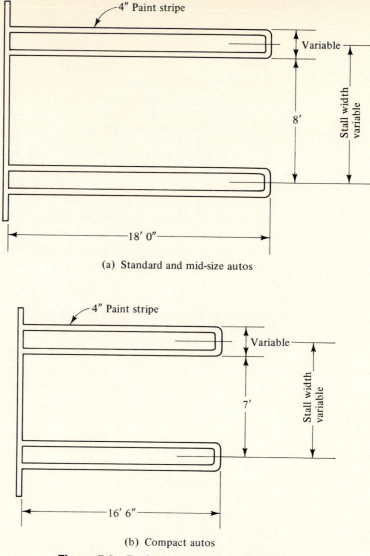

(a) Standard and mid-size autos

(b) Compact autos

Figure 7-9 Preferred striping of parking stall.

ensure that the full sidewalk width is available for pedestrian movement. A similar treatment should be provided where the parking is immediately adjacent to a building. It should be noted that the full depth of the parking stall is provided but that the curb line is 2.5 feet back from the front edge of the parking area. The same provision must be provided with interior planting strips (see Figure 7-11) and parking spaces at the outside margin of a parking lot (Figure 7-12, p. 200). When angle parking is used, the minimum overhang provided should be 2.2 feet for 60-degree and 1.8 feet for 45-degree parking.

In large parking lots, a planter strip should be provided every three or four parking bays in order to prevent high-speed movement diagonally across the parking lot (see Figure 7-13, p. 201). End islands should be used to delineate the on-site circulation roadway at the edge of the parking lots and protect the autos parked at the end of each row from turning vehicles. They also provide a location for landscaping, which enhances the esthetic value of the development by providing visual relief from the large expanse of paved area.

Curbs which serve as wheel stops should not exceed four inches in height in order to avoid damage to the increasing number of small cars equipped with air dams.

When end-stall parking is permitted, as illustrated in Figure 7-14 (p. 202), sight distance is severely limited by parked cars. The use of painted end islands is not an

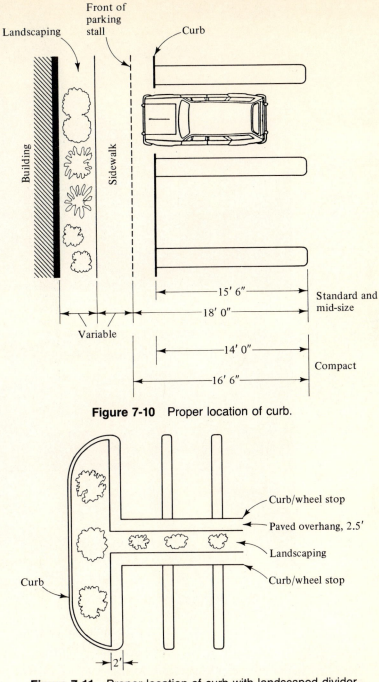

Figure 7-10 Proper location of curb.

Figure 7-11 Proper location of curb with landscaped divider.

effective means of ensuring that the necessary sight distance will be available to drivers, since drivers often park in painted end-island areas. The problem is especially severe near store or shopping-mall entrances. In many cases, vehicles parked in these painted areas encroach upon the aisle and/or the circulation (collector) roadway—especially when the parking angle is less than 90 degrees. Use of raised, landscaped islands (Figure 7-15 (p. 202)) avoids the problem and contributes to the aesthetics of the development.

Nunez and Parsonson [7] reported an average speed of about 20–23 mph on circulation (minor-collector) roadways at the approach to intersections with the parking aisles. The average of the 85th percentile speeds, which is appropriate for design, was reported to be 25 mph. The minimum sight distance required by the approaching vehicle to stop

Figure 7-12 Paving the area under the front overhang facilitates maintenance of landscaped areas.

if a vehicle pulls out from an aisle is about 150 feet using AASHTO criteria and slightly over 100 feet for a 20-mph speed.

The sight distance required for a vehicle to turn right from an aisle into the path of a vehicle approaching from the left is over 100 feet; it assumes that the approaching vehicle is traveling at 25 mph and the driver has a 2-second perception–reaction time and decelerates at 6 to 8 feet per second squared while the turning vehicle accelerates at 3 to 4 feet per second squared. For an approach speed of 20 mph, the sight distance required is at least 75 feet.

Typical end-island designs are illustrated in Figures 7-16 and 7-17 (p. 203) for 90 and 60 degrees, respectively. When the island is landscaped to the back of the curb, the ground cover adjacent to the curb is commonly trampled (see Figure 7-18, p. 204). Paving a strip two to three feet wide adjacent to the back of the curb will avoid this problem.

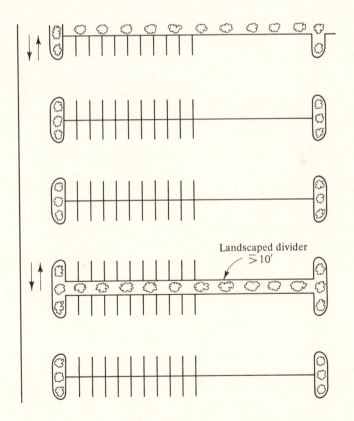

Figure 7-13 Use of interior planted strip to prevent high-speed diagonal movement.

Curbs. The standard 6-inch vertical curb has been commonly used for all applications — including end islands and landscaped barriers within parking lots and the curbs at the margin of parking lots. A 4-inch curb is ample as a wheel-stop and for end islands.

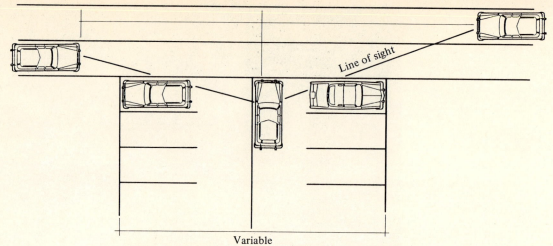

Figure 7-14 Minimum sight distance obstructed when end-stall parking is permitted.

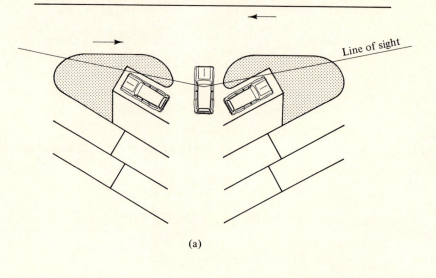

(a)

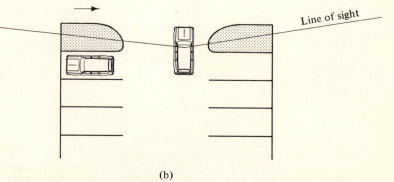

(b)

Figure 7-15 Curbed end islands preclude parking within the sight triangle.

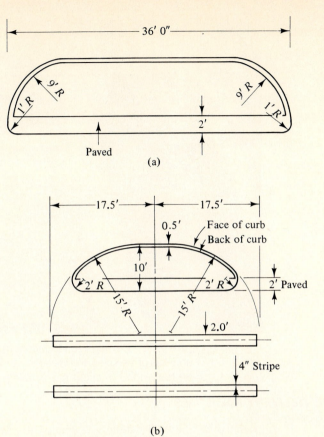

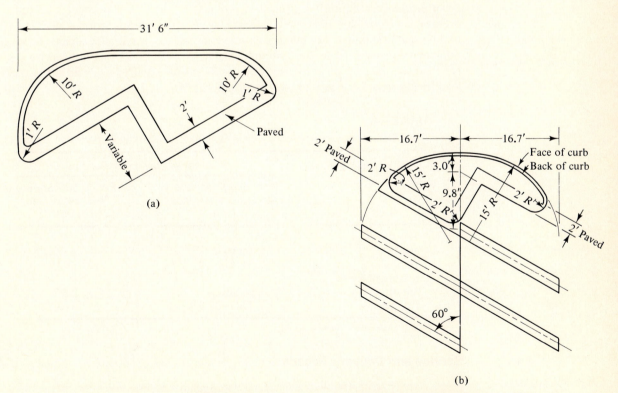

Figure 7-16 Typical end-island designs for ninety-degree parking.

Figure 7-17 Typical end-island design for sixty-degree parking.

Figure 7-18 Damage to landscaping in end islands. Persons getting in and out of vehicles trample the landscaping. Paving a strip two to three feet wide will avoid this problem.

SERVICE AND DELIVERY FACILITIES

Relatively little information is available concerning the service and delivery requirements of commercial office and retail development.

Christiansen [3] reported that the number of deliveries to office buildings and department stores during the peak delivery hour of the day was about 1.25 times the average hour and that nearly all deliveries were made during normal working hours (9:00 a.m.–5:00 p.m.). The number of deliveries per day per 10,000 square feet of gross floor area is given in Table 7-8. Assuming that the arrivals of delivery and service vehicles are random, queuing analysis (see Chapter 8) can be used to evaluate the number of loading positions necessary to meet selected criteria.

TABLE 7-8

Truck Deliveries Generated by Office Buildings and Retail Department Stores

	Number of Deliveries Per Day	
	Per 10,000 Square Meters Gross Floor Area	Per 10,000 Square Feet Gross Floor Area
Office Buildings:		
Mean	22.7	2.11
Range	16.1–25.8	1.5–2.4
Department Store:		
Mean	25.5	2.5
Range	15.1–39.8	1.4–3.7

SOURCE: Dennis L. Christiansen [4].

Service and Delivery Access

Large activity centers should be designed with separate access drives for trucks. The truck circulation system should be designed to discourage use by automobile traffic, so that the internal truck circulation patterns will not interfere with automobile and pedestrian movements or with parking in proximity to the building.

Truck docks should be located away from the areas of pedestrian movement and screened from view from parking areas, adjacent properties, or adjacent streets. Rear access is commonly used for deliveries and service; it is most suitable where parking and customer access is from one, two, or three sides (Figure 7-19). Since the service area is out of view of the customers, little if any attention is given to aesthetics. In many cases, litter and poor maintenance are common problems. Most municipal ordinances require that a fence be erected to screen the view of the rear of commercial buildings from view of adjacent properties.

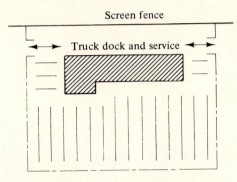

(a) Rear dock — three-sided center

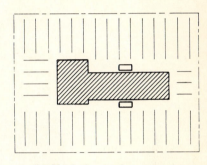

(b) No dock — curb access only

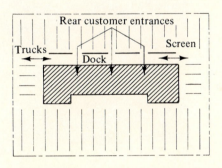

(c) Screened dock with controlled pedestrian access

Figure 7-19 Truck delivery and service.

Over-the-sidewalk delivery and service should be used only as an auxiliary method.

Court access (Figure 7-20 (p. 206)) is a popular treatment where all of the building sides are exposed. Common applications include: regional shopping centers where the building is surrounded by parking; office buildings, hotels, hospitals, and other development where the service area/truck dock is visible from a street or pedestrian mall; planned unit development; and "high-tech" industrial facilities.

Truck delivery tunnels are used in some large, high-density development. Their very high cost is a major limitation.

Design of Service-Vehicle Facilities. Rear loading/unloading is much more efficient and convenient than side loading. The truck circulation pattern and loading position should be designed for a left-side back-in maneuver (see Figure 7-21, p. 207). This allows the driver to sight along the left side of the vehicle when backing. The apron space (see Figure 7-22) should be adequate to allow the truck to back in and pull out in one continuous maneuver. When semi-tractor-trailer combinations may be expected, the WB-50 vehicle (50-foot wheelbase—eighteen wheeler) should be used for design. Di-

(a)

(b)

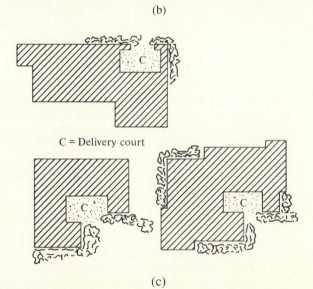

C = Delivery court

(c)

Figure 7-20 (a) and (b) Examples of delivery courts. (c) Typical court arrangements.

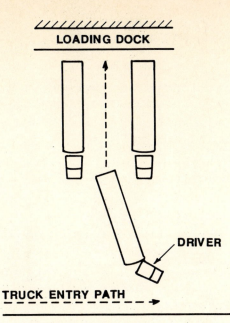

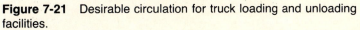

Figure 7-21 Desirable circulation for truck loading and unloading facilities.

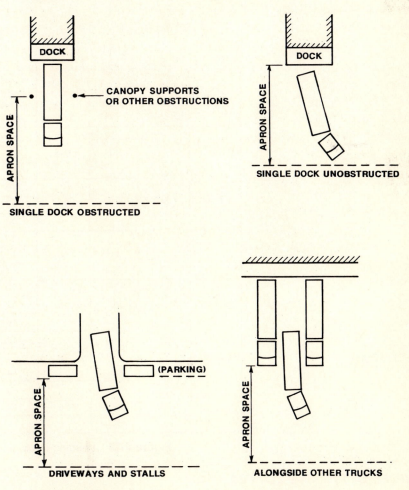

Figure 7-22 Loading-dock configurations.

mensions for 90, 60, and 45-degree facilities are given in Figure 7-23 for both a WB-50 and a WB-40.

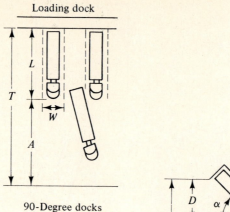

90-Degree docks

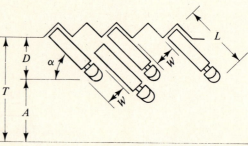

Sawtooth docks

Design vehicle	Length in feet (L)	Dock angle (α)	Clearance in feet (D)	Berth width in feet (W)	Apron space in feet (A)	Total offset in feet (T)
WB-40	50	90°	50	10	63	113
				12	56	106
				14	52	102
		60°	44	10	46	90
				12	40	84
				14	35	79
		45°	36	10	37	73
				12	32	68
				14	29	65
WB-50	55	90°	55	10	77	132
				12	72	127
				14	67	122
		60°	48	10	55	103
				12	51	99
				14	46	94
		45°	39	10	45	84
				12	40	79
				14	37	76

Figure 7-23 Loading-dock dimensions.

EXAMPLES OF PARKING-LOT FEATURES

Figures 7-24 through 7-31 illustrate various features of parking-lot design. See pp. 210–212.

REFERENCES

1. Alan M. Voorhees and Associates, Inc., "Parking Requirements for Shopping Centers," *Technical Bulletin 53,* The Urban Land Institute, 1965.

2. Barton-Aschman Associates, Inc., "Parking Requirements at the Regionals," *Urban Land,* May 1979.

3. Christiansen, Dennis L., "Off-Street Loading Facilities in Downtown Areas, Requirements and Design," *TRB Record 688,* Transportation Research Board, 1978.

4. Highway Research Board, "Parking Principles," *Special Report No. 125,* 1971.

5. Institute of Transportation Engineers, *Parking Generation,* 1985.

6. Keneipp, Jean M., "Design for Small Cars in New Buildings and Old Ones," *Parking,* July 1980.

7. Nunez, Andres Jr., and Parsonson, Peter S., "Safe Design of Parking Lots for Regional Shopping Centers," paper presented at the 1980 annual meeting of the Institute of Transportation Engineers.

8. Parking Standards Design Associates, *A Parking Standards Report,* Volume 1, March 10, 1971.

9. Strickland, Richard I., "Parking Design for Downsized Cars," *ITE Journal,* November 1960.

10. The Traffic Institute, Northwestern University, course notes.

11. ULI—The Urban Land Institute, *Shared Parking,* a study by Barton-Aschman Associates, 1983.

12. Urban Transport Branch "Parking Standards" *Report U10/10/15,* Department of Transport, Republic of South Africa, March 1980.

13. Whitlock, Edward M., *Parking for Institutions and Special Events,* Eno Foundation for Transportation, 1982.

14. Wilbur Smith and Associates, Inc., *Parking Requirements for Shopping Centers,* The Urban Land Institute, 1981.

Figure 7-24 Painted end islands are ineffective. Painted end islands are frequently used as parking spaces. This results in inadequate sight distance.

Figure 7-25 Poor landscaping. The vegetation shown in this photograph must be periodically trimmed. Moreover, it has been allowed to grow to an excessive height so that it seriously restricts the sight distance of drivers exiting the circulation isle. Vegetation should be no more than 24 inches, preferably no more than 18 inches, high.

Figure 7-26 Effective end islands. Raised end islands provide delineation of the on-site circulation roadway, protect the cars parked in the end stalls, ensure an adequate sight triangle, and add to the appearance of the site. Landscaping materials should be carefully selected in order to ensure that the vegetation will not interfere with the sight triangle and to minimize maintenance. The planting material used is appropriate; it has a small trunk, no low branches, needs only infrequent maintenance, and is native to the area.

Figure 7-27 Large paved areas promote hazardous circulation. Large, open paved areas are conducive to high-speed, random maneuvers, such as those being made by the drivers of the two autos in the center of the photograph. Concrete pillars are effective in preventing light posts from being damaged. However, inspection will reveal that they are often hit by vehicles. Incorporation of the lighting into appropriately designed landscaping will improve the circulation and site appearance as well as protect the lighting.

Figure 7-28 Esthetics may lack function. This landscaping design contributes to esthetics; however, it has no circulation function. Speed bumps have been added in the circulation aisles in an attempt to control speed. Drivers simply avoid the speed bumps by driving through the parking spaces.

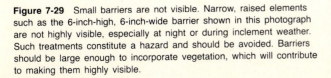

Figure 7-29 Small barriers are not visible. Narrow, raised elements such as the 6-inch-high, 6-inch-wide barrier shown in this photograph are not highly visible, especially at night or during inclement weather. Such treatments constitute a hazard and should be avoided. Barriers should be large enough to incorporate vegetation, which will contribute to making them highly visible.

Figure 7-30 Underground truck delivery. Underground truck delivery minimizes truck–auto conflict and facilitates deliveries of this regional shopping center in the northeast United States.

Figure 7-31 Example of deceleration turn bay to private development adjacent to a major arterial. As illustrated in this photograph, access drives to development along this arterial have right-turn deceleration bays. This design limits the speed differential between ingress vehicles and through traffic to about 10 miles per hour.

8

Drive-In Facilities

DRIVE-IN SERVICES

Drive-in services continue to become increasingly popular. Included in this category are drive-in banks, savings and loan institutions, fast-food restaurants, car washes, and liquor stores. The site design incorporates a drive-thru facility either as part of the initial design or as an addition to an existing establishment. As a result, many new and unique site-design problems have evolved. In other cases circulation problems have developed on or in the vicinity of drive-thru facilities as a result of increased business activity.

As with other types of development, the traffic engineer/planner should be involved in the project from its inception. However, the addition of the drive-thru operation adds a dimension to the analysis and design. Parking and circulation considerations which are unique to drive-thru facilities include:

- Separation of the drive-thru traffic from the other site traffic and parking
- Clear identification and delineation between the drive-thru and parking-lot circulation
- Provisions for adequate queue storage that prevents queue interference with pedestrian or other vehicular movement
- Provision of an "escape" route — especially where waiting times may be long or experiencing considerable variation
- Simple and easy maneuver into and through the drive-thru service positions
- Flexibility in operations to meet a range of demand conditions
- Opportunity to expand in order to adapt to changing conditions

213

Storage requirements, waiting time, and the effect of the number of service positions and service time on the drive-thru operations can be evaluated utilizing queueing analysis discussed at the end of this chapter.

FINANCIAL INSTITUTIONS

Drive-in banking at full-service as well as at savings and loan establishments has become increasingly popular. Consequently, the design of drive-thru facilities, either as an integral part of the site or as a satellite facility, has become a significant concern.

Drive-In Window Arrangements

There are three basic configurations for drive-in windows, as illustrated in Figure 8-1.

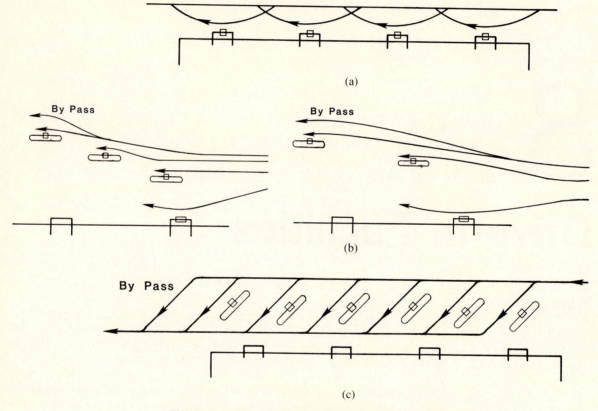

Figure 8-1   Drive-in bank service and teller configurations (a) one teller/one position, (b) one teller/two positions, (c) two tellers/three positions.

Configuration A.   This configuration is the least desirable of the three, as it makes inefficient use of building storage and tellers. An excessive building frontage is required so that vehicles can pull into and out of the individual service positions. Even with 60 or 70 feet between teller positions, it is not convenient for a driver to properly enter into a service position. The excessive separation results in a ratio of one teller to one window, and the teller's time is not productively used when waiting for the next vehicle to stop at the window.

Configuration B.   Configuration B is commonly operated with one teller for two service positions. This results in longer service times for customers. However, as the facility becomes larger, the distance from the teller to the customers becomes very long, and personal eye contact between the teller and a customer is lost. This "depersonalizes" the service and increases transit time for the carrier. It also requires more area per teller window than Configuration C and does not lend itself to one-lane or two-lane approach and departure design.

Configuration C. This arrangement is designed to operate with two tellers serving three customer positions. This makes for efficient use of teller personnel as well as short service time for customers.

Orientation of the service islands at an angle to the building facilitates the exit maneuver (when properly designed) and places the customer being served within eye-contact distance of the teller. A variation of this design is to orient the service islands perpendicular to the building. As a result a 90-degree left turn is required when exiting. Proper design will allow this maneuver to be easily made; however, the service island will be farther from the teller than with the angled orientation. The distance between tellers is less with the 90-degree design, and less building frontage is required. The choice between a 90-degree and, say, 60-degree design may be dictated by the dimensions of the tract.

Demand Forecasts for Banks and Savings and Loan Institutions

Traffic planning for a financial institution may involve a facility on a new site or expansion of an existing facility. Although the procedures are somewhat different in each of these situations, the following considerations are involved:

- Estimation of the drive-in and lobby traffic generation
- Analysis of the number of drive-in windows needed to meet design conditions
- Analysis of the number of parking spaces required for customers and for employees
- Evaluation of the existing and future traffic conditions and the impact which the development will have on the streets in the vicinity of the site
- Development of a functional system of access, circulation, parking, pedestrian flow, and drive-in storage

Analysis of New Facilities

When a new bank or savings and loan is planned, the floor area of the proposed building is used as the basis for the forecast of employee and lobby customer parking and drive-in requirements. (The floor area of the proposed facilities, internally, should be based on a market survey.)

Traffic Generation. The most desirable procedure is to use trip-generation rates developed from traffic counts of existing facilities which are as similar as possible to the proposed facility.

Forecasts are usually prepared for the design hour, which may be the highest one-hour period (or an hourly flow rate based on a 10- to 30-minute count) on the day selected for design. In the case of banks, this generally will be the afternoon of those Fridays which are paydays.

In absence of local area information, the rates contained in the ITE manual, *Trip Generation Rates* [3] may be used. A quick review of the reported data reveals considerable variation. Scifres [8] reported that the lobby traffic-generation rate decreases with floor area (see Table 8-1). This probably contributes to the range in trip-generation rates.

Some of the trips generated by banks are traffic which is already on the adjacent street (e.g., passer-by traffic). Lalani [5] reported that 14% of the total trips (lobby and drive-thru) generated by banks having drive-thru windows during the afternoon peak of the street (4:30 to 5:30 p.m.) is "passer-by" traffic which is already on the street. Hence, the p.m. peak trip generation should be discounted for traffic impact analysis. Thus, the p.m. peak traffic generation would be multiplied by 0.86 (say 0.85 rounded) to obtain an estimate of the traffic added to the street by the proposed bank.

TABLE 8-1

Design-Hour Lobby Traffic Generation for Banks with Drive-In Windows

Gross Floor Area Used by Bank	Hourly One-Way Traffic Generation (per 1,000 sq. ft.)
5,000 to 20,000 sq. ft.	15 to 20 vehicles
20,000 to 40,000 sq. ft.	10 to 15 vehicles
Over 40,000 sq. ft.	5 to 10 vehicles

SOURCE: Peter N. Scifres [8].

Parking. It is desirable to have as much traffic as possible use the drive-in windows. Petersen [7] reported a 50–50 split between lobby and drive-thru customers when the drive-thru facilities are not unduly congested. Customer parking duration averages about 15 to 20 minutes. During the peak period, parking demand should not exceed 90% of the parking capacity if customers are to be able to find a parking space without excessive delay. Scifres [8] reported customer parking requirements as given in Table 8-2.

TABLE 8-2

Design-Hour Lobby Customer Parking Requirements for Banks with Drive-In Windows

Gross Floor Area Used by Bank	Customer Parking Requirements (per 1,000 sq. ft.)
5,000 to 20,000 sq. ft.	2.0 to 2.5 Spaces
20,000 to 40,000 sq. ft.	1.5 to 2.0 Spaces
Over 40,000 sq. ft.	1.0 to 1.5 Spaces

SOURCE: Peter N. Scifres [8].

Drive-In Window Requirements. The number of service positions required is a function of the average service time and the demand. The technique contained in the section "Analysis of Service Times," presented later in this chapter, can be used to calculate the average time in the system and the average time in the queue for different operating conditions (number of service positions, number of tellers, average service time, and demand) in order to help evaluate proposed designs.

Bank officials commonly underestimate service and waiting time; therefore the average service time should be obtained through observation of similar facilities in the local area, since wait time and, theoretically, storage requirements are fairly sensitive to the parameter.

Table 8-3 gives guidelines for the number of drive-in windows as a function of lobby size. These guidelines assume an average service time of approximately 2 minutes and that 50% of the bank customers will use the drive-in windows. These typical values might be used where a more detailed (and expensive) analysis is not warranted.

TABLE 8-3

Lobby Size Versus Drive-In Window Requirements

Lobby Sizes (sq. ft.)	Number of Drive-In Windows
5,000 to 10,000	2 to 3
10,000 to 20,000	3 to 4
20,000 to 30,000	4 to 5
30,000 to 40,000	6 to 8
40,000 to 50,000	8 to 10

SOURCE: Peter N. Scifres [8].

As demand approaches capacity, some drive-in customers will be required to wait in a storage area immediately in advance of the service positions. When demand exceeds the capacity of the drive-in windows, the queue of waiting vehicles theoretically will become infinite. However, customers will not use the facility if the wait is too long and will exercise the option of using the lobby, making the transaction at another time of the day, or moving their account to a less congested institution. Therefore, it is not necessary to provide the storage calculated by queueing analysis when the wait time also is long. As service rate increases, longer queue lengths (more required storage) will involve acceptable wait time. Generally, storage for more than 30 vehicles is not necessary. Tables 8-4 thru 8-6 provide guidelines for drive-in window requirements and storage.

TABLE 8-4

Drive-In Window Configuration Capacities

	Vehicle/Window/ Hour	Vehicles/Teller Hour
One teller/window (A)	30 to 35	30 to 35
One teller/two windows (B)	25 to 30	50 to 60
Two tellers/three windows (C)	35 to 40	52 to 60

SOURCE: The Traffic Institute, Northwestern University [10].

TABLE 8-5

Drive-In Window Storage Requirements

Number of Windows	Acceptable Waiting Time			Recommended Storage
	10 Minutes	12.5 Minutes	15 Minutes	
2	12	15	18	12–18
3	18	22	26	18–26
4	23	29	35*	23–30
5	29	36*	44*	25–30
6	35*	—	—	25–30
7	—	—	—	25–30
8	—	—	—	25–30

SOURCE: The Traffic Institute, Northwestern University [10].

*It is generally not necessary to provide more than 30-vehicle storage.

TABLE 8-6

Storage Requirements Based on Queueing Theory

Number of Drive-In Windows	Desirable Design Storage (vehicle/window)	Total Storage (vehicles)
2	10	20
3	7	21
4	5	20
5	4	20
7	3	21
9	2	18

SOURCE: The Traffic Institute, Northwestern University [10].

Analysis of an Existing Facility

In planning the expansion of a bank, the following data should be obtained for the existing facility on the peak day:

- Traffic counts by 15-minute periods of customers using the lobby

- Interviews of lobby customers to ascertain:
  - Parking location (bank lot, curb, other—explain).
  - Mode of travel (drive, passenger, walk, has a bicycle).
  - Reason for not using the existing drive-in or walk-up facilities (too congested, transaction cannot be completed, other).
  - Would customer use the drive-in windows if service and wait time were less (fewer cars waiting for service, other—explain).

- Parking duration, turnover, and accumulation of customer lot. Similar data on curb parking if present. Collect data by license-plate survey every 5 or 10 minutes.

- Directional traffic counts on the adjacent streets and bank access drives using mechanical counters recording by 15-minute (or more frequent) intervals to determine the time and volume of peak street traffic and the peak of the bank.

- Manual counts to obtain turning movements at all intersections of bank access drives and direction of approach and direction of departure.

- Number of teller transactions by one-hour intervals for lobby and drive-in/walk-up windows. The peak day may be identified by comparing total transactions over several days.

- Employee parking demand.

Unless a major restructuring of the hours of operations and/or service is planned, the design peak hour is assumed to be similar to the peak hour on the day of data collection. The lobby interviews provide a basis for estimating the number of transactions which might be transferred to an upgraded drive-in facility or walk-up windows or automatic tellers. The total existing demand on these facilities will be the existing demand plus the latent demand of the present lobby customers.

The ratio of projected number of transactions (not deposits) to the present number of transactions is then used to factor up the customer parking, lobby, drive-in, walk-up, and automatic teller demands as illustrated:

$$\text{Future peak-hour drive-in demand} = \frac{\text{Future transactions}}{\text{Present transactions}} \times \text{Present drive-in use plus existing latent lobby demand for drive-in}$$

$$\text{Future peak-hour customers parking demand} = \frac{\text{Future transactions}}{\text{Present transactions}} \times \text{Present lobby use less existing latent lobby demand for drive-in}$$

Examples and Case Studies

Modification of an Existing Bank. An example that embodies the concepts presented regarding the design/redesign of a bank drive-in facility is given in Figure 8-2.

- Employee parking is segregated from the customer parking lot.
- The area designated as future parking is to be landscaped until the parking demand calls for additional space.
- Storage for the drive-in facility is removed from the public roadways, thus ensuring that vehicles will not back up onto the public roadways. More than adequate storage is provided for the four drive-in windows.
- The drive-in facility also serves walk-up customers. The drive-in was an expansion of the present banking operation. In the past the main building was open from 9:00 a.m. to 3:00 p.m. Monday through Friday, and 9:00 a.m. to 1:00 p.m. on Saturday. The bank officials wanted to increase their hours of operation by the use of the walk-up/drive-in facility from 7:00 a.m. to 6:00 p.m. Monday through

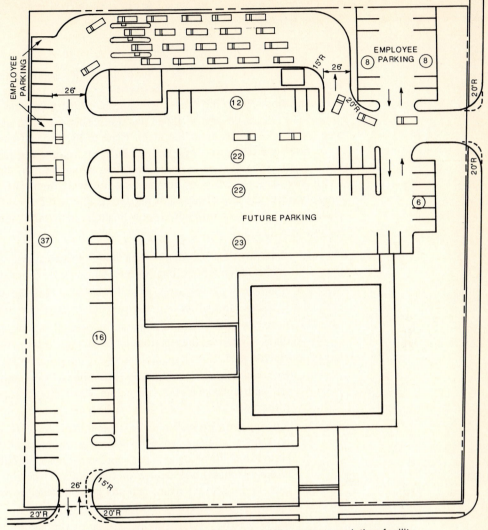

Figure 8-2 Addition of drive-in/walk-up to an existing facility.
SOURCE: The Traffic Institute, Northwestern University [9].

Saturday. Note the good pedestrian access from the parking areas to both the walk-up and the main building.

- Parking circulation and access to the site can easily be comprehended by the driver.
- Changes in curb radii and width at the access drives were recommended to better accommodate the traffic volumes.

FAST-FOOD RESTAURANTS

A fast-food restaurant is any restaurant with more than 25 seats serving the majority of its food in disposable containers, for consumption on and off the premises. A growing number of fast-food restaurants are being constructed, most of which provide drive-up services for customers who arrive by automobile. Drive-thru facilities are planned for new sites or are modifications that are being made to existing fast-food restaurants.

Efficient site access and internal circulation plus sufficient parking and drive-thru stacking space are essential to minimizing the traffic impact to the adjacent roadway. When a new restaurant is planned, these features can be readily provided. When a drive-thru facility is to be added to an existing restaurant, the options or alternative solutions are greatly reduced.

Factors Affecting Site Access

Factors which will affect access to the proposed development are the location of the site, the roadnet available to serve traffic moving to and from the site, and the ability to obtain adequate access from the roadways adjacent to the site. Adequate access requires the provision of entrance–exit facilities that are properly located and designed to accommodate traffic movements from the major route to the site and vice versa.

Fast-food restaurants rely on high business volume and fast turnover of customers. With a high percentage of customers arriving by automobile, they should be adjacent to a roadway that provides good area access, relatively high traffic volumes, and adequate capacity. Data about roadway elements can be obtained from field observations and from discussions with local officials responsible for area traffic operation. These elements include:

1. *Roadway classification* — functional classification, normally included as part of the Thoroughfare Plan in the community's Comprehensive Plan.
2. *Roadway cross section(s)* — right-of-way width, the number and width of traffic lanes, special turning and parking lanes, and roadway drainage.
3. *Access control* — restrictions on driveway locations, barrier or mountable medians, signalized intersections in the vicinity of the site, and other traffic-control conditions.
4. *Existing driveway and parking conditions* — location of driveway opposite the site and adjacent to the site within 300 feet, on-street parking locations and restrictions.
5. *Existing traffic conditions* — current average daily traffic volumes (ADT), peak-hour volumes typically occurring during peak business periods (lunch periods and the roadways' peak traffic periods), posted speed limits, peak-hour turning volumes and degree of congestion at nearby intersections, available gaps in the traffic stream, and any sight-distance restrictions.
6. *Future traffic conditions* — planned improvements on adjacent or nearby routes, traffic signal installations or modifications, other planned land use developments.

Customer data include estimates of the percentage of drive-in or walk-in patrons. Elements to be considered are nearby land uses (schools, shopping centers, or other employment considerations), pedestrian activity, and areawide travel patterns.

Site-Traffic Generation

The volume of vehicular traffic generated by a development is determined primarily by the size and type of the land use. With respect to fast-food restaurants, other considerations include surrounding land uses, traffic on adjacent roadways, whether or not drive-thru facilities are to be provided, and what percent of the roadway traffic will be diverted to the site. The principal concern is what volume of new traffic will be generated instead of the total volume that will enter and leave the site.

Peak Traffic Periods. The lunch period, Monday through Saturday, is typically the time period during which both inbound and outbound traffic volumes are the highest. During this period, through traffic on the adjacent roadways is usually not at its highest volume; therefore, the peak site traffic period is normally not critical with respect to roadway capacity conditions. However, if the restaurant is proposed for a site in close proximity to a large shopping center, the Saturday noon hour may become a critical period.

Noon-hour traffic conditions should be studied when considering site access and internal conditions. The availability of gaps in the traffic stream, the lack of special turning lanes and traffic backups on the site that block parking or drive-thru lanes can make the noon hour critical.

The period of time that coincides with the evening peak traffic hour should also be analyzed. This period, usually occurring sometime between 4:00 and 6:00 p.m., is when the combination of adjacent street and site traffic is the highest. Site traffic is relatively low but the time period is considered critical by the public and most site-plan review agencies. Figure 8-3 indicates results of one study of the peaking characteristics of fast-food restaurant traffic.

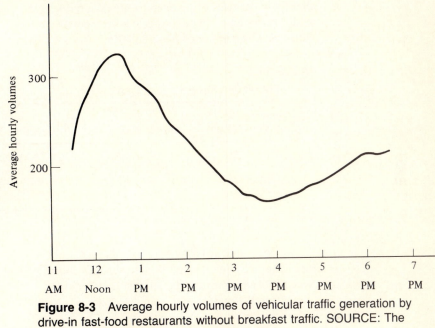

Figure 8-3 Average hourly volumes of vehicular traffic generation by drive-in fast-food restaurants without breakfast traffic. SOURCE: The Traffic Institute, Northwestern University [9].

Site-Traffic Volumes. Estimates of site-generated traffic are typically based on the size of the restaurant and are computed on the basis of the number of vehicular trips per 1,000 square feet of gross floor area. The available data based for site-generated traffic volumes is relatively small. In order to provide a point of beginning, Table 8-7 summarizes the results of several studies of existing fast-food restaurants. The average rate for inbound and outbound trips is indicated plus the recorded range in the site-generated trips.

Although Table 8-7 can be used to obtain an estimate of total site traffic, it will not provide an estimate of the total new traffic that will be added to traffic on the adjacent roadway. Total site-generated traffic is necessary to determine ingress and egress require-

TABLE 8-7

Site-Traffic Generation Rates (trips per 1,000 sq. ft.)

Time Period	Inbound	Outbound	Range in Total Trips
Monday–Friday:			
12:00–1:00 p.m.	39	38	40–150
5:00–6:00 p.m.	24	23	20–70
Saturday:			
12:00–1:00	44	41	—

Source: The Traffic Institute, Northwestern University [10].

ments. However, since restaurant patrons are made up of those who travel on the roadways specifically to visit the facility, plus those who are drawn to the site from the passing traffic, the total site traffic should be decreased to estimate new or additional volumes.

Diverted Traffic. The percent of total site traffic that is diverted from the traffic flow passing the site will vary dependent upon time of day, site location, and the type of nearby land uses. A survey conducted by the Planning Department of Newark, Delaware, [6] indicated that approximately one-third of the patrons of a fast-food restaurant came to the restaurant specifically to eat and then returned to their place of origin. The remaining two-thirds of the patrons stopped to eat at the restaurant while on a multipurpose trip.

Table 8-8 indicates the results of a study of several McDonald's [1] which shows slightly lower rates of diverted traffic than the Virginia study. These rates can be considered conservative, since the results of another extensive market survey by McDonald's indicated diversion rates of up to 67%.

TABLE 8-8

Generated Versus Diverted Site Traffic

Time Period (p.m. Weekdays)	Generated Traffic	Diverted Traffic	Total Site Traffic
12:00–1:00	48 to 65% 56% average	35 to 52% 44% average	100%
4:00–6:00	45 to 64% 53% average	36 to 55% 47% average	100%

Source: The Traffic Institute, Northwestern University [10].

Site-Traffic Distribution. Each restaurant has its own geographic area of influence. The size and shape of the area depends upon the available roadnet, type and location of nearby land uses, and population distribution.

Once the market-area boundaries are established, the directions from which traffic will approach or depart a restaurant can be determined. The directional distribution of traffic already on the street should be used to estimate diverted traffic, while the location of schools, shopping areas, and employment centers and the distribution of households will determine the direction of approach of new or additional traffic. Each land use within the market area should be evaluated with respect to (1) size and location, (2) the probability of generating customers from the land use, and (3) the efficiency of the available street system.

Effect of Drive-Thru Facilities

Typically, drive-thru facilities do not add a significantly higher volume to site-generated traffic. This is true whether a drive-thru window is part of the initial construction or is an add-on to an existing restaurant. Owing to the uniqueness of each site, and the ranges in traffic-generation rates, the values indicated in Table 8-9 can be applied to new restaurants with drive-thru windows or to an existing restaurant to which a drive-thru is to be added.

When a drive-thru window is to be added to an existing facility, some increase in site traffic can be expected. Studies of McDonald's restaurants [1] indicate that an increase in sales of 10% to 14% can be expected when a drive-thru is added, with some increases upwards of 25%. Although the difference between 10% and 25% may seem high, the total increase in inbound or outbound trips would be in the range of 20 to 30 vehicles per hour. Table 8-9 indicates the representative percentage of total entering site traffic that uses the drive-thru facility at McDonald's. Results of the McDonald's studies also indicate that approximately 30% of the total site traffic will utilize the drive-thru window and that the addition of a drive-thru window will decrease customer parking demand by approximately 20%.

TABLE 8-9

Drive-Thru Window Use

Time Period (p.m. Weekdays)	Drive-Thru Window Use (Percent of Total Entering Site Traffic)
11:00 to 12:00	38% to 43%
12:00 to 1:00	30% to 35%
1:00 to 2:00	40% to 45%
4:00 to 5:00	36% to 42%
5:00 to 6:00	40% to 45%
6:00 to 7:00	42% to 48%

Source: Barton-Aschman Associates, Inc. [1].

Unpublished data for Burger King restaurants also indicate that the addition of a drive-thru window will, in addition to increasing sales, decrease the accumulation of parked vehicles on the site by about 25% and that drive-thru customers amount to approximately 45% of the restaurant's total business.

When analyzing the effect of adding a drive-thru window to an existing site, traffic counts should be taken at the existing restaurant during peak business hours, and the volumes (inbound and outbound) should be increased by the appropriate percentage.

On-Site Circulation and Parking

When preparing a site plan for a proposed restaurant or when modifying an existing plan to allow for the addition of a drive-thru window, consideration should be given to building size and location, entrance ways, and the location of the drive-thru window to ensure that required parking and drive-thru stacking areas can be accommodated. Figures 8-4 and 8-5 illustrate drive-thru elements that were poorly designed.

Figure 8-4 Example of inadequate horizontal geometry and inadequate delineation. The restrictive horizontal curvature at this fast-food restaurant does not permit vehicles to conveniently negotiate the turn. The problem is compounded by the poor delineation of the roadway leading to the drive-thru window. The tire marks indicate that some drivers failed to negotiate the turn. The difference in elevation in the vicinity of the light pole is over 3 feet.

Figure 8-5 Poor design of drive-thru. Poor delineation and inadequate separation between the shopping-center ring road and the roadway from a fast-food restaurant (upper photo) results in vehicles driving across the curb. The problem is compounded by the short distance to the intersection with the arterial street (center photo). The lower photo shows the evidence of several hard hits.

Parking Requirements.   The peak parking demand typically occurs during the noon hour, with Saturday frequently being the critical day. Since parking demand varies considerably based on site location and the percent of walk-in and drive-thru business, studies of comparable restaurants should be made. Many existing zoning ordinances for restaurants were adopted before drive-thru services of fast-food restaurants reached their current popularity and thereby frequently require more parking spaces than will realistically be needed. The McDonald's study recommends 17.5 spaces per 1,000 square feet of building area and assumes an average 20-minute parking duration.

Driveway location and design greatly affect internal circulation. Site access, one-way or two-way circulation, parking-stall angles, and the location and length of stacking areas for drive-thru windows must all be closely coordinated.

Stacking Space.   The adequacy of on-site reservoir space to permit the stacking of vehicles waiting to be served at a drive-thru window is an important factor when designing or reviewing plans for drive-thru facilities. Sufficient reservoir space should be provided to eliminate conflicts with parking vehicles and to avoid interference with the flow of traffic on the adjacent roadway.

The length of necessary stacking space is a function of the number of anticipated drive-thru vehicles, the service time from when a customer places his order until he receives his order, and the window time necessary to complete the pick-up transaction. The stacking space should be separated into the distance in advance of the order point (menu board) and the distance between the order point and the pick-up window.

If the site is an existing facility that is to be expanded, the volume can be obtained by counting the existing inbound volume and factoring it to include a drive-thru window. If the site is to be used for a new restaurant, the number of vehicles to be stored can be obtained from design guidelines established by the various fast-food establishments. The Fairfax County study [2] indicates the average number of vehicles accommodated between the pick-up window and the order point is four; and the average number of spaces provided in advance of the order point is also four.

Burger King has a customer service standard that permits a 3-minute maximum allowable total service time per customer. This is the time from when a customer enters the drive-thru line until he gets his order. They also have a service standard that permits a maximum acceptable window transaction time of 30 seconds. This is the time from when the customer stops at the pick-up window to when he receives the order. Burger King restaurants are periodically tested and graded to insure they meet the requirements.

Review of the available data indicates that between 4 and 14 vehicles can be expected to arrive at the order boards during a 15-minute period. These data also indicate a total service time ranging between 2 and 3 minutes per customer.

As a "rule of thumb," the distance between the order board and the pick-up window should be sufficient to store four cars (not including the vehicles at the pick-up window and menu board). Storage for at least four vehicles should also be provided in advance of the menu board so that the queue does not interfere with the dining-room traffic.

Driveway Capacity.   Intersection capacity analysis should be made for driveway traffic. A methodology to determine the level of traffic service provided at unsignalized intersections is available from the Transportation Research Board, or gap studies can be conducted in the vicinity of the site access points. These studies will determine if the number of acceptable gaps are sufficient to accommodate entering and exiting site traffic.

Driveway Pavement Marking and Signing.   Noticeable and easily understandable marking and signing are the best way to communicate to driving customers and to minimize confusion. Parking stalls (standard and handicapped), aisles, and access lanes should be clearly marked. The direction of traffic flow and, in the case of drive-thru facilities, entrances to stacking areas should be designated by pavement marking and signs. Areas of restricted horizontal or vertical clearances should be signed to prohibit use by vans and other large vehicles.

APPLICATIONS OF QUEUEING ANALYSIS

Providing an adequate and well-defined storage area for drive-thru traffic is particularly critical, especially at fast-food restaurants and drive-thru bank facilities where queues can, and do, become quite long. Waiting vehicles should be stored on private property clear of driveways so that traffic back-up does not interfere with movement on the arterial street. At fast-food restaurants, the menu board should be installed upstream of the service window to permit drive-thru customers to place their orders prior to their arrival at the service window. Preparation of their order can then begin before they reach the service window, thus minimizing their time at the service window. A well-defined storage area for the waiting traffic should be located so that the waiting vehicles do not block or impede the movement of driveway traffic.

Where a single service position is involved, the situation is referred to as a *single-channel problem. Multiple-channel problems* arise when two or more service positions are available. Such problems commonly arise with bank tellers (indoor as well as drive-in windows), entrances and exits at large parking lots and garages, at passenger pick-up areas at transit stations and taxi stands, truck terminals or loading/unloading areas, supermarket checkout counters, telephone calls, building entrances, and transit-station turnstiles. The assumptions of Poisson arrivals and negative exponential service time are commonly acceptable and used for both single- and multiple-channel problems. Thurgood [11] found these assumptions to be representative of drive-in facilities.

Customers arriving randomly at a drive-in facility may enter into service immediately or may have to enter the queue until they can be served. Waiting lines occur whenever the immediate demand for service exceeds the current capacity of the facility providing that service.

Basic Notation and Terminology

The following notation is employed throughout this section:

n = number of customers in the drive-in system

M = number of customers in the queue waiting to be served (number of customers in the system minus the number being served)

$P(n)$ = steady-state probability that exactly n customers are in the queueing system

$P(0)$ = probability that zero vehicles are in the queueing system

N = number of parallel service positions

q = mean average arrival rate of vehicles into the system (vehicles/hour)

Q = mean average service rate per service position (vehicles/hour/position)

Avg (t) = $60/Q$ = mean service time expressed in minutes per vehicle

ρ = q/NQ = coefficient of utilization

$E(m)$ = expected (average) number of customers in the system

$E(n)$ = expected (average) number of customers waiting in the queue

$E(t)$ = expected (average) waiting time in system (includes service time)

$E(w)$ = expected (average) waiting time in queue (excludes service time)

The equations employed in the analysis of queueing problems are given in Table 8-10.

Jones, Woods, and Thurgood [4] have developed a graph (Figure 8-6) for determining the probability that there will be no customers in the system — values for $P(0)$. They also developed graphs for determining the average number of waiting customers (Figure 8-7), the average waiting time (Figure 8-8), and average queue length (Figure 8-9). These figures avoid the necessity to perform the time-consuming, although simple, queueing-analysis calculations. See pp. 228–30.

TABLE 8-10
Queueing System Equations

Equation Number	Variable	Equation
(8-1)	Coefficient of utilization	$\rho = \dfrac{q}{NQ}$
(8-2)	Probability of no customers in the system	$P(0) = \left[\displaystyle\sum_{n=0}^{N-1} \dfrac{\left(\frac{q}{Q}\right)^n}{n!} + \dfrac{\left(\frac{q}{Q}\right)^N}{N!(1-\rho)}\right]^{-1}$
(8-3)	Mean number in the queue	$E(m) = \left[\dfrac{\rho\left(\frac{q}{Q}\right)^N}{N!(1-\rho)^2}\right]P(0)$
(8-4)	Mean number in the system	$E(n) = E(m) + \dfrac{q}{Q}$
(8-5)	Mean wait time in queue (hours)	$E(w) = \dfrac{E(m)}{q}$
(8-6)	Mean time in the system (hours)	$E(t) = E(w) + \dfrac{1}{Q}$ $= E(w) + \text{Avg}\,(t)$
(8-7)	Proportion of customers who wait	$P[E(w) > 0] = \left[\dfrac{\left(\frac{q}{Q}\right)^N}{N!(1-\rho)}\right]P(0)$
(8-8)	Probability of a queue exceeding a length M	$P(x > M) = (\rho^{N+1})P[E(w) > 0]$
(8-9a)	Queue storage required	$M = \left[\dfrac{\ln P(x > M) - \ln E(w) > 0}{\ln \rho}\right] - 1$
(8-9b)*	Queue storage required	$M = \left[\dfrac{\ln P(x > M) - \ln Q_M}{\ln \rho}\right] - 1$

*Q_M is a statistic which is a function of the utilization rate and the number of service channels (service positions); see Table 8-11. The table of Q_M values and use of Equation (8-9b) greatly simplifies the calculations compared to those using Equations (8-9a).

Use of the equations and the graphs may be illustrated by the following example of a drive-in bank.

Conditions:

Number of drive-in windows, $N = 3$
Demand on the system, $q = 70$
Service capacity per channel, $Q = 28.6$ for an average service time, Avg $(t) = 2.1$ minutes

Solution Using Graphs:

- Coefficient of utilization $= 70/(3)(28.6) = 0.816$
- Probability that there are customers waiting in the system, Figure 8-6: $P(0) = 0.05$
- Expected average number of customers waiting in the queue, Figure 8-7: $E(m)/N = 1.0$; and the average number $E(m) = (3)(1.0) = 3$

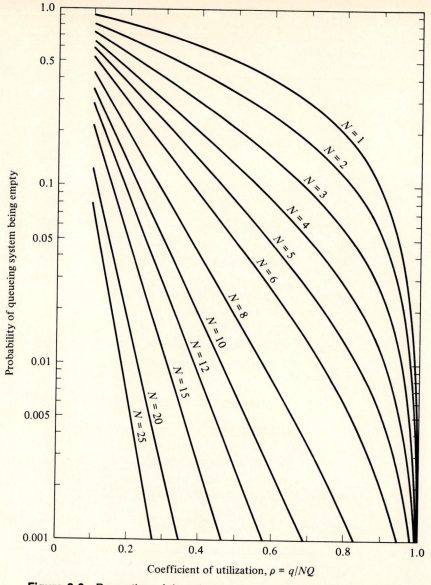

Figure 8-6 Proportion of time there are no customers in the system [$P(0)$ values]. SOURCE: Jones, Woods, and Thurgood [4].

- Expected average time that a customer will have to wait in the queue, Figure 8-8: $E(w)/\text{Avg}\,(t) = 1.2$; and the average waiting time $E(w) = (1.2)(2.1 \text{ minutes}) = 2.5$ minutes

Solution Using Equations:

$$P(0) = \left[\frac{(2.45)^0}{0!} + \frac{(2.45)^1}{1!} + \frac{(2.45)^2}{2!} + \frac{(2.45)^3}{3!(1 - 0.816)}\right]^{-1} = 0.0505$$

$$E(m) = \left[\frac{(0.816)(70/28.6)^3}{3!(1 - 0.816)^2}\right]0.0505 = 2.97$$

$$E(n) = 2.97 + 70/28.6 = 5.42$$

$$E(w) = 2.97 \div 70 = 0.0424 \text{ hours or } 2.55 \text{ minutes}$$

$$E(t) = 0.0424 + 1/28.6 = 0.0774 \text{ hours or } 4.64 \text{ minutes}$$

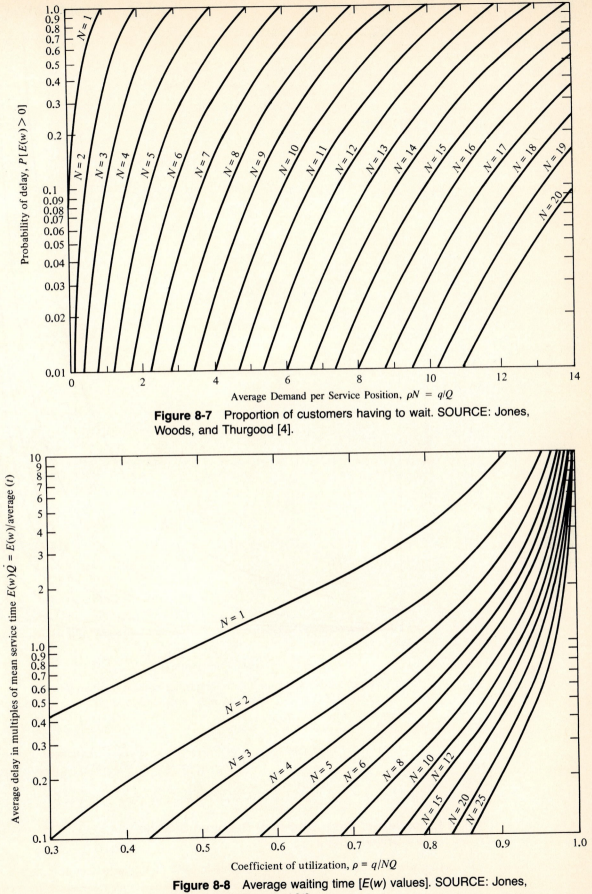

Figure 8-7 Proportion of customers having to wait. SOURCE: Jones, Woods, and Thurgood [4].

Figure 8-8 Average waiting time [$E(w)$ values]. SOURCE: Jones, Woods, and Thurgood [4].

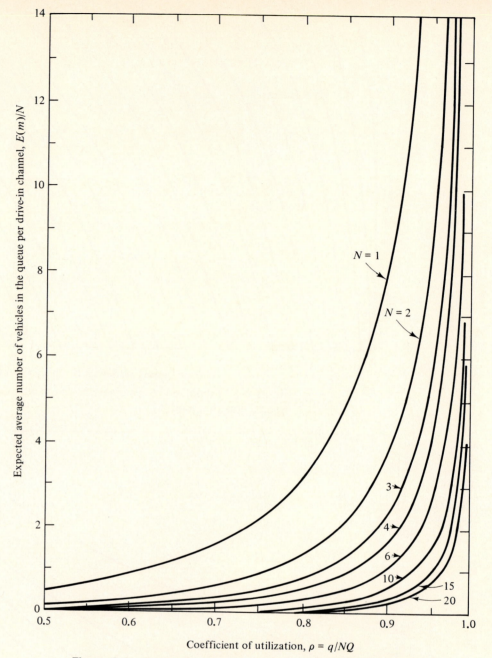

Figure 8-9 Average queue length per service position [$E(m)/N$ values]. SOURCE: Jones, Woods, and Thurgood [4].

Comparison:

Variable	Graphs	Equations
$P(0)$	0.05	0.0505
$E(m)$	3	2.97
$E(w)$	2.5	2.55

Example and Case Studies of Required Storage at a Drive-In Bank

Consider the following example of a drive-in bank facility as a demonstration of the use of queueing analysis. Review of a site plan for a proposed bank shows there are six drive-in window positions plus space to store 18 vehicles waiting to be served. In view of its location, a 5% probability of back-up onto the adjacent street is judged to be acceptable. Demand on the system for design is expected to be 110 vehicles in a 45-minute period. Average service time was expected to be 2.2 minutes. Is the queue storage adequate?

Such problems can be quickly solved using Equation (8–9b) given in Table 8-10 and repeated below for convenience.

$$M = \left[\frac{\ln P(x > M) - \ln Q_M}{\ln \rho} \right] - 1$$

where:

M = queue length which is exceeded p percent of the time

N = number of service channels (drive-in positions)

Q = service rate per channel (vehicles per hour)

$\rho = \dfrac{\text{demand rate}}{\text{service rate}} = \dfrac{q}{NQ}$ = utilization factor

q = demand rate on the system (vehicles per hour)

Q_M = tabled values of the relationship between queue length, number of channels, and utilization factor (see Table 8.11)

TABLE 8-11

Table of Q_M Values

	N = 1	2	3	4	6	8	10
0.0	0.0000	0.0000	0.0000	0.0000			
0.1	.1000	.0182	.0037	.0008	.0000	0.0000	0.0000
.2	.2000	.0666	.0247	.0096	.0015	.0002	.0000
.3	.3000	.1385	.0700	.0370	.0111	.0036	.0011
.4	.4000	.2286	.1411	.0907	.0400	.0185	.0088
.5	.5000	.3333	.2368	.1739	.0991	.0591	.0360
.6	.6000	.4501	.3548	.2870	.1965	.1395	.1013
.7	.7000	.5766	.4923	.4286	.3359	.2706	.2218
.8	.8000	.7111	.6472	.5964	.5178	.4576	.4093
.9	.9000	.8526	.8172	.7878	.7401	.7014	.6687
1.0	1.0000	1.0000	1.0000	1.0000	1.0000	1.0000	1.0000

$\rho = \dfrac{q}{NQ} = \dfrac{\text{arrival rate, total}}{\text{(number of channels)(service rate per channel)}}$

N = number of channels (service positions)

Solution

Step 1: $Q = \dfrac{60 \text{ min/hr}}{2.2 \text{ min/service}} = 27.3$ services per hour

Step 2: $q = (110 \text{ veh/45 min}) \times (60 \text{ min/hr}) = 146.7$ vehicles per hour

Step 3: $\rho = \dfrac{q}{NQ} = \dfrac{146.7}{(6)(27.3)} = 0.8956$

Step 4: $Q_M = 0.7303$ by interpolation between 0.8 and 0.9 for $N = 6$ from the table of Q_M values (see Table 8-11).

Step 5: The acceptable probability of the queue, M, being longer than the storage, 18 spaces in this example, was stated to be 5%. $P(x > M) = 0.05$, and:

$$M = \left[\frac{\ln 0.05 - \ln 0.7303}{\ln 0.8956} \right] - 1 = \left[\frac{-2.996 - (-0.314)}{-0.110} \right] - 1$$

$$= 24.38 - 1 = 23.38, \text{ say 23 vehicles.}$$

The number of vehicles in the queue would be expected to exceed 23 more than 5% of the time. Since the site plan will accommodate a queue of 18 vehicles, the storage is not sufficient for the conditions stated.

It is important to realize that, for any $P\ (x > M)$ value, the queue length required increases very rapidly for values of $\rho > 0.85$ (see Figure 8-9). When $\rho > 1.0$, the solution is indeterminate and the queue length theoretically becomes infinite.

Analysis of Service Times. In many instances it is effective to demonstrate that a proposed design not only is inadequate to store vehicles waiting for service but will result in unacceptable wait times as well. The necessary equations are given in Table 8-10.

For purposes of checking computations it is convenient to know that the limit of $P(0)$, as the number of channels approaches infinity (in practical terms when $N > 10$), is:

$$\lim_{N \to \infty} P(0) = e^{-\lambda} \qquad \text{where } \lambda = q/Q$$

Drive-In Bank Example: Under the site-development approval requirements, representatives of a bank presented a site plan for the construction of a new bank having three service positions. Information provided by bank officials and observations at other local banks provided the following data:

- Expected average arrival rate during the design hour (4:30–5:30 p.m. on Fridays) = 70 vehicles per hour (vph)
- Average service time per customer = 2.1 minutes

Does the site plan provide for sufficient storage to accommodate all vehicles arriving 95% of the time?

$$q = 70 \text{ vph arrival rate}$$

$$Q = \frac{60 \text{ minutes per hour}}{2.1 \text{ minutes per service}} = 28.6 \text{ vph service rate}$$

$$\rho = \frac{70}{(3)(28.6)} = 0.816$$

$$\frac{q}{Q} = \frac{70}{28.6} = 2.45$$

$$Q_M = 0.674 \text{ by interpolation from Table 8-11}$$

$$P(x > M) = 1.00 - 0.95 = 0.05$$

By Equation (8-9b)

$$M = \left[\frac{\ln 0.05 - \ln 0.674}{\ln 0.816} \right] - 1 = \left[\frac{-2.996 - (-0.396)}{-0.203} \right] - 1 = 11.8, \text{ say } 12$$

Thus, it would be necessary to store 12 vehicles, exclusive of the three service positions, in order to accommodate the arriving vehicles 95% of the time; or alternatively, to have waiting vehicles extending back into the adjacent street no more than 5% of the time between 4:30 and 5:30 p.m. on Fridays. Since the site plan provides for six spaces, the site plan as submitted is inadequate and should be disapproved.

A solution to the problem would be to increase the storage, or if this is not possible add a service position in order to reduce the average service time.

Addition of a service position would reduce the number of storage spaces needed to three (three storage plus four service positions)—assuming the same arrival rate and service time:

$$M = \left[\frac{\ln 0.05 - \ln 0.301}{\ln 0.612} \right] - 1 = 2.7, \text{ say } 3$$

A redesign to provide four service positions would have the additional benefit of substantially reducing the expected waiting time (from over 4 minutes to less than $\frac{1}{2}$ minute) for the bank customers using the drive-in windows:

With Three Service Positions:

$$q = 70 \text{ vph}$$

$$Q = 28.6 \text{ vph}$$

$$\frac{q}{Q} = 2.45$$

$$\rho = \frac{70}{(3)(28.6)} = 0.816$$

$$P(0) = \left[\frac{(2.45)^0}{0!} + \frac{(2.45)^1}{1!} + \frac{(2.45)^2}{2!} + \frac{(2.45)^3}{3!\left[1 - \left(\frac{2.45}{3}\right)\right]} \right]^{-1}$$

$$= [1 + 2.45 + 3.00 + 13.37]^{-1} = 0.0505$$

$$E(m) = \left[\frac{(0.816)\left(\frac{70}{28.6}\right)^3}{3!(1 - 0.816)^2} \right] 0.0505 = 2.97$$

$$E(n) = 2.97 + 70.28.6 = 5.42$$

$$E(t) = \frac{2.97}{70} = 0.0424 \text{ hours or 2.55 minutes}$$

$$E(w) = 0.0424 + \frac{1}{28.6} = 0.0774 \text{ hours or 4.64 minutes}$$

With Four Service Positions:

$$q = 70 \text{ vph}$$

$$Q = 28.6 \text{ vph}$$

$$\frac{q}{Q} = 2.45$$

$$\rho = \frac{70}{(4)(28.6)} = 0.612$$

$$P(0) = \left[\frac{(2.45)^0}{0!} + \frac{(2.45)^1}{1!} + \frac{(2.45)^2}{2!} + \frac{(2.45)^3}{3!} + \frac{(2.45)^4}{4!\left[1 - \left(\frac{2.45}{4}\right)\right]} \right]^{-1}$$

$$= 0.0783$$

$$E(m) = \left[\frac{(0.612)(2.45)^4}{4!(1 - 0.612)^2} \right] 0.0783 = 0.48$$

$$E(n) = 0.48 + 2.45 = 2.93$$

$$E(t) = 0.007 + \frac{1}{28.6} = 0.042 \text{ hours or 2.51 minutes}$$

$$E(w) = \frac{0.48}{70} = 0.007 \text{ hours or 0.41 minutes}$$

However, the service time would increase somewhat unless an additional teller were also added. Nevertheless, an increase to 2.5 minutes, or more, would still reduce the storage space required and result in better service (less time in the system). Besides, time spent being served is less irritating to the customer than an equal time spent waiting.

Conversion of a Residence.   An existing single-family residence was situated on a 2.5-acre tract fronting on the major north–south arterial in the urbanizing fringe of a metropolitan area of 100,000 population. The 85th percentile speed exceeded 50 mph; however, it was anticipated that the speed limit would be reduced to 45 mph as further urbanization occurred.

Requests for rezoning from single-family residential to general commercial had received negative recommendations from the Planning and Zoning Commission and denied by the City Council. Nevertheless, the fact that changing conditions in the vicinity of the site were making the property less desirable as a single-family residence was generally recognized. Therefore, when an application was submitted for a Conditional Use Permit to establish a private school using the existing residence for classrooms, the Planning and Zoning Commission was very favorably disposed to the request. The applicant provided the following information prior to the public hearing.

1. The completed application for a conditional use
2. A statement that the intended use was for a Montessori school using the existing structure
3. A site plan as required for all proposed development, other than single-family and duplex residential development, before a building permit will be issued for a new structure and for remodeling of an existing one

The following information was presented at the public hearing by the applicant:

1. At least 40 students would be enrolled before any change would be made in the site circulation.
2. Eighty percent of the students were expected to be picked up within a 20-minute period — a substantial additional fee was to be charged for children picked up more than 30 minutes after school.
3. A strong parent–school relationship was intended, so that average pick-up time of at least 2 minutes and visits of 5 minutes or longer would not be unusual.

The following were agreed upon at the public hearing:

1. The probability of vehicles backing up onto the main lane of the major arterial should be negligible, less than 1%.
2. The site plan, with no change in the circulation pattern, would provide for four service positions and three storage positions.

Based upon these conditions, the following analysis was performed using Equation (8-9b):

$$M = 3$$
$$N = 4$$
$$Q = 60 \text{ minutes per hour} \div 2 \text{ minutes per service} = 30 \text{ vph}$$
$$q = (40 \text{ students}) (80\% \text{ in } 20 \text{ minutes}) \left(\frac{60}{20}\right) = 96 \text{ vph}$$
$$\rho = \frac{96}{(4)(30)} = 0.8000$$

$P(x > 3) = 0.01$ (a 1% chance of vehicles backing up onto the arterial)

$$Q_M = 0.8585, \text{ from Table 8-11}$$
$$3 = \left[\frac{\ln P(x > 3) - \ln 0.5964}{\ln 0.8000}\right] - 1$$
$$3 = \left[\frac{\ln P(x > 3) - (-0.5168)}{-0.2231}\right] - 1$$

Then,

$$\ln P(x > 3) = (4)(-0.2231) - 0.5168 = -1.4092$$

and

$$P(x > 3) = e^{-1.4092} = 0.244 \text{ or } 24\%$$

Thus, the calculated probability that the queue could back up onto the arterial is 24% (given the stated conditions), which is considerably greater than the acceptable probability of less than 1%, and the application was denied. The Planning and Zoning Commission suggested various compromises of redesign of the site and issuance of a conditional use permit for a school (under the ordinance, a school can be located in any zoning district by condition) with the condition that the maximum enrollment would not exceed 24 students, which is the number necessary to achieve a value of $P(x > 3) < 0.01$. All such proposals were rejected by the applicant. The site was subsequently rezoned to the Administrative and Professional District (a restricted office district) and is now being used as a dentist's office.

REFERENCES

1. Barton-Aschman Associates, Inc., *McDonald's Site Traffic Analysis Manual,* 1980.

2. Fairfax County, Virginia, *Stacking Space Standards for Drive-In Windows At Fast Food Restaurants,* 1980.

3. Institute of Transportation Engineers, *Trip Generation Rates,* 1976.

4. Jones, Robert L., Woods, Donald, L., and Thurgood, Glen S., "Drive-In Banking: Managing for Maximum Service," *ITE Journal,* publication pending.

5. Lalani, Nazir, "Factoring 'Passer-By' Trips Into Traffic Impact Analyses," *Public Works,* May 1984.

6. Lopata, Roy H. and Jaffe, Stuart J., "Fast Food Restaurant Trip Generation: Another Look," *ITE Journal,* 1980.

7. Petersen, David O., "Bank-Savings and Loan Traffic and Parking Analysis," unpublished internal memorandum, Barton-Aschman Associates Inc., February 1974.

8. Scifres, Peter N., "Traffic Planning for Drive-In Financial Institutions," *Traffic Engineering,* September 1975.

9. The Traffic Institute, Northwestern University, Selected Studies of Burger King Restaurants.

10. The Traffic Institute, Northwestern University, short course notes.

11. Thurgood, Glen S., "The Application of Stochastic Queueing Theory in the Development of Suggested Traffic Design Guidelines for Drive-In Service Facilities," doctoral dissertation, Texas A&M University, December 1975.

Index